GRIEF AND GRIEVANCE
the Assassination of Yitzhak Rabin

Dr Rena Moses-Hrushovski with
the collaboration of Dr Rafael Moses

MINERVA PRESS
LONDON
MIAMI RIO DE JANEIRO DELHI

GRIEF AND GRIEVANCE: *The Assassination of Yitzhak Rabin*
Copyright © Dr Rena Moses-Hrushovski with the collaboration
of Dr Rafael Moses 2000

All Rights Reserved

No part of this book may be reproduced in any form
by photocopying or by any electronic or mechanical means,
including information storage or retrieval systems,
without permission in writing from both the copyright
owner and the publisher of this book.

ISBN 0 75411 243 8

First Published 2000 by
MINERVA PRESS
315–317 Regent Street
London W1R 7YB

Printed in Great Britain for Minerva Press

GRIEF AND GRIEVANCE
The Assassination of Yitzhak Rabin

*To my/our children and grandchildren
with love and hope for a peaceful future.*

ACKNOWLEDGEMENT

I would like first of all to thank Sheldon Roth, MD, who read chapter after chapter of this manuscript, sending me his insightful and constructive comments which often helped clarify my thinking and improved my writing.

I am grateful to Norma Schneider for her superb work as the first editor of this book. She cared not only for the technical aspects but was also deeply involved in the matters discussed in the book.

I am indebted to Sarah Leeman whose accurate typing and constant availability I appreciated greatly.

I also want to thank Ms Rebecca Ward and Karen Patient, our publications managers and her editor as well as Angelina Anton, the managing director, Kate Dale, the publications director and Alison Thomas, the managing editor.

My special thanks are due to my husband Rafael Moses who collaborated with me in many ways while accompanying me in my way of writing.

FOREWORD

I first met Rena Moses-Hrushovski nearly twenty years ago when we worked together facilitating an extended process of unofficial Arab–Israeli dialogues. Through a six-year series of meetings involving psychiatrists, psychoanalysts, diplomats, high-ranking military and government officials, and other representatives from Israel, Egypt and Palestine, we sought to understand the complex and intertwined psychological relationship of an individual, his or her nation, and those who were considered their enemies. Our work in these dialogues, and our reflections on our personal and clinical experiences, revealed innumerable intricate connections between the psychological defences utilised by individuals in response to past trauma and anxiety, and the collective behaviour of large groups such as national, ethnic, religious or cultural entities.

After the dialogues came to an end, we both continued to independently and collaboratively investigate the parallels in the conscious and unconscious mechanisms used by individuals and the collectives that bind them together and set them apart. I therefore was not surprised when Dr Moses-Hrushovski told me that she was endeavouring to write a book about the psychological and societal phenomena that were revealed and concealed in the tragic assassination of Yitzhak Rabin.

I talked to Dr Moses-Hrushovski shortly after the traumatic event. She had watched on television the peace rally that Rabin had been attending when he had been fatally shot by Yigal Amir, and was still grieving the tragic loss of the revered Israeli leader. But this was not the only loss that confronted her. Rabin's assassination reactivated in her mind memories of her own and her family's trauma as Jews in Europe during the Holocaust, and the emotions that pertained to events that occurred fifty years earlier were uncontrollably tied to those that were unfolding in front of her.

As she began work on this book, she was well aware that focusing on grief and grievance, and their psychological and societal manifestations and consequences, would therefore involve a complex 'mourning task'. But although this task would be difficult, it also promised rewards: her psychoanalytic insights into her patients' conscious and unconscious responses to loss and experiences of injustice would be enhanced; she could contribute to the crucial understanding of psychosocial and psychopolitical phenomena, and she could also create a personal monument to the memory of Yitzhak Rabin.

From early in her life, Rena Moses-Hrushovski has had a sense of mistrust for people who could not blend and express their rational thoughts and appropriate emotions. During a conversation, she reminded me of the statement by the German commander of a concentration camp in France: 'I did these things without feelings. This is the way I was brought up.' The ability of human beings to dissociate thoughts and actions from feelings and emotions, the specific psychic mechanisms they employ, and the individual and societal ramifications of this process are at the heart of this book. She beautifully combines her empathic and emotional sense of the world around her with creative scientific exploration of human nature, especially its aggressive components – the result is a book that is not only professionally enlightening but also emotionally moving.

The crucial theoretical core of this book is the author's description and application of 'deployment', a rigid pattern of defensive behaviour she introduced in *Deployment: A Narcissistic Character Defence* (1994). Individuals who utilise this character defence, often in response to overwhelming and humiliating traumas, possess an exaggerated sense of mission to escape disruptive aspects of their internal world. The result is that their perceptions, feelings and choices are restricted, often leading to self-defeating behaviour. As Moses-Hrushovski has observed, it is analogous to 'remaining in the Ark long after the flood' or 'staying in the bunker long after the war'. Deployment, therefore, is the antithesis of mourning, and reflects unconscious efforts to harden oneself and deny loss. The individuals' endless vigilance, repeated activities, frozen perspective, sense of righteousness and use of violence and counter-shame strategies enable them to control emotions associated with guilt, humiliation, uncertainty, sadness and fear at the expense of empathy, sympathy, and responsibility.

Deployment, therefore, has created serious and intractable impediments to peace in the Middle East through its *egotism of victimisation*. Yitzhak Rabin, however, presented an alternative strategy and served as a role model for all sides through his long struggle for viable relations between Arabs and Israelis. Only after decades of tireless work was he able to lessen the utilisation of deployment among Israelis, which made any communication or compromise with Palestinians and other Arabs unthinkable, thereby paving the way for the possibility of peace. Yet the phenomenon of deployment was so severe among some that it could not be ameliorated, resulting in his death at the hands of an Israeli extremist.

Rena Moses-Hrushovski's book seeks to address both sides of this event. On one hand, she investigates the nature of Rabin's personality in order to understand what drove him to champion peace in spite of the tremendous opposition he constantly faced, how he was able to succeed in his political mission, but also the shared trauma that his assassination caused. On the other, she disentangles the ideological and personal pathological roots of Yigal Amir's act of terrorism. She discusses the nature and extent of Amir's use of deployment, his resulting rigid and fanatical thoughts and behaviour, and other factors that led to his act of terror. She also discusses terrorism in general, and explains both the individual and societal factors that have made it a chronic part of life in the region. *Grief and Grievance: The Assassination of Yitzhak Rabin* therefore contains both clinical psychoanalytic data as well as relevant psychopolitical and social applications that illustrate the full spectrum of the manifestations of deployment, the parallels between individual and group behaviour, and the complex vicissitudes of mourning induced by a traumatic event. Clinically oriented material is presented that carefully illustrates the rigid and difficult barriers characteristic of deployment, but the author also discusses therapeutic strategies such as recognising transference manifestations of deployment and methods to soften or modify this character defence. Theoretical and clinical findings are then applied to more general strategies such as education, dialogue, and open communication that can be applied to young people in order to encourage them to utilise appropriate emotions, defuse anger and frustration, and facilitate compromise rather than perpetuate the cycle of violence and victimisation.

This book is an excellent example of how a dedicated, sensitive and courageous clinician can, as Freud long ago envisioned, take psychoanalysis beyond the couch and apply it in relevant, provocative, vigorous and sound ways. Rena Moses-Hrushovski, an extremely competent analyst, illustrates how she has taken the insights gained from the internal world of her patients and utilised them to evolve a deeper understanding of the external world, especially the chronic societal violence that has plagued Israel and its relationships with its neighbours. In doing so she emerges as an outstanding theoretician and perceptive humanitarian.

Vamik D. Volkan

Contents

Acknowledgement		v
Foreword		vii
Introduction		xiii
I	Trauma and the Phenomenon of Grief: the Assassination of Yitzhak Rabin	1
II	Ways, Tasks and Stages of Mourning	17
III	Deployment in the Individual	44
IV	Some Aspects of Deployment in the Social and Political Arena: from Grievance to Grief, Mourning and Change	67
V	Grievance, Fanaticism and Terrorism	92
VI	The Assassination in the Shadow of Oblivion: the Failure to Adequately Mourn the Death of Yitzhak Rabin and the Increase in Jewish Fundamentalism	113
VII	Fundamentalism among Ultra-Orthodox Jews: Deployments against Change	132
VIII	Postscript	154
Bibliography		187

INTRODUCTION

Rabin's openness to the perception of changing circumstances – and to the change in attitudes of our neighbouring countries – brought about a substantial shift in his thinking. His open mind in the last years of his life enabled him to realise that the existential threat to Israel no longer existed. His courage to reconsider his political views and bring about revolutionary change, his determination and sincere commitment to do all that can be done to fight violence and embark on the peace process, all became for many of us a symbol for the readiness and capacity to redeploy forces and apply them in new directions. New directions, according to changing conditions, needs, interests, beliefs and perceptions.

We are now at the writing of this introduction, four-and-a-half years after the assassination of Yitzhak Rabin and a year after the elections in Israel which brought Ehud Barak, Rabin's spiritual successor, to power. Barak poses three major goals: to bring security to Israel and to the area by means of a network of peace agreements as long as they do not harm Israel's vital interests; the closure of social gaps in the country, especially between the rich and the poor; and to bring about unity within the nation of Israel. But the conflicting and complex psychological, social and psychopolitical processes continue as this book goes to press. Between crisis and hope, it is hard to tell where we actually are.

I would like to explain why I, an Israeli psychoanalyst, felt the need to write this book. I had prepared myself to write a book on grief and grievance as experienced in my clinical work with certain difficult patients. However, after Rabin's assassination, I could not do anything other than write about the immense grief and mourning in which I was both a participant and an observer. Though I believe that a systematic interdisciplinary study based on psychoanalytic, psychopolitical, psychohistorical and sociological knowledge would do more justice to dealing with the background and meaning of these events and what followed, I felt and feel that there is a special value also to an impressionistic study, carried out and written directly after the events, when everything was still so immediate and intense. We know that emotional elements tend to fade as time passes, making it difficult to reconstruct them later on.

Another motivation was to try and apply my clinical experience to social and political phenomena. There are political forces that impact on what happens to the individual and similarly, there are psychological and emotional factors which influence political behaviour and events. At the same time, the writing of this book was for me a way of mourning Yitzhak Rabin who had fought for peace and against violence.

A vitriolic political climate gave rise to the murder of Yitzhak Rabin. How can we try and avoid the repetition of history? This question relates to multi-layered psychic and political realities that underlie political behaviour. In this book, we try to explore the various obstacles to peace and reconciliation in both ourselves and our neighbours, between men and women and between other conflicting groups. We look at this through the lens of both temporary and pathological deployment. We believe that paying attention to deploymental phenomena and understanding their complex dynamics can facilitate the processes of change in our country – and perhaps universally – as happened recently in Northern Ireland.

A central theme in this book relates to the effect of traumas on feeling, thinking, behaving – and thus on the entire organisation of our lives. The deep influence of a traumatic experience on a man's life, feelings, thoughts, attitudes and behaviour is illustrated by the following: it was the morning of 19 March 1944 when the Gestapo came to take Joseph's father. He was twelve years old. His father quietly put on his clothes, kissed Joseph and said, 'Either I shall see you again or I won't.' They never saw each other again. Since then, all that Joseph thinks and does in his life is determined by this moment. This also determined the relationship of Tommy Joseph Lapid, journalist turned politician, to the state of Israel. For him, Israel and what it stands for is his answer to this and other traumatic acts.

We in Israel can all feel how the injured self-image associated with the mental representation of a shared traumatic event is deposited into the next generation together with the unconscious expectation that the children will be able to mourn the losses which their parents could not mourn; and perhaps that the children will reverse the humiliation that they, the parents could not overcome. As usually happens with traumas in individuals with regard to past traumas, the trauma of Rabin's assassination brought to the hearts and minds of Israelis the memories of other national traumas – the Holocaust, the wars of independence, the Yom Kippur War and the Gulf War. Some of these became or may yet become 'Chosen Traumas' in the sense of Volkan (1991).

Traumatised people cannot resume the normal course of their lives, because the trauma repeatedly emerges long after the dangers of the trauma have passed. They relive the event as though it were continually recurring in the present, not only in their dreams and thoughts, but also in their actions. Often they re-enact the traumatic moment in fantasy life or reality, wishing thereby to change the traumatic encounter retroactively, so that they can, as it were, overcome it differently this time. Or they may wish to obtain redress from the other to correct the helplessness they had experienced at the time. Thus it becomes clear that much of their efforts and psychic energy goes to deal with the past rather than with the present or the future.

David Grossman (1995), a leading Israeli author, says that when thinking about the Holocaust, the dominant emotion is a bitter and inconsolable humiliation that such things were done to people. The humiliated person is rooted in helpless indignation. An entire generation suffers from an emotional handicap and lives in constant preparedness for a new Holocaust.

A deep existential anxiety motivates Israeli society in its relationship to the Palestinians. It turns into a major motive, building our protective entrenchment. It is traumas and cumulative traumas which have such effects on individuals and nations. But the actualisation and the peacefulness of the individual as well as the nation are determined no less by patterns of dealing with traumas. I think that it is the mission of all to remember the Holocaust and to do everything possible to avoid a recurrence of the tragedy. But when this becomes a narrow mission which allows no mental space to think about the present, to reassess the situation and reconsider pre-existing beliefs, then such a mission becomes dangerous indeed.

In zealous, ideological missions by extremists, realistic fears are often blended with apocalyptic fantasies, and existential anxiety is at times, consciously or unconsciously, used for political purposes. Extreme groups always tend to find a straw man to frustrate peace and reconciliation processes whenever myths about the enemy die. Often they are prepared – ahead of time – to watch for the catastrophe to come about. Many deployed individuals do so in order to avoid being surprised by a sudden shock or attack. Sometimes, they assume such a stance to prove that they were indeed right. Often, this becomes a self-fulfilling prophecy, either through a pre-emptive attack or because mistrust leads to the breakdown of negotiations.

When I organised my thinking about the distinct emotional disturbance represented by my traumatised patients – called difficult or stuck patients in the literature – I felt, like Herman (1992), that diagnostic categories used by psychiatrists for mentally ill people do not fit them. Like Herman, I see the survivors of extreme situations as suffering from complex post-traumatic stress disorder. I thought similarly about those of my patients who had not profited from previous classical psychoanalytic or psychotherapeutic treatment. These patients had in common a configuration of feeling, thinking and doing that prevented them from acting in their best interests and making maximal use of their resources, this because of strong unconscious trends of protest, revenge and a desire to retroactively 'correct' the past. All had been traumatised in their pre- or post-oedipal stages. They suffered from power abuse, sexual abuse or emotional abuse and from other traumas such as death or illness in the family. I called this configuration 'deployment'. I chose this name because it entails a rigid self-programming into a system of attitudes, positions, roles and behaviour aimed at protecting one's self-esteem and dignity, consoling one for what one had experienced as self-annihilation and humiliation and correcting the injustices done to one. Such a person has been beautifully described in the literature by the German writer, Heinrich Kleist (1808, 1967), in his 'Michael Kohlhaas'. In psychiatric and psychoanalytic terminology, this is considered a disturbance of the self, a predominantly narcissistic pathology.

A common motivation in these persons was never to forgive or forget, never to agree to a reconciliation before the other side admits their share of responsibility for the wrong done. From my clinical work, I learned a great deal about being stuck in despair and grievances. I found these to be remarkably akin and alike to the reactions of groups and nations to psychopolitical events, especially as they relate to power conflicts concerned with injustice. A common denominator is the difficulty in containing conflicts or trying to resolve them. This difficulty often leads to a tendency to enact and re-enact conflicts and thus repeat the history of helplessness and violence.

Looking now at both the individual and the group, society or nation, we can say that if mourning means staying with the variety and complexity of feelings resulting from loss, abuse, neglect, or infringement of one's rights, then the behaviour of deployed individuals or groups represents the antithesis of mourning, change and development.

I will not repeat here what I have written about the deploymental perspective and phenomena (1992, 1993, 1994, 1996, 1999, 2000). I do intend here to describe briefly the main characteristics of deployment in individuals and in nations – as they were expressed in my patients on the one hand and in our nation, especially after the traumas of the Holocaust and Rabin's assassination. The first characteristic is a dissociation of feelings from thoughts and ideas: deployed individuals instantly cut themselves off emotionally, severing meaningful connections in states of stress in order to avoid feeling hurt, weak, shamed, blamed and confused. They do so when they perceive a threat or an insult to their self-esteem – or even before such a threat is observed. Used as a temporary coping mechanism such as described by Moshe Dayan (one-time Israel Minister of Defence) it is quite effective. When he spoke in the Israeli Knesset and the opposition was hurling abuse at him, he went on with his speech while withdrawing emotionally, a sensation which was familiar to him from the battlefield. He then felt like being in a fog: it was unreal as had been the bursting of shells when he crossed a field of fire in battle.

On the other hand, when dissociation becomes a way of life, it interferes with intrapsychic and interpersonal communication and is thereby likely to become dangerously destructive. Persons may become oblivious to the implications of their deeds when their feelings are so totally separated from their actions. This is true both for individuals and for nations or societies. Deployed individuals who have adopted dissociation as a regular mechanism and then go on to withdraw emotionally will often disclaim responsibility for such action, and cease communication, assuming the position of the 'offended one'. Only as a result of exploration of this pattern of behaviour in therapy or analysis, i.e. exploring what they were feeling, when, why and how they reacted to an event, can they gradually realise that there are other ways of reacting than remaining stuck in their rigid position.

Grievance is a second feature of deployment. In contrast to grief, grievance is a wrong perceived, real, experienced or imagined. It is considered grounds for a constant complaint against an unjust act, circumstance or relationship. It becomes the mission of those deployed in grievance to notice injustices committed by others and to focus on what needs to be corrected in others. This is at the expense of looking at what is or might be wrong in their own perception, thinking or behaviour. Of course, they then do not search how to invest in themselves in order to understand, perhaps to own, previously unacceptable thoughts or feelings and to bring about change. The obstinate demand to wait until the other takes responsibility reminds us of the soul-searching that took place after the assassination of Rabin. It was usually the searching of the other's soul rather than one's own.

A third characteristic of deployment relates to the dominant part of shame and guilt and the use of counter-shame and counter-guilt strategies. Among these, we find self-hardening and violence in order to try and protect oneself from the paralysing threats of feeling – yes, actually feeling – guilt, humiliation and shame. Deployed persons would like to remove these terms from the dictionary. The concept of the Israeli-born 'Sabra' is said to symbolise this: it denotes a prickly pear, symbolising the prickliness and hurtfulness from the outside, yet the softness and sweetness on the inside.

A form of counter-shame strategy lies in unconsciously assuming and being stuck in the position of the victim. Shulamit Aloni, politician and one-time minister in an Israeli government, wrote that Golda Meir, one-time Prime Minister, accused her: 'How can you say we are conquerors? There are no Jewish conquerors.' Aloni comments bitterly: 'So we, the Jews, are always the victims, always the persecuted side, the robbed, entitled to be pitied and therefore the just.' To espouse the role of the victim is one form of deployment which then becomes a common cause for failure and maladjustment. The unconscious motivation is mostly to mobilise others to now, at last, provide what they felt they had been entitled to receive long ago.

I want to describe here one more important feature of deployment. The deployer has a drive to automatically switch on a form of corrective programming, aimed at fighting any threat of being miserable, weak or inferior. Much of the Sabra mentality was derived from the wish to be the opposite of the mentality of the Diaspora Jew, perceived as weak and helpless. A leading value was to win and not to be a 'sucker' or a 'loser'. For these and other reasons, pride, arrogance and superiority were unconsciously substituted. To this day these qualities cause the bitterness of grievances, especially of those ethnic groups that came after the establishment of the state.

The last feature of deployment I will mention is that of 'being prepared'. This means to be constantly on guard and in control to avoid the exposure of weakness, failure and mistakes, especially so that the calamity should not appear unexpectedly. There is an overlap here among the various features of deployment: preparedness, exerting control, dissociation, grievance, corrective programming, one-dimensional mission and one-track-mindedness must not be viewed in isolation, but rather in relation to each other and to the total they present.

There are many schools in psychoanalysis, each of which reflects a limited perspective. We feel that adding the deploymental perspective may increase our understanding and help us deal with hindrances to negotiations, reconciliation and peace.

In the postscript to this book, we present some thoughts about how to use our professional knowledge and sensitivities to help find ways of understanding and handling conflicts, grievances, frustrations and everyday pressures. They, after all, are the seedbed of violence and terror. It is our belief that the more each one of us becomes aware of and can own his mixed, conflicted and confused feelings, the less is there a need to project them onto or into others outside oneself; the less will there also be a need for splits between opposing views or camps in a nation.

We discuss in the postscript the changing of attitudes: education towards openness, sensitivity, autonomy, flexibility and pluralism. There is a constant tension and interaction among these goals and values. The task of each individual and each group is to crystallise goals and values according to their choice.

In the light of the violence, terror and mental or religious fundamentalism, the feeling of many of us is that we must try to remove the blind spots that do not allow us to see the whole picture in a more complex light: to come to terms with the reality of coexistence; to relinquish imposing irrational, omnipotent fantasies on reality; to create within ourselves a mental space to be rather than do (i.e. act), a space for reflection, for critical judgement and for tolerance of those with different views. If we cannot manage to carry out these important tasks, the blind spot may turn into a black hole that will swallow us all.

A goal of psychoanalysis is to facilitate the individual's capacity to feel like her- or himself while being with a multiplicity of many authentic selves, each seeking expression and needing to be heard and taken into consideration. Could we not think similarly about the nation being one, yet consisting of many subgroups and variegated identities, each with legitimate, authentic parts needing to be heard? This could be a good basis for solving problems and resolving conflicts. In these times, we move not only from the individual to the group and to the nation, but also to the world as a whole. Globalisation is not only an economic phenomenon, but can be seen as a factor in the fight against violence and terror.

Rena Moses-Hrushovski

Chapter I
TRAUMA AND THE PHENOMENON OF GRIEF: THE ASSASSINATION OF YITZHAK RABIN

In my clinical work with narcissistic patients over the years, I have been struck by a specific configuration that I eventually conceptualised as *deployment*. In my definition, deployment entails a rigid self-organisation into a system of attitudes, roles and behaviours aimed at protecting one's self-esteem and dignity, at consoling or compensating oneself for what one has experienced in the past as unfair, painful, and humiliating. The major characteristics of the forms of deployment, which are described elsewhere (1992, 1994), will be discussed in Chapters 3 and 4.

As I have discussed in *Deployment: Hiding Behind Power Struggles as a Character Defence* (1994), many of my patients who are deployed into grievance spend a great deal of time complaining, inwardly or explicitly, and find themselves unable to live free, creative or happy lives. Most of these individuals are compulsively driven to prove their special worth, as if constantly compelled to justify their existence. It is as if such patients keep protesting against those who did not behave, think or feel as they should have done in the past, when the person was hurt by or failed to receive succour from them.

My treatment of these patients has revealed that, as children, most of them underwent traumas such as a death in the family, the transition to another country, physical or sexual abuse, or emotional neglect. Since they were deprived of or could not make use of the opportunity to feel the full pain of their grief, aided by emotionally available parents, they have spent the rest of their lives weighed down by unbearable tension and anger, the seeds of self-defeat or self-destruction.

After some years of treating patients like this, it has become clear to me that these people are carrying the burden of a grief they lack the ability to express and even to feel. They seem to be awaiting an opportunity to be brought closer to their real feelings so they can begin the mourning process that should have taken place years and years ago, although they are strongly resistant when they are encouraged to confront that which has been so unbearable.

For some years I had been planning to write a book about grief and grievance in the patients I have treated – on how we analysts and therapists can help them recapture the traumatic moments as they were originally experienced, and enable them to see how much of their power has been invested in attempting to make certain that they will not be there again, whether in reality or in memory. I planned to include a discussion of the attitudes and methods I use to reach the grief their grievances are aimed at keeping hidden and the painful situations in which they unconsciously remain frozen.

Then, suddenly, on 4 November 1995, the Israeli Prime Minister Yitzhak Rabin was assassinated. As we in Israel are still in the process of mourning his death (as well as the deaths of almost a hundred more innocent people killed in the spate of terrorist bombings which took place thereafter), I have come to realise that my book on grief and grievance could not help but relate to the feelings of grief and the mourning process in which all Israelis are still involved as a nation. I also feel that Yitzhak Rabin's international reputation as a seeker of peace could help bring the phenomenon of grief and mourning into the broader context of similar tragedies being suffered by people throughout the world.

This is not an objective study of reactions to a tragic murder and the ineffably intense and emotional grief and mourning phenomenon that have followed. It is more an impressionistic study of the ways in which the Israeli people are experiencing this grief, based on observations in both clinical and non-clinical settings, on its reverberations in everyday life. As such, it is concerned with a wide range of subjective experiences – emotional, psychological and somatic – in the social context of one particular society.

It may be too early to describe or try to understand the deeply felt trauma into which we have all been thrust. A systematic interdisciplinary study based on psychoanalytic, psychopolitical, psychohistorical and sociological knowledge might do more justice to this phenomenon of grief and mourning. Nevertheless, I find it important to note and comment on what has happened while it is still fresh, direct, immediate and intense, since emotional elements tend to fade as time passes, making it difficult to reconstruct them.

Moreover, were I to present the reactions to these ghastly events in an abstract manner, for example, by listing the reactions of helplessness, shock, panic, paralysis, dissociation, restlessness, apathy, despair, sadness, loneliness, somatisation, shame, guilt and other responses – the depth of the emotional substance would not be conveyed. In order to describe the mourning as precisely and experientially as possible, I have found it necessary to present many illustrations of the variety of reactions in concrete detail, often in direct speech. There will, no doubt, be some overlapping since the range of issues that have affected the process of grieving interrelate. What follows reflects my own perception of the web of interpretations, experiences and circumstances that surrounded the assassination. While writing about the different reactions to Israel's traumatic experience, I felt as if I were going through a mourning process myself, as if the echoes that filled me were resonating to different voices. Indeed, these voices have become increasingly integrated and 'mine' through the writing process.

The Assassination: Trauma and the Experience of Grief

The term 'grief' refers to the wide range of experiences, behaviours, feelings and thoughts that arise following the death of a beloved or emotionally significant individual. It is always difficult to disentangle the complex range of experiences associated with grief. Here I shall try to describe them from the perspective of a psychoanalyst who is a participant–observer in the mourning situation.

All Israel was shaken to its core and shattered to the depths of its soul by the announcement of Yitzhak Rabin's assassination. The shock was universal. It was a black day for the whole nation (except for the relatively few extreme nationalists, whom I shall discuss later).

The bullets that killed Yitzhak Rabin were fired at the peak of exaltation, at a rally for peace and against violence, just after the normally shy Prime Minister had joined in singing the 'Song of Peace' and experienced waves of sympathy from the huge crowd flow over him.

'There is no doubt in my mind that this mass meeting demonstrates to all Israelis and Jews all over the world, and to many in the Arab world, that the people of Israel are serious in their desire for peace,' were the words Rabin had just finished uttering. 'Today, you are demonstrating that the people really want peace and oppose violence. Violence can only erode the foundations of Israeli democracy. It must be condemned and isolated. This is not the Israeli way...' (Ben-Meir 1996:183).

Upon hearing of Yitzhak Rabin's death, many, if not most, Israelis – adults, children and youths – burst into tears. In the first hours after his death, shock and disbelief were on faces everywhere, in the voices and speeches of Israeli citizens, as well as those of the country's newscasters and leaders. Many people were unable to stop crying for two or three days, finding it very difficult to bear the experience of grief.

In this outpouring of emotion, the previously silent majority was crying out, crying together. This included restrained people who do not usually react in an outwardly emotional way, who were surprised to find tears welling up in their eyes whenever Rabin was shown on television, talked about, or remembered in their own minds. Some of these people reported that this had not been the case even when their parents had died. Others wondered how they could react this way towards somebody they did not know personally. Many were afraid of the intensity of their emotions and their seeming inability to control them.

It was amazing to see how everybody seemed to relate to the tragedy personally. In the remembrance book (Stavi 1995) in which Israeli authors wrote down their feelings and reactions to

Yitzhak Rabin and his assassination, there are many images of Rabin the restrained person with his half-smile, of Rabin on the stage at the demonstration in support of the peace process at which he was murdered, of Rabin embracing his former Labour Party rival, Shimon Peres, of Rabin speaking warmly and enthusiastically against violence and in favour of peace.

One of these authors, Yehudit Hendel, wrote that the only words one could hear in the streets were: 'It can't be!'; 'Everyone's eyes were red. It felt as if time stood still. There is only before and after' (Stavi 1995:68–70). Another Israeli writer, Yoram Kaniuck, said that he cried for Rabin the tears that he did not have for his mother (Stavi 1995:78).

This universal outburst of tears was particularly striking in view of the long-held Israeli cultural pattern of restraining the expression of grief in public. Until recently, it was considered inappropriate, in fact taboo, to cry or show one's grief (Moses 1982) even when Israeli soldiers were killed. It was regarded as a sign of weakness and unacceptable behaviour (Baram 1995). When soldiers began to weep at the funerals of their comrades some years ago, a number of Israeli politicians vented their feeling that this was against our nation's code of public behaviour. Thus journalist, Gideon Samet, overheard our previous Prime Minister, Itzhak Shamir, complain that in his time soldiers did not cry. Shamir represents an ideology that viewed softness not only as giving in or defeat, but as something that would lead to a subversion of the nation's power (Samet 1995).

This attitude of restraint disappeared on 4 November 1995, when the Israeli nation publicly expressed its grief in a manner without precedent. From the songs whispered as memorial candles were lit, to the soft voices of the groups that gathered in Rabin Square to mourn, it was clear that the entire nation was together in experiencing the tragedy. Israeli citizens of all ages, status and ethnic backgrounds felt a strong drive to be part of the greater community. This community was mourning for Yitzhak Rabin and for their country, which they felt was at risk if such a tragedy could happen.

Hundreds of thousands of people, from schoolchildren to kings, presidents and heads of state from more than eighty countries came to pay tribute to Yitzhak Rabin, the international statesman. 'I think that, more than anything else, the eighty representatives of countries from all over the world who came today to pay their last respects to Yitzhak, symbolise Yitzhak's achievements in life,' said President Ezer Weizman at the funeral.

'Allow me to say to the people of Israel: look at what you have achieved – reclamation of the desert, building a flowering democracy in a hostile environment, victory in battles and in wars, and now a victory in peace…' was part of the commemorative speech of President Bill Clinton. 'God commanded Abraham to sacrifice his son Yitzhak… but then God had mercy on Yitzhak. This time God has put our faith to an extreme test, and he took our Yitzhak from us. Shalom Haver' (friend in Hebrew), said President Clinton with tears in his eyes.

King Hussein, who together with Rabin had succeeded in developing normal contacts between Israelis and Jordanians in many sectors of industry, health, tourism and commerce – a great story not yet told (Rami G Hori 1996) – said: 'The faces of my people, the citizens of Jordan, are sad today… we pray that God will guide us… to do all that is in our power for the sake of a better future, according to the wishes of Yitzhak Rabin. Up to the day that my time comes, I will be proud that I knew him, that I worked with him, as a brother, as a friend, as a human being' (Ben-Meir 1996:186).

For many, Noa Ben Artzi Filosof's eulogy of her grandfather symbolised both the horror of the murder and the admiration that many Israelis, especially young people, felt towards their Prime Minister, whether as the image of their father or their grandfather. Noa's words moved hearts in Israel and throughout the civilised world. Some sections are given below.

> Please forgive me, for I do not want to talk about peace. I want to talk about my grandfather. One always wakes up from a nightmare. But ever since yesterday, I have only awakened to a nightmare – the nightmare of life without you. And this is beyond my grasp. The television stations show your pictures constantly and you are so alive and tangible that I can almost touch you. But only 'almost' because

I no longer can. Grandpa, you were the pillar of fire before the camp; now we are left with just a camp. Alone, in the dark, we are so cold and sad. I know that people are talking in terms of a national disaster, but how can one possibly comfort a whole people or let it share in our own private grief, with Grandma crying incessantly, while we are speechless, feeling the enormous void without you? And I could do nothing to save you. I have no feeling of revenge because my pain and loss are so big – too big... Your half-smile, which always conveyed so much to me. That same smile that is no more. It is frozen with you forever...

Israeli author, Yitzhak Orpaz, said that he went to the place where Rabin was shot to touch the ground where he fell and to try and get a sense impression of what had happened, but that he was still unable to grasp its enormity. He wanted to cry, feeling that only tears could melt the iceberg which lay like a dead weight on his heart, but no tears came. It was only when Rabin's granddaughter Noa spoke about her grandfather, her voice suffused with tears as she described how he used to caress her head, that Orpaz burst into tears (Stavi 1995:74).

Personal mourning merged with national and international mourning. It was said that 25,000 letters were sent to Rabin's home between the news of his assassination and the end of the seven days of mourning. This was in addition to the thousands of people who paid *shiv'a* calls at his home, including many who had not known him personally or who were not in favour of his drive for peace.

As relations and close friends traditionally gather at a *shiv'a* in the home of the deceased, a large segment of the Jewish nation felt the need to come together to mourn their late Prime Minister as a community. The wish to be together, to receive and share information about Rabin as political leader, as soldier, as father – Rabin in the manifold roles he filled in his life – was overwhelming for most Israelis.

Sitting hypnotised near the radio or in front of the television, hearing and seeing – and belonging – was a way of taking him inside ourselves, of building a coherent narrative to unite the tear, of separating from him gradually. Here, the proliferation of images, messages and codes disseminated through the phantasmagoria of the mass media was of key importance.

Unending crowds thronged the Knesset Plaza where Yitzhak Rabin lay in state, the graveside, as well as the spontaneous mourning sites across Malchei Israel Square – now Rabin Square – where the Prime Minister was cut down. For seven days and seven nights, hundreds of youths stood or sat on the ground there, staring vacantly into space or at the memorial candles they had lit in his name, crying, singing, playing the guitar or writing.

A flower-bedecked memorial appeared on the spot where Rabin was murdered. It was a poster with the white dove of peace imposed on black, surrounded by circles of the memorial candles, inscriptions and handwritten goodbye notes, many of them composed as if to a beloved father. A teacher from Haifa wrote that the sound of 'Rabin's Song', 'The Song of Peace', played and sung at the demonstration minutes before he was shot – with his unprecedented participation, for he knew that he could not carry a tune – will echo in our hearts forever. One of the inscriptions read: 'Three bullets were fired. Two hit Yitzhak Rabin. One has died. Six million have been injured.'

Leah Rabin said that the public's grief helped ease her own. She felt that it expressed appreciation to a great man who had not received the gratitude he had deserved while he was still alive. 'This is where he stood only a week ago. Here he was happy,' Leah Rabin said at a mass meeting in Rabin Square on 11 November 1995, the seventh day after her husband's death. 'Yitzhak... I want to believe that this disaster, that has befallen us... has not been in vain, and that we shall rise from this nightmare to a different world... because everybody knew you were their hope for peace' (Ben-Meir 1996:190).

The *shiv'a* was extremely difficult for Leah Rabin. Her feelings of emptiness, sorrow, and loss, especially at night, were complicated by her bitterness towards Israel's far-right, who she (and many others) felt had brought about her husband's death through their attempts to delegitimise him and the peace process he fought to keep alive. Leah Rabin participated in many meetings, conveying her emotions about her husband's death honestly, weeping openly, without losing her composure. Many bereaved parents who came to visit her during the *shiv'a* told her that they had not cried as they were crying now since the deaths of their own sons.

The most difficult memorial meeting for Leah Rabin was the one that took place at the Central Committee of the Labour Party, which Yitzhak Rabin had headed. She said that listening to the songs sung in his memory by some of Israel's most popular entertainers, and seeing the huge picture of Rabin looking down on those gathered, broke her heart.

Every time she joined the young people gathered together in harmony at Rabin Square, Mrs Rabin was moved to tears. Especially heartbreaking to her was the red rosebud she was handed by two young men along with a note saying: 'We will not be silent anymore.'

Reactions to Rabin's death came from all over the world, from Arabs, Christians and Jews. I shall present only a few to convey their spirit.

Hasan Abdel Rahmu, the head of one of the PLO's offices, said that he had come to the funeral as an expression of his sympathy for the Israeli people and government and to give his condolences to Mr Rabin's family; as well as to pay respect to the man who had joined hands with PLO leader Yassir Arafat on behalf of Israel and who had been Arafat's partner in the effort to effect reconciliation between their two peoples.

Ronald and Diane Wintraub from Tucson, Arizona, 'were on a cruise ship on its way from Kota Kinabalu in Malaysia to Ho Chi Minh City in Vietnam.' They reported that 'a Catholic priest and a Jewish passenger organised a combined service to commemorate Mr Rabin's life.'

Mordechai Pasternak-Hagel from Germany was stunned to see an old man in his town, a former soldier in General Rommel's Afrika Korps, burst into tears upon hearing of Rabin's assassination. As a Jew, Pasternak-Hagel was profoundly moved by this emotional reaction to Rabin's murder, which he could not help but contrast with the 'unnatural morally deficient' response of ultra-nationalist Kahana Chai members.

One month after the assassination of Yitzhak Rabin, the sense of trauma still reigned strong in Israel. 'It has only begun,' said poet Haim Guri. 'And it will never really end.'

Thirty days after the assassination journalists, Biranit Goren and Ronit Zach, studied reactions to the trauma. They were particularly interested in what those who had witnessed the assassination in person had been feeling during the past month: whether and how the trauma had changed their daily lives; what, if any, memories kept returning to their minds. The reactions of the three people presented in detail below are representative of those experienced by a wide range of Israelis.

Aliza Goren, the Prime Minister's spokeswoman, was standing near Rabin when he was shot. When interviewed by Goren and Zach, she said that she found herself unable to recover from the experience. Ever since the murder she had had no strength and found it difficult to breathe. During the first week she found herself crying several times every day. Although this had now passed, she still felt as if she was hovering, not quite 'there'. She kept asking herself what the Israeli people were doing to themselves. And she could not help but explode when she heard anyone using the kind of inciteful language that had allowed Rabin's murderer to feel that his act of assassination was legitimate.

Knesset Member, Ophir Pines, had also been standing near Rabin when he was shot. He had heard the announcement of the Prime Minister's death while interviewed on Israeli television, and had burst into tears in front of the nation and the world. Many people told him later that they had cried along with him. Others said that they could allow themselves to cry after they saw him. As Pines watched the tape of his television interview, he was amazed to find that he did not remember what had happened. It was as if he were experiencing it for the first time. 'A crisis occurred here for all of us,' he said, 'and the scar will last forever.' Since the murder Pines had become more actively involved in political life. He has begun to read books about religious education and had decided to write about the murder.

Miryam Oren could not get Yitzhak Rabin's image out of her mind. She was shown on Israeli television immediately after he was shot, saying that she had heard the shot but that the Prime

Minister was safe. When interviewed by Goren and Zach, Oren said that that was what she had thought or wanted to believe. She felt embarrassed and guilty for having misled the nation. Miryam was ill and was running a high fever. She felt that her world had collapsed. Scenes of Rabin kept flooding her head; for example, the one in which he had thrown away his cigarette after a group of young people at the peace rally had begged him to do so, after which she had extinguished her own cigarette as a sign of identification. Miryam was filled with fear. It was as if she was haunted by an ongoing nightmare. People suggested that she see a therapist, but she decided she was strong enough to deal with her trauma on her own.

The Cumulative Trauma

What caused this unprecedented nationwide outpouring of emotion? What made the experience of grief so powerful?

Rabin's death was so sudden, so unexpected, so untimely and so disorienting that it was impossible to come to terms with the trauma or digest it, particularly because he was assassinated by a Jew and not an enemy terrorist. The sense of helplessness that often accompanies traumas that occur suddenly and that one can do nothing to avoid was overwhelming. Above all, it was the abrupt loss of innocence, the intense shock related to the collapse of belief that political assassination was anathema here, a shock that a man who had survived three wars without being injured could be shot down by another Jew, that the fabled Israeli security services had not been able to prevent the murder of the nation's leader.

Leah Rabin said that her husband had never entertained the notion that this might happen to him. That was one of the reasons he had refused to wear a bullet-proof vest.

'But the feeling that "this could never happen to us" has been experienced by Jews several times in the past, most conspicuously in the case of the Holocaust, a trauma that has still not been digested half a century later. And, when that happened, we also wondered how a person could do this to others without the heavens darkening. We vowed that we would never let this happen to us again.'

The trauma of Rabin's assassination brought to heart and mind other national traumas that could not be or were not mourned sufficiently at the time; for example, the Yom Kippur War for which Israel was totally unprepared, and the Gulf War, when we were huddled in sealed rooms in what we now know would have been a failed attempt to protect ourselves from Iraqi Scuds and their poison gas.

Although many now say that the handwriting has long been on the wall, we did not believe in our hearts that a Jewish citizen of the Jewish state could take the life of any public official. Our conscious and unconscious feeling that Jews are not murderers is still so strong that we experienced Yigal Amir's dastardly act as an unbearable wound and narcissistic injury.

Particularly wounded by the Orthodox law student's act were members of the National Religious Movement, who were just as stunned as the rest of the Israelis, but who were immediately blamed for having spawned Amir, and were even attacked for wearing *kippot* (skull caps).

Vamik Volkan tells us, as Freud had written in 1917, that repressed anger is one of the causes of pathological mourning (Volkan 1988:157). He says that when anger does not appear in the first stage of mourning, it may be displaced and directed towards others. As Littlewood (1990:989) puts it, it is through the affective experience of anger that some persons tend to discharge their feelings in the service of a mastery of shock, panic and grief. But, since this particular trauma took place 'within the family,' it was particularly difficult to find legitimate outlets for our rage, especially since that might foster a civil war.

There was a great sense of injustice for someone who fought for peace then dying for it, of someone being cut down in the midst of his battle for a life free of war and terrorist attacks. This exacerbated the feeling familiar from previous traumas that we cannot trust anyone, that the 'bad ones' had won again, that there is no justice in this world.

Rabin's assassination, by one of us, also violated our belief that it is safe to fantasise or even to express one's feelings of fury and fantasy verbally, as long as we do not act upon these feelings – that we can safely distinguish between fantasy, feelings and action. For Yigal Amir and his advisers destroyed our belief that there are basic rules of respect and decency, of order and security, of what is and is not permissible.

There was a previously unimaginable contrast between the rally's slogan 'For Peace and against Violence', and the tragic way it ended. Rabin's partner in the peace process, Shimon Peres, said that he had never seen Rabin happier, softer and more at peace with himself than he had been at the rally. Everyone there and most of those watching on television could sense the bond of harmony as the hope for peace had been celebrated with the 'Song of Peace'. When this moment was turned upside down, at the peak of exaltation, it caused a horrible break. The bullets that killed Yitzhak Rabin penetrated all those who hope for peace. Our innocent belief in a better world, one without the horror of bloody wars or the cruelty involved in occupation, was cruelly shattered.

Volkan suggests that it is more difficult to mourn a loss like murder, brought about through human agency, than a natural disaster. For, when a human being commits such an act, it brings injury to the group, which often suffers a loss of self-esteem based on guilt, humiliation and shame, in addition to its pain. The guilt is over acts of omission, over not being present at the death, or for not being available, or understanding, or kind enough to the person when he was still alive. When such rational guilt is mixed with irrational factors, it may constitute a chronic complication of the bereavement process.

Guilt and Shame

What Israelis felt after Rabin was killed was more than a newly discovered affection for a fallen Prime Minister. We also felt guilt. Guilt for supporting the peace process in silence; for permitting the streets to be taken over by the dissenters; for standing by silently while hundreds of Israelis called their leader a traitor and a murderer; for indirectly and inadvertently allowing a cancer to grow in our society that snuffed out the life of the man who had come to symbolise the country's best hopes (Slater 1996:611).

Some people think that the Israeli obsession with Rabin and his family stems from a desire to right the wrong. 'Thank you for coming,' Leah Rabin says to the endless thousands who are still paying condolence calls. 'But where were you when demonstrators were calling Rabin a murderer?' This thought had struck many Israelis even before Leah Rabin's accusatory words. Many of us felt guilty and ashamed – adults, youths and children. Rational and irrational reasoning was intermixed. Miryam Oren felt the need to talk with Mrs Rabin, to apologise, although she knew that she herself had done everything possible to encourage Yitzhak Rabin in his search for peace. 'Maybe I could have done something. Maybe I could have jumped on the murderer. There was such a tiny distance between Rabin and me when he was murdered, and I'm big. That runs through my head all the time.'

'Only a crazy person could commit a murder in the name of religion,' said a Haredi (ultra-Orthodox) Jew from Hebron upon hearing that many Israelis were identifying those who wear skull caps with the assassin (Keinon 1995). 'We are so ashamed. We have lost our self-esteem. What has happened to us? Will we ever be able to feel proud again?' was another common reaction.

Many Israelis expressed their feeling of shame that this could happen here. 'The heart refuses to accept that this could happen in our country. And by a Jew!' Children and youths came to ask Leah Rabin's forgiveness, as if they had failed in having protected the Prime Minister, whom – especially after his death – they saw as a beloved father figure. One five-year-old's initial reaction to the murder was that she should have died instead. 'He was such an important man... the Prime Minister.' Similar reactions remind us of the survivor guilt from the Holocaust with which so many Israelis are still afflicted. They feel that they must live with this sorrow and guilt for the rest of their lives to absolve themselves for not having done enough for those who did not, like themselves, manage to survive. An enormous number of Israelis, on both the right and the left, are now accusing themselves of complacency at the threats that were hurled at Rabin, and of silently condoning the atmosphere that enabled his delegitimisation by those opposed to the peace process. Israeli television broadcast the statements of many political leaders and others in the public eye who said that their pain, shame and guilt at this realisation could never be erased.

Others began to berate themselves for having been bystanders, for not having stood with Rabin at the crucial moment, for not having provided the political and emotional help that might have facilitated his work towards peace, for allowing fanatics to fill the arena with their hysteria. Now these people are asking Rabin's (and their country's) forgiveness for having remained silent, for having allowed a murder to occur that will forever remain a blot on the Israeli people. Now, too, the 'decent' people who opposed Rabin's policies to the point where they did not protest signs and cries to the effect that he was an enemy of Israel and a murderer – or even called him a murderer themselves out of nationalist frenzy or fear – are saying that they did not really 'mean' murderer, that it never entered their minds that their silence would lead an unstable fanatic to feel that he had a duty to *murder* 'the murderer'.

Practically every Israeli could echo the words of the person who said: 'We watched while he was carrying out the mission that was imposed upon him, and that he accepted so wholeheartedly. We did not realise that this mission also obligated us who asked him to carry it out on our behalf.'

I was struck by the poetic expression that Naomi Ragen, an author from Jerusalem, gave in her confession, in the piece 'Too Late' (24 October 1996). I could feel her transformation of grievance into deep grief and remorse:

> I was one of those awful people who shouted at Yitzhak Rabin and called him a traitor. The nearest I can get to describe my true agenda was that I needed, almost physically, to shout out loud that the situation could not go on. Bombings, shootings, kidnappings. Blood all over Jerusalem's streets and the vile doublespeak of elected officials who called the victims 'sacrifices for peace' articulated our outrage at the latest government action. Finally, when it was almost too cold to bear, someone announced: 'He's coming.' He was in the back seat of his car facing me. I could see the blood rush to his face as the shouts and insults came through the window. He looked out at us. I could see

> the muscles in his jaw flinch. The words froze in my throat.
>
> To say that I felt ashamed would be true, but not precise. I felt as if I had physically harmed someone I know well, someone I had grown up with and admired…

That evening, Naomi Ragen recalled an article that described how Rabin had often been left alone as a little boy as his mother went off to work for yet another important cause. This made her want to cry. On the eve of Yom Kippur, 1996, she walked to Mount Herzl to find Yitzhak Rabin's resting place. 'I sat down on the cold stone,' Ragen writes. 'The dead can't hear our pleas for forgiveness or see our tears. Only the living. And when I finally got up to face a day of fasting, prayer and hope for atonement, I understood for the first time the devastating finality of the words "too late".'

Chapter II
WAYS, TASKS AND STAGES OF MOURNING

Mourning is a universal process that helps people adapt to loss, change and transition. Mourning a loss helps to restore ego equilibrium because it forces us to adapt to the fact that we have, indeed, suffered that loss. The manner in which we express our grief, and mourn, is determined by our individual, social, cultural and historical situation.

Forms of Mourning

RITUALS TO WORK THROUGH HELPLESSNESS AND DESPAIR

Rituals help the bereaved and support society in general. When Yitzhak Rabin was assassinated, people sought out rituals to help themselves face the traumatic reality, to help themselves express the feeling of being there at a tragic moment of history. As professor of anthropology Tzali Gurevitch put it, rituals helped the individual Israeli 'become part of a people that experienced this emotion' (Kaunber 1995). During the first days of mourning, the Israeli nation witnessed the strong drive of its citizens to become part of the collective, to fuse with it. The thousands of Israelis who gathered at Rabin Square and other sites reminiscent of the tragedy, symbolically attempting to repair the tear by bringing the trauma and the life together. These integrative rituals aimed to restore the social balance. Sociologist Moshe Lissak views them as a prescription for the long-term future, an injection to help cure our sick political system (Allison Kaplan-Sommer and Netty C. Gross, 10 November 1995).

There are both similarities and differences in how individuals and groups react to loss (Volkan 1981, 1988). One of the similarities is that both attempt to relive their memories of the lost one, and revive affects appropriate to these memories by identifying with people close to the deceased, or trying to maintain contact with the deceased through television and other mass media. According to Volkan, both individuals and groups utilise shared linking objects that represent what has been lost as a way of mourning it. The writing of elegiac poetry, letters and graffiti, which are shared, binds group members together as well as connecting them, the living, with the dead.

CREATIVE EXPRESSIONS INCLUDING ARTISTIC PERFORMANCES AND PRODUCTIONS AS MAJOR WAYS OF MOURNING

When Israeli sculptor, Dani Karavan, came to the place where Rabin was assassinated, he was amazed to see how that secular square had been turned into a temple of art (Karavan, 29 November 1995). He felt that the intensity and sincerity of the masses gathered there represented an outpouring of prayer. Karavan was so moved that he had to return to Rabin Square time and time again, during the day and the night, to observe and participate in the experience. What particularly struck him was that this harmonious unity, with all its endless variation, had come about without a directing hand.

In attempting to ascertain what had given birth to this spontaneous creation, he wondered whether it was the fear and doubt the assassination had stirred in those who returned there over and over, or the hope and wish to overcome the impossible death. What was clear to him, however, was that the restraint and internalisation so evident in Rabin Square was so powerful that what was created there would never be erased from the consciousness of the Israeli people.

The late film-maker, Louis Mallé, told those assembled at the Venice Film Festival that he had not worked through his shock at the injustice, hypocrisy and cruelty of the adult world, over the death of a Jewish school friend, until he had made the film *Au Revoir Les Enfants*. That film, for which he received an Oscar, was based on what happened to a young Jewish boy who had been given shelter in Mallé's school during the Holocaust, but who was betrayed to the Nazis by one of its employees and was sent to a concentration camp where he died.

Music became the primary focus of the Israeli nation's mourning for its lost leader and an attempt to heal itself. The joining together to sing popular songs, especially the 'Song of Peace', created a feeling of community and continuity. *Jerusalem Post* reporter, Allison Kaplan-Sommer, was overwhelmed by songwriter Shlomo Gronich's unforgettable performance at the memorial ceremony that closed the seven-day mourning period. Gronich had had doubts that he would be able to perform beneath the huge picture of Rabin, and in front of Rabin's family. As he began to perform, he had to fight back tears. He felt like he was floating. Finally, he performed a moving version of 'Bab-el-Wad', a song that portrays the love and mourning for the soldiers who fell in Israel's War of Independence.

When Gronich asked himself how he garnered the strength to sing, he realised that it was the desire to pray, to combine his mourning and feelings with those of others. Kaplan-Sommer said that Gronich could have been speaking for the whole country. 'The creative product may reflect the mourning process in theme, style, form and content, and it may itself stand as a memorial. These creative attempts may be conceptualised as restitution, reparation, discharge or sublimation' (Pollock 1989:114).

HUMOUR AND BLACK HUMOUR

Some people protect themselves from the trauma of tragedy through black humour (Volkan 1996:271). These jokes are a psychological outlet for unbearable tensions when no other options seem available. Among the spate of jokes that followed Rabin's death were some that dealt directly with the concerns and fears. For example: 'why did Shimon Peres appoint Rabbi Amital, a political moderate from outside the existing parties, as Minister Without Portfolio? So there would be at least one rabbi in the country without a police file.' (This was a reference to the several Israeli rabbis, at least one of them a Member of Knesset, under police investigation.) Among the dozen or more political jokes that emanated from the tragic circumstances of the murder is that told by Chanan Morrison from the Orthodox settlement, Mitzpe Yericho: 'Rabin dies and is disappointed that he is being led to Hell. He complains: "But I fought for peace!" "True," he is told. "You deserve better. But I can't send you to paradise because you have given it away."'

Another political joke redolent of black humour concerns Shimon Peres: when a bank clerk serving a long line of people asks, 'Who's next?' another person in line shouts out, 'Peres!' and everyone else in line bursts out laughing. This clearly indicates the need to discharge the unbearable tension of those days.

Volkan describes (1996:272) how the black humour that results from disaster serves the function of lessening the sadness of those who have survived. It allows anger to be expressed indirectly, and helps survivors displace their guilt over having survived and initiate mourning in an acceptable and shared way.

Another *Jerusalem Post* reporter, Greer Fay Cashman (4 March 1996), wrote about the macabre humour that followed the deadly Hamas suicide bus attacks in Jerusalem, when eighteen people were killed on bus number 18, exactly one week after another suicide bomber had taken twenty-five lives on the same line:

> Residents of Jerusalem's Katamonim area spent yesterday afternoon consoling each other and wondering why hamas suicide bombers had targeted the number 18 bus that goes through their neighbourhood. Neighbourhood resident ayala sabag repeated a macabre joke circulating throughout the neighbourhood: 'Depressed people who want to commit suicide don't have to hang themselves. They just have to get on any bus travelling from the katamonim to own.'

RECONSTRUCTION OF EMOTIONAL MEANINGS AND MENTAL REPRESENTATIONS AS A WAY OF DEALING WITH A TRAUMATIC EVENT

Building a narrative of the deceased is a way of separating from the outer figure and forming an inner remembrance of him or her. It is an important part of the mourning process for both individuals and groups as it helps them understand the significance of who and what has been lost, recognise the reality of the loss and discover its meanings for their world-view. One of our mourning tasks in Israel, therefore, was to try and understand what Yitzhak Rabin had represented for us and what we had lived through him; in short, what it was in him that we had appreciated and what functions he had fulfilled for us, consciously or unconsciously. My aim in what follows is not to present an outline of Yitzhak Rabin's personal or leadership qualities, but to bring together the feelings and thoughts about how he was perceived which I absorbed from the 'mourning environment'.

Volkan (1988:159) writes that successful mourning is said to occur when there is a predominance of feelings of love towards the lost object. The spirit of many of the loving letters written to newspapers about Rabin was: 'Let us embody the best of Rabin's qualities and the vision and determination he showed us. For he gave us hope.' Like the majority of Israelis, I too felt a strong drive to fill myself with information about Rabin and his life, to obtain a fuller picture of the lost object by formulating a narrative that would help me integrate the shock and the loss in myself, to bridge the dissonance that followed the trauma.

During his life, Rabin had not enjoyed the great love that he gained after his death. How did the outpouring of love and gratitude exhibited in the mourning period and afterwards come about? How was the legend and the myth of Rabin, the quiet hero, created so quickly. Was it a protest against those who had opposed the peace process, the group from which the assassin had come? Was this demonstration of love and even idealisation related to the 'Isaac syndrome', through which everything is viewed in terms of Abraham's readiness to sacrifice his son, Isaac, to the will of God? Was the heart of the Israeli nation going out to the innocent Yitzhak (Isaac), who had been sacrificed in the service of peace? Or was it guilt? A prayer? A secular religion? What was it that we discovered after Rabin's death that we had not grasped previously?

It seems that, after Rabin's death, the nation learned things about the late Prime Minister from his family, friends and comrades that showed a side he had never allowed the public to see during his lifetime. Thus, whereas he had often been criticised in life for being insensitive, uncommunicative and abrasive, the stories being broadcast now concentrated on illustrating his sensitivity, softness and humanness. Israeli writer Amos Oz said (Stavi 1995) that Rabin was an emotional yet shy person who felt that his feelings should remain private. 'But,' Oz continued, 'behind his toughness one could sense the softness that he almost never exposed and which many people recalled only after his death.'

'Beyond the tip of the iceberg was a man who was very warm,' reminisced Joseph Sisco of the US Department of State, who had been in close contact with Rabin when he was the Israeli Ambassador to the US, and who Sisco felt had become a real friend.

'He never forgot those who died in the war, or their families,' said Eitan Haber, Director of the Prime Minister's Office. It was particularly appreciated how, on the flight to Warsaw for one of the Israeli missions to the Nazi death camps, Rabin made a point of acquainting himself with all the Holocaust survivors on board, whom he had invited to join him on the pilgrimage.

When a mother who lost both her son and her husband in a terrorist attack bitterly assailed Rabin for being ready to free terrorists as part of the peace process, Rabin listened silently but conveyed his grief through his facial expression. As the grieving mother continued to berate him, he asked her quietly what she would do if she were Prime Minister in his stead. The woman said afterwards that while the exchange had not changed her opinion about Rabin's policy, it had changed her feelings about him.

Most impressive was Rabin's commitment and determination. As he said in his Nobel Prize speech, he had not had the same vision of his life when he was given a rifle to defend his country that he had during the peace negotiations. But he did have the same commitment to defend his country in both war and peace. 'Like any native-born Israeli who grew up in this country, I was brought up with the knowledge that we have a mission in life. I grew up fully conscious that, by our very existence and our achievements in this country, we are fulfilling and laying the basis for something momentous.' The Israeli poet, Natan Zach, commented that it was only after his death that we came to know the real Yitzhak Rabin.

> Many Israelis saw in Rabin a brave and strong man who allowed us to hope that we could change the course of our lives. Young people, in particular, felt that he was all that stood between them and the next war, between them and the disaster of an ongoing occupation (Stavi 1995). At the September 1993 declaration of principles with the PLO in Washington, Rabin said: We have come to try and put an end to the hostilities so that our children and our children's children will no longer have to experience the painful cost of the war, violence and terror. We have come to secure their lives and to ease the sorrow of the painful memories of the past, to hope and pray for peace. We will begin a new reckoning in relations between parents tired of war, between children who will not know war... Normalisation is life itself. This is the peace of which we dreamed, peace in its day-to-day embodiment.

Rabin took steps which previous Israeli governments had deemed unthinkable. By coming to an agreement with the PLO, he inspired the hope that what had seemed insurmountable could indeed be achieved. His impressive commitment and determination to fight for peace represented a major transformation in himself and in the life of the nation.

First of all, Yitzhak Rabin personified the spirit of the 'New Israel' that seeks solutions rather than salvation. As the first native-born Prime Minister, he came to the post with a vastly different view of Israel and of the essence of the Jewish people, than his predecessors. Whereas the cornerstone of the political faith of Menachem Begin and Yitzhak Shamir had been that the Jewish state was a powerless victim at the mercy of outside governments that were all tainted by some degree of anti-Semitism, this mode of feeling and thinking was alien to the sabra Rabin.

Embodying the independence and self-sufficiency of modern Israel, Yitzhak Rabin's orientation was towards openness, pluralism, universalism and democratic values. Moreover, whereas previous Prime Ministers viewed a Palestinian state as a mortal threat to Israel's existence, Rabin was confident that the Israeli army could cope with any dangers that such a state might cause. His life experience was of a Jew who was empowered on his own behalf. As such, he did not view the Arab world as one frightening mass, but as individual states that could be approached separately in accordance with the interests of each. And he felt that there was a social matrix of readiness to seek new directions for ending the stalemated confrontation between Israelis and Palestinians.

Rabin was not restricted by the ideological or religious structures that sometimes inhibit flexibility in dealing with the problems involved in peacemaking. His open mind prepared him not only to absorb new verities but to shed old conventions when the time was right, including those he had held himself. According to Menachem Brinker (1996), the process of testing intentions, the strictness with which he examined the details, as well as the gradual abandonment of his suspicion regarding the Palestinians was a central source of credibility for the peace process. Rabin tried to overcome the rigid philosophical premises of the Israeli political culture of the previous fifteen years (of which he had been a part) and to redefine Israel's priorities.

He said that he had continued to fight so long as he saw no chance of peace, but that once the possibility opened up he realised that Israel 'must take advantage of it on behalf of those living here, as well as those who have fallen in battle – and they are many.'

Rabin felt that we must do all we can, including the taking of calculated risks, to stop the bloody wars. In his July 1992 speech to the Knesset, he told Members of Parliament that the Israeli public needed to overcome the sense of isolation that had held us in thrall for almost a century; that we needed to stop thinking and behaving as if the whole world was against us, and that we needed to become part of the movement towards peace, reconciliation and cooperation that was sweeping the entire globe.

Rabin's openness to the fact that conditions had changed, his readiness to re-examine and reflect on his former beliefs, his willingness to break stereotypes, effect an about-face in order to build a new reality, all contributed to the adoration that enveloped him just before his assassination. What was less apparent at the time, however, was the fear of those who identified with the assassin's ideology and their feeling of outrage that Rabin was not listening to them.

One of the major factors that contributed to Rabin's willingness to change was his gradual realisation that the *intifada* could not be suppressed by force. After beginning by saying that he would 'break the legs' of the demonstrators, or transmitting the message that force had to be used, he came to realise that the use of power was disastrous for both victims and victimisers. He began to see that it was impossible to continue to rule over or control the 2.5 million Palestinians under Israeli rule. And he also became increasingly aware of the problems and moral deterioration of the Israeli soldiers forced to act as occupiers. Also of great impact were the results of a study of a large number of Palestinian prisoners, that what had made them join the *intifada* had not been so much Arab nationalism as the pain of insult and humiliation they had been suffering at the hands of Israeli police, soldiers and security services.

After much inner debate and conflict, which he shared with only a few friends and colleagues, Yitzhak Rabin arrived at the conviction that a different solution had to be found – that peace required concessions. Once convinced of this, and of the chance to attain peace through dialogue, he invested himself completely in achieving this goal and navigating the peace process. 'It is my ultimate responsibility as Prime Minister, as well as our responsibility as a government, to examine every possibility for peace.' It was his attitude of taking the lead in this process that corresponded to the Israeli people's need for a strong and protective father figure.

Once Rabin decided that ending the occupation and adopting a policy of peace was in Israel's interest, he did not allow his opponents' threats or doubts to deflect him from following the new course. There is little doubt that, had he not been cut down in the middle of these efforts, his courage, commitment, investment and creativity would have led to political change.

Throughout his efforts to reach an agreement with the PLO, Prime Minister Rabin retained an image of credibility. The strength, courage and self-confidence he radiated stemmed from his foresight and his thoroughness. Because he was a proven warrior, many Israelis believed that they could trust him to not concede too much at the expense of security and therefore began to view returning territories as a sign of strength instead of weakness. In this respect, his image as one who kept security constantly in mind, and particularly his ability to be tough when dealing with Arab violence at the same time that he continued to strive for peace appealed to Israelis (Slater 1996:429).

People felt that if a conquering hero was willing to return territories for peace, he must be convinced that reconciliation is possible. Roni Somek, an Israeli writer (Stavi 1995), relates the story of a woman who told Rabin that ever since he had become Prime Minister she could cover herself with a blanket and sleep peacefully. To which the Prime Minister is said to have replied that ever since he had become Prime Minister he had been sleeping without a blanket. Truth or metaphor? There is no telling. But his alleged response seems to indicate that he was constantly prepared to leap up to protect the Israeli people.

Past enemies on the left were appreciative of the inner revolution that Rabin had undergone. After his death, well-known Israeli writer, S Yizhar, said that Rabin had remained honest, faithful, responsible and analytic in a rational matter-of-fact way – that one had always been able to rely on him (Stavi 1995). And Peace Now activist, Professor Theodore Friedgut, wrote that Rabin, who had led the Israeli Defence Forces to their victory in the Six Day War, now viewed leading Israel through the peace process as the historical completion of that event (Friedgut 1995:78).

At the ceremony for the signing of the Israeli–Palestinian declaration of peace in Washington, Rabin told Yassir Arafat:

> We are destined to live together on the same land. We, the soldiers who have returned from battles stained with blood, we who have seen our relatives and friends killed before our eyes... we who fought you, the Palestinians, say today in a loud and clear voice: 'No more tears, no more bloodshed! Enough!' We do not feel hatred toward you, we do not want revenge. We, like you, are people who want to

build, to plant trees, to love and to live side by side with you in dignity, in harmony, as human beings, as free men and women.

And Shlomo Avineri, a professor of political science, argues that few people knew what was in the back of his mind when Rabin responded to the *intifada* with an iron fist policy in 1987. Rabin felt it would be disadvantageous to disclose his complex strategies publicly – in other words, Rabin knew even then that Israel would have to return territories for peace, but that he had to reach such agreements from a position of strength. To attain this, he had to first raise the morale of the IDF after its trauma of the Yom Kippur War, to rehabilitate the diplomatic and psychological status of the nation, to see a deepening in the American commitment to Israel, and to convince the Arabs that Israel was not offering concessions to attain peace in the Middle East out of weakness, but out of strength.

Rabin had strong personal and political motivations to turn to diplomatic negotiations in place of military confrontations. As Health Minister Ephraim Sneh said after the Prime Minister's death, it was Rabin's moral authority that helped convince Israelis of the unique opportunity to embark on the path of peace.

Although he was criticised for relying on only a few loyal colleagues whom he considered experts on the issues involved, and did not encourage broad discussion of his policies, Yitzhak Rabin possessed both the talent and the authority to negotiate in his own way. Taciturn, introverted and with little patience for small talk, he had an analytic mind and a clear instinct for what had to be done. He could grasp information, store it, and then use it at the right moment. As Rabin put it in 1994:

> A century of hatred doesn't dissolve suddenly with a handshake in Washington. Peace will be built slowly, day by day, through modest deeds and countless spontaneous details... We are going slowly and cautiously, one step at a time... Extremists on both sides are lying in wait for us, and we Israelis and Palestinians must not fail. At every step we must consider and weigh, check – and beware.

Israeli author, A B Yehoshua, points out (Stavi 1995) that Rabin's success in overcoming personal rivalries was another gift which people came to see only after his death. The fact that the peace process, which involved a dispute between two related peoples for the same land, was made by two men who had been bitter political and battle front rivals, Rabin and Arafat, and who succeeded in constructing some form of personal relationship in the process, added strength to the negotiations (Stavi 1995). In the same vein, the fact that Yitzhak Rabin and Shimon Peres were able to overcome the long-term personal rivalries, narcissistic injuries and tensions between them in the service of a cherished common goal, symbolised the possibility that the same might be achieved between Israelis and Palestinians.

Stages of Mourning

This process is generally considered to have several stages, each of them characterised by specific phenomena and mechanisms.

The acute stage of the mourning process begins with a denial: 'This cannot be!' Then come the reactions that follow immediately upon the loss of the object: shock, grief, anxiety and pain at the separation. Then begins the internal object de-cathexis that comes with recognition of the loss.

As the acute stage progresses, the chronic stage gradually takes over. In this stage, the adaptive mechanisms attempt to integrate the experience of the loss with reality so that life activities can proceed. Such adaptation involves reviving the moment of trauma, finding appropriate ways to remember and mourn the pain and loss, as well as the continued integration of newer demands to reconnect with oneself and one's present and future life (Herman 1992). This enables the ego to withstand the more immediate effects of the loss and furthers the reparative aspect of a more lasting adaptation. From a psychoanalytic perspective, the last stage of ordinary mourning is resolution, that is, acceptance of the loss, continued de-cathexis of the object and re-cathexis of a new object.

Veikko Tähkä (1984) speaks of remembrance formation after a good amount of mourning has taken place. He sees this as a form of internalisation.

In the Jewish tradition, there are five stages of mourning, which I shall summarise within a psychoanalytic frame of reference. The first stage occurs between death and burial, when despair is most intense and social amenities and major religious requirements are foregone in recognition of the mourner's troubled state. This stage closely corresponds to the acute phase of the intrapsychic mourning process. The second stage occurs during the first three days after the burial, when the seven days of mourning (*shiv'a*) have begun. These are days of intense grief and pain, devoted to weeping and lamenting, shared with family. The grief and pain phase in this second stage corresponds closely to those of the acute intrapsychic mourning process. The third stage, which overlaps the second, is the period of the *shiv'a*, when friends and neighbours continue to fill the house of mourning in addition to the family, to grieve with the mourners and reminisce about the deceased. This helps the mourner to begin to emerge from the stage of intense grief. By talking about the loss, and accepting comfort from others, the inner freezing that comes with the death of the lost one now begins to thaw. The fourth stage, leading up to the *shloshim* or thirty days following burial, signifies the official end of the acute mourning period. During it, the mourner is encouraged to begin rejoining society. In the fifth stage, twelve months after the death, when the headstone is set on the grave, life returns, more or less, to the pre-loss state (Pollock 1989:257–258).

Rabin's Legacy

Some of the questions that occupied the minds of many Israelis after Rabin's death were: how can we project Rabin's importance?; how can we maintain his memory constructively?; and what direction should we take to continue building on his legacy for peace? Leah Rabin declared that 'the fire Rabin left will never be extinguished!' All those who eulogised him laid stress on the importance of Rabin's legacy of 'fighting for peace'. The voice of the majority was that Yitzhak Rabin could not be allowed to have died in vain, that the peace he had fought and died for must come to fruition! Youth from the Peace Now movement translated the 'Song for Peace' into Arabic and English so they could sing it together with all those who believed in Rabin's vision of peace. To continue in his path, no matter the obstacles, was their motto. This was how they would execute the legacy with which their movement had always been identified.

Yitzhak Rabin had been determined to survive under any circumstances, with self-esteem and pride. The Israeli people would, therefore, correct the self-injury caused by his murder and not be defeated by it. We would show that we were strong enough to win peace. This too was Rabin's legacy: a psychological sense of invulnerability adopted as a sustaining force.

The determination to not be defeated by despair and helplessness was expressed in a variety of ways. Many who missed Rabin began to seek ways to turn his sacrifice into an ongoing search for peace so that his death would not have been in vain. 'Hard-liners on both sides oppose peace. But we shall not reward them by breaking down. We must continue on the road to peace as the Prime Minister would have wanted,' wrote Palestinian peace advocate M Hamed Hanan Hemet. Teaching about democracy and finding ways to enable meaningful mourning, not only on the cognitive level, was another idea of commemorating Rabin.

At the state ceremony marking the end of the thirty-day mourning period, Shimon Peres said that Rabin had trod a path upon which we would continue to march along with determination, and that he, Peres, saw this as his task.

Rabin symbolised the spirit of the 'New Israel'. The question every Israeli now faces is: how will we construct our moral, national and cultural world in a modern and democratic manner? How can we synthesise the many different poles represented while still maintaining our uniqueness, integrity and inner peace? Modern versus traditional; liberal–national versus national–messianic; a democratic society that strives towards the will and rights of the individual and society versus a *halachic* (theocratic) state in which democracy can be dispensed with – choosing one's space among the different poles, and being tolerant of other views while not losing oneself, requires a constant struggle to define and redefine one's identity.

There has been much discussion about what should remain at Rabin Square. The erection of memorials is part of the shared work of mourning. Different cultures accomplish this work in different ways. Some people have suggested that a monument or a statue is in order; others say that statues are unJewish and that a plaque may be more appropriate. *Jerusalem Post* reporter, Allison Kaplan-Sommer (1996), described a happening that reflects the wish to commemorate Rabin and the problems involved:

> About two and a half months after Rabin's assassination, teenagers from the desert town Sderot came to the site where Prime Minister Yitzhak Rabin was gunned down. They were contemplating the pile of stones, memorial candles and fresh flowers placed at the square to commemorate Rabin. Then the youths looked at the graffiti which had been written on the walls of the Tel Aviv municipal building before, pulled out their pens and wrote down their own thoughts. All over the walls their pain and anger following Rabin's murder is expressed. There are some ugly scrawls of graffiti on the wall, some small intimate writings, some pictures and drawings.
>
> Knesset Member Mordechai Virshubski, who was in charge of art and culture in the city of Tel Aviv, caused a stir when he called for a major cleaning of the municipality wall. What Virshubski viewed as dirt others saw as a spontaneous outpouring of affection and a meaningful symbol, a testament crying out against the horrible deed. It was a spontaneous reaction to grief. 'It is all we have left of Rabin,' said S as she carefully traced her tribute onto the wall. Publicly there was a backlash of opposition to Virshubski's response. The feeling was that it was too soon to wipe away the traces of the national trauma.

Changes Following Yitzhak Rabin's Murder

The months after the murder of Yitzhak Rabin brought about changes among intellectual circles in Arab countries, the major one being that – until the May elections – Israel was no longer perceived as a monolith whose main aim is the suppression of Arabs. The sight of Jordan's King Hussein and Egyptian President Hosni Mubarak alongside the leading Arab figures who came to Jerusalem to eulogise Yitzhak Rabin was a critical element in melting the emotional ice in which Israeli-Arab contacts had been frozen, wrote Youssef M Ibrahim (1995). The fact that a Jewish religious fanatic had murdered an Israeli war hero and Prime Minister for seeking peace opened new vistas to the Arab world, most of which had never realised how risky a business it would be for any Israeli politician to give up land.

The main revelation was that many Israelis, like many Arabs, looked outward from the mainstream with fear at their own extremists. 'Maybe this is the end of stereotypes of Arabs and Jews,' wrote Hazem Sagieh, a *Le Janese* columnist, a few days after the assassination. 'Maybe this is the incentive to create the counter-party, "The Peace Party" of Arabs and Israelis.'

The mutual will for stability and a better quality of life, transmitted by the image of Rabin, also succeeded in bringing Israeli Arabs and Jews closer to one another. A poll conducted by Professor Sammy Smooha of Haifa University following Rabin's assassination revealed that ninety-five per cent of Israeli Arabs generally vote for Labour and the left as the government that will fulfil both their nationalist interests and Israeli civic needs.

About three months after the assassination, Shimon Peres called for early elections to renew the mandate for peace forged by Rabin and himself. Peres called for a short, civilised campaign, without epithets like 'murderer and traitor', one of the hard lessons learned from the death of Rabin. He opened the campaign by recalling in detail the night of Rabin's assassination, scenes that are still with us.

The problem was how to remember Rabin and all he meant to us without making political misuse of his death. Peres listed the achievements of the Rabin government and of the government since Rabin's death: achievements in the educational system, a drastic cut in unemployment, new roads that opened up the country, the successful administration of Palestinian elections – the most democratic elections in the Arab world to date. It seemed, in February 1996, that the prophets of doom had been proven wrong. Even those who had poured scathing criticism on the Oslo Accords grudgingly admitted that the Accords were the only path to peace (Honig 1996).

Three months after the murder of Rabin, the right-wing parties were still suffering from an image of illegitimacy among a good part of their traditional supporters (Shragai 1996). Thus, the organisers of the first decidedly anti-government right-wing rally, held in Jerusalem on 20 January 1996, made a determined effort to restrict extremist declarations and epithets. And the fact that Uri Ariel, head of the Council of Jewish Communities in Judea, Samaria and Gaza, one of the organisations behind the rally, was quoted as saying that fifty ushers had been hired to ensure that extremists would not hijack the rally with inflammatory signs, leaflets or chants showed that the right had learned from the Rabin assassination. Ariel was referring to the extreme right-wing elements which had not been stopped at previous demonstrations from raising the banned Kach (Kahana Group) banner, distributing inflammatory literature showing Rabin wearing a Nazi uniform or calling him a traitor and murderer.

Even Moshe Arens, Defence Minister in the Likud government, was enthusiastic about the coming elections, which he saw as a turning point in the conflict over the peace process. In his view, democracy brings with it values that are inseparable from the democratic way of life, including freedom, equality, human rights, the reign of the law, tolerance towards minorities and restraint from using violence. He also felt hopeful that the Palestinian elections would serve as catalyst for the democratisation of the Arab world (Arens 1996).

Attempts at Realising Rabin's Legacy in Jordan

In his eulogy of Yitzhak Rabin, Jordan's King Hussein said: 'He had courage. He had vision and he had a commitment to peace... Standing here I commit myself to you, and before my people in Jordan and before the world, to do the utmost to ensure that we shall leave a similar legacy.'

Some of the factors involved in realising Rabin's legacy, which also became the legacy of King Hussein, were a strong commitment to and a determination to fight for peace. King Hussein, who had generally eschewed the rhetoric of fundamentalism and hatred, took constructive steps to prepare selected segments of his kingdom to become acquainted with their Israeli neighbours. Moreover, by refusing to endorse a previous boycott against Israel, he led the way to a real peace between his country and Israel. Reporter Steve Rodan (1996) reported on Hussein's public change of gears: 'We are taking a look at ourselves,' the King said, 'of where we have been, and to see what we can do to move ahead; to make this country hopefully an example to others in terms of democracy, respect for pluralism and respect for human rights.'

In February 1996, Hussein decided to bring the Jordanian bureaucracy in line by appointing a thirty-one member cabinet headed by pro-Western technocrats, and to give them a clear mandate to overcome all obstacles to full cooperation with Israel. He said that Jordan's 'wait and see' policy towards full, peaceful relations with Israel had changed with Rabin's death. Hussein's move towards liberalisation and normalisation has brought many of those in Jordan who were silent to voice their support for peace (Rodan, February 1996).

'Rabin was born again and he's amongst us,' said Jordanian farmer Abdul-Kader, referring to his new-born baby son whom he named after Rabin in recognition of the slain Israeli Prime Minister's work for peace. Abdul-Kader said he was fond of Rabin because he broke the psychological barrier between Jordanians and Israelis in October 1994, when he signed the peace treaty with Jordan. 'When my wife was pregnant I prayed to God to have a baby boy so that I could name him Yitzhak Rabin after the soldier of peace,' Abdul-Kader told a reporter. 'When I saw this man fall dead on television at the hands of the enemies of peace, I was doubly determined to give his name to my son. My wife encouraged me. When she delivered, she shocked the doctors by saying without hesitation that she named the newborn Yitzhak Rabin.' For some months Abdul-Kader paid for this decision. He was beaten by neighbours and denied employment. He even experienced difficulty in registering the name officially. On 23 March 1996, we in Israel heard on the news that the name had been recorded and that Abdul-Kader was now a happy man. This example shows how a single man in Jordan fought courageously and persistently to continue Rabin's legacy, using his King as his example.

Commemorating Rabin, Perpetuating his Name and Fostering his Achievements and Legacy

As the days, weeks, and months passed since the infamous 4 November – the date of Rabin's assassination – it became important to decide how best to perpetuate the name of the leader 'who crossed the great historical watershed,' first by recognising the PLO as the legitimate representative of the Palestinian people and then by launching peace negotiations with Yassir Arafat to end the protracted conflict between our two peoples. A law has been passed to determine how best to perpetuate Rabin's name and the special place he has earned in our history (Dan Leon, 25 January 1996).

Leah Rabin, who has come under considerable criticism in connection with her request for a government allocation to enable her to respond to the mass outpouring of sympathy following her husband's assassination, played a special role in fostering Rabin's achievement. She was enveloped with love, as if she had been charged with carrying out the royal task of representing her husband in the peace for which he had given his life.

Although Yitzhak had paid the ultimate price for his dream of peace, Leah said, she was certain that he had not died in vain. As journalist Tom Segev wrote, many Israelis follow the myth that Leah Rabin fosters and symbolises, since peace needs a hero that is larger than life (Segev, 10 January 1996). Yuval Rabin, Leah's and Yitzhak's son, who never before had been politically oriented, became politically active after his father's assassination, and headed the Dor Shalem Doresh Shalom (A Whole Generation Calls Out For Peace movement).

There is no precedent for us to follow here, wrote Dan Leon (25 January 1996), since no Israeli Prime Minister has ever been murdered before. Leon suggested that a non-profit body could be attached to an Israeli university, and warned against random memorial projects that might cause Rabin's name to be cheapened instead of honoured. Volkan writes that when the painful mourning process has been completed, our loss may be transformed into substantial gain (Volkan 1988:159). In this regard, the mourning task of soul-searching may play a part in determining whether a tragedy will remain a 'chosen trauma' that turns people into helpless victims-who-are-entitled, or whether people will utilise the loss as the basis for a new beginning. Which will the Israeli people choose?

Soul-Searching: Self-examination and Attempts at Integration

I find Hagman's way of thinking in terms of mourning tasks relevant to what I see taking place after the assassination of Yitzhak Rabin. His perspective on bereavement proposes that, rather than being process-oriented, mourning is an adaptive response to specific task demands that arise from loss, which must be dealt with regardless of individual, culture or historical era. To him, it is these mourning tasks with which the bereaved person must contend rather than a set of ready-made goals (Hagman 1995:909–920). Hagman's model encompasses elements of the mourning process that are distinct yet interrelated. This means that there is some overlapping. Several of these tasks have been discussed as I followed the mourning work of the Israeli nation. For example, full expression of traumatic memories; reconstitution of a coherent narrative of the trauma, with all the associated feelings; integration of the traumatic story into one's personal and national history, including the working through of previous breaks and reconnection or reconciliation with one's self and reintegration into one's normal life. There is also the important task of 'soul-searching', which easily turns into searching the souls of others rather than self-examination.

Who was to blame for the assassination of Rabin? Whose hands spilled his blood? What were the different areas of responsibility of each of us? Where was our neglect? How can we facilitate the coexistence of different political groups and overcome the destructive splits among our multiple ethnicities? What can we learn from the tragedy? I shall endeavour to describe the soul-searching as it took place in individuals and groups, as well as the atmosphere in which this mourning task was carried out.

Israelis on both sides of the peace issue blamed the security services for failing to protect our Prime Minister. The Shamgar Commission concluded that K, the head of General Security Service, was at least partially responsible for the fateful security failure. It is ironic that K's appointment to the post in 1994 was criticised because he had concentrated on Jewish underground movements and reputedly lacked experience in countering Arab terrorism; for the man, who was considered an expert on Jewish extremists, had failed to follow up information about a possible attempt on the life of an Israeli official but had had great success in containing Arab terror since his appointment.

It seems that the security authorities had received information from a reserve soldier that a small man of Yemenite origin was planning to assassinate Yitzhak Rabin. But the General Security Service was convinced that no Jew, no matter how extremist, would attempt to murder the Prime Minister.

K resigned as head of the GSS after ten months on the job. In his letter of resignation, he said that although he was stepping down because of the security service's failure which resulted in the terrible murder, he did not consider himself personally responsible for that failure and would continue efforts to clear himself.

The GSS failure was not confined to its information failure or to the inability of its bodyguards to protect Rabin. There was something wrong from the outset in the way that GSS agent Avishai Raviv, who was planted in extremist groups, was used by his handlers. The GSS had crossed the line between the legitimate placement of an informer and the unacceptable use of an *agent provocateur* who himself incited violence in that group and committed crimes.

An atmosphere of fear and hatred, especially towards right-wingers, filled the air immediately after the assassination. Israeli Doves blamed the overheated rhetoric of right-wingers and the National Religious or ultra-Orthodox for incitement to murder. They also excoriated parties on the right for condoning this rhetoric and the accompanying violence. The right wing and the National Religious camp responded by deploying themselves into defensiveness and ending whatever soul-searching they had begun to engage in.

One of the most important lessons learned after the murder is that both the Israeli security services and police have tended to either turn a blind eye or 'go easy' on Jewish zealots who act against the law. In this respect, Judge Richard Goldstone, who is investigating the murder of entire peoples in Yugoslavia and Rwanda, reports that his investigation has opened his eyes to the dangers of thinking that only emotionally disturbed people are capable of such atrocities. People forget that it was 'normal' people who perpetrated previous genocides against Jews and Gypsies in World War II and the Armenians in the early years of the twentieth century. Goldstone now realises that the same demonisation of 'the other' that allowed such abominable crimes to occur is still at work. He concludes that the best way to prevent these crimes against humanity is to be open to the needs and grievances of all sectors of society, the fostering of civil rights of all peoples and the active involvement of the mass media in decrying such outrages (Melman 1995).

Since 4 November 1995, the powers in Israel have taken steps to bring the fullest strength of the law down on those who threaten to destroy the fabric of society through zealotry, dogmatism or the language of hate. For the country has finally realised that democracies must take action against those who exploit or misuse freedom of speech. It is not easy, however, to determine where freedom of speech ends and incitement begins, when inflammatory speech is likely to lead to violent deeds and when it is a legitimate verbal protest that will reduce the chance of violent acts. For letting off steam verbally is an essential part of free expression, and fervency an integral part of the political message.

In the immediate aftermath of Yitzhak Rabin's assassination, these questions were sometimes thrust aside amidst the suspicion, blaming and finger-pointing against right-wingers and religious nationalists. The verbal – and sometimes physical – incitement against the radicals among them spread to the religious sector from which the murderer had come.

Novelist Meir Shalev said that there are two camps in Israel: that of peace, compromise and hope, and that of violence and hate, and that there are religious and secular people, young and old, Ashkenazim and Sephardim in both camps. But, Shalev pointed out, in only one of these camps are there murderers. And the tragedy is that the camp with the murderers believes that it is carrying out the will of God. On the other hand, Robert Avraham of Jerusalem, who considers himself a 'centrist,' wrote that while he too was deeply shocked by the murder of Rabin, he was just as deeply disturbed by 'the subsequent witch-hunt in which anyone who is religious or in the opposition is labelled a murderer.' Like Goldstone, Avraham concluded that the Israeli government must lead the way in defusing this situation by showing respect and sensitivity to all its citizens (*Newsweek*, 12 November 1995).

As difficult as it was to carry out adequate self-examination tasks while all of Israel was still in a state of shock over Rabin's murder and still subject to terror from without and polarisation within, a majority of the Israeli public on all sides of the political spectrum did begin re-examining their attitudes, behaviour and beliefs. At meetings at Bar-Ilan University, where Yigal Amir had studied law, as well as in other religious settings, people began to search their souls and deal with the failure of their system to impart complex ideas that cannot be solved by clichés or simple answers. 'For us who not only are teachers in this university, but who also consider ourselves part of the people who carry the flag of tradition and religion,' said one of the Bar-Ilan staff, 'it is hard to bear the feelings of guilt and shame that national bigotry and religious fanaticism extract from *halakhic* sources.' Both the President and the Rector of Bar-Ilan expressed the university's determination to lead soul-searching within the religious Zionist community. And officials of the National Religious Party spoke of weeding out the 'wild offshoots who misinterpret' Halakhah and distort the image of Judaism.' As will be shown in Chapter 5, such a process of soul-searching was a challenge not easily accepted.

Modern Orthodox Rabbi, David Hartman, of the Shalom Hartman Institute in Jerusalem suggests that the trauma of Rabin's assassination provides an opportunity for internal renewal in Israel's religious camps, such as the separation between religion and politics and the fostering of such democratic values as pluralism and freedom of conscience.

Orthodox rabbis of liberal orientation called on National Religious elements to embark on a course of soul-searching. Lord Immanuel Jacobovitz, former Chief Rabbi of the United Kingdom, speaking at the Conference of Jewish Ministers and Members of Parliament held in Jerusalem, said this was not the first time that 'an ideologically motivated murder with catastrophic consequences for Israel as a whole has emerged from the National Religious element... Recovery can only follow a reassessment in which traditional priorities replace temporary aberration.' Lord Jacobovitz believes that Orthodox Jews can best serve their country, as well as religion, by concentrating on the quality of the land rather than on its extent.

Rabbi Shmuel Goldin, a founder and chairman of Shvil Hazahav (Golden Path), a group of moderate Orthodox rabbis, educators and lay leaders, wrote that his group has been speaking for years about what they perceive as the 'hijacking' of religious Zionism by the radical right, but that there has been no complex and systematic thinking as to how to deal with the problem on the part of Orthodoxy in general.

Likud Member of Knesset, Tuvia Blumental, declared that 'this is an hour of group searching for all of us. We all have to ask ourselves how we can go on after the disaster, and how we can change.'

There seems to be general agreement on the part of a great many Israelis that what is needed now is to distinguish between a legitimate and loyal opposition, and extremists, whose acts must be condemned, delegitimised, and who must have their financial support cut off. A frequently expressed wish was that Jewish law will eventually be differentiated from civic law in Israel – unlike after the 1996 elections.

Etan Broshi of Kibbutz Gevat (20 November 1995) said Rabin's assassination obliges the entire kibbutz movement to conduct soul-searching into where it stands on the issue and what it has done to influence public opinion. Broshi stressed that this should include not only an investigation into the past, but on how to proceed in the future.

Soul-searching was not only carried out within groups, but also between them. 'Suddenly it seems that half of Israel is involved in a dialogue with people from the other side,' wrote *Jerusalem Post* reporter Ruth Mason (19 January 1996). Professor Aviezer Ravitzky, Chairman of the Hebrew University's Department of Jewish Studies, views this explosion of dialogue as a 'medicine' for the nation's aching soul.

I shall briefly describe several of these inter-group dialogues – some of which began prior to Rabin's assassination, but most of them afterwards – to convey the variety of settings in which they are taking place.

Three hundred army officers took part in the democracy seminars at Elul, a religious studies centre in Jerusalem where religious and secular people study together. Although these seminars have been going on for years, and have left many depressed at the seemingly insurmountable gap between them, there have been renewed efforts to find a common language.

Seventy police officers took part in workshops aimed at helping them understand and deal with religious extremists.

Bus loads of young people from left-wing kibbutzim have gone to Yeshivot on the West Bank to begin a dialogue, or at least strike up an acquaintance, with those who have different ideas about how life should be lived in the Jewish state.

Religious settlers spent a *Shabbat* at the secular left-wing kibbutz Mizra. The aim was to see if it is possible for people with values if at opposite ends of the political and religious spectrum to find common ground to communicate with one another. Some did, others found it too hard to bridge the differences.

Six hundred religious and secular Nahal soldiers (who serve most of their time in the army on kibbutzim) spent two days discussing their differences in an effort to understand each other's political ideology and lives.

Left-wing university students in Jerusalem formed a circle with hesder yeshiva students (who serve in the army while studying) from Judea and Samaria.

A right–left dialogue group, originally intended for group leaders of Gesher, an organisation that promotes meetings between religious and secular youth, has been opened to the general public.

Members of the Ratz (Citizens' Rights) Party and religious-nationalist settlers from Ophra on the West Bank, who originally met to discuss the pros and cons of the Oslo Accords, continue to meet after Rabin's murder, even though this meant overcoming great resistance on both sides.

Hala, a new group of religious and secular high school students that formed in Jerusalem shortly after the assassination, and that hopes to go national, began meeting outside the Prime Minister's residence in Jerusalem during the first week of mourning and continues to meet bi-weekly. Though this kind of group did not follow its original plan, other groups have been formed as will be described in the Postscript.

The leaders of Peace Now and the settler's movement began talking to each other for the first time in years. One of the results has been the realisation of their deafness to one another and the failure of both groups to be open to change. Another is that some of their demonisation of each other abated through meeting and talking.

The attempt to understand, to achieve communication based on respect, tolerance and acceptance, are the hallmarks of all the above dialogues. One of the first things that happened at every such encounter was that stereotypes began to fade. Thus, even if these groups do not continue meeting, they will have sowed the seeds for an understanding that could eventually spread to others in the groups they represent.

To meet the human being behind the stereotype, to find what Aviezer Ravitzky calls 'a common cultural language', were some of the goals of these encounters. By this Ravitzky means realising that 'I understand your pain and you understand mine', discovering what they have in common while listening respectfully to their differences, as well as discussing the critical issues that have arisen in these dialogues.

The relationship between Judaism and democracy, one of the

most crucial issues in today's Israel, was raised in many of the dialogues held between religious and secular groups. Although there are certainly differences of opinion on this issue, the discussions evinced the desire to create some kind of communication and understanding between those who feel that democracy must come first and those who insist that the Jewish nation must be ruled in accordance with *Halakha*, whether or not its decrees accord with democratic values and practices.

Less than four months after Rabin's assassination, Hamas terror groups struck again, killing more than sixty people and wounding more than a hundred within a week. This ongoing terror has, no doubt, had a negative effect on attempts at dialogue within Israel – as it had on the outcome of the 1996 national elections. I began the first chapter of this book with a review of the trauma caused by Jewish terror in which our Prime Minister was assassinated, and I am ending it with the terror of Hamas activists. Before we can achieve a cessation of such terrorist acts, we must understand that both Jewish and Palestinian fanatics truly believe they are carrying out the will of God.

'Hamas is an idea, not an organisation,' states the new General Security Service Head Ami Ayalon. 'There are hundreds of Palestinians waiting in line to die as martyrs.' We must hope that this is not the case with Jews who believe in the Greater Israel at any cost. In an effort to see what we can learn from the field of psychoanalysis about terror, violence and fundamentalism, we shall look at *deployment* – one of the character defences related to the social and political climate of violence.

Chapter III
DEPLOYMENT IN THE INDIVIDUAL

I shall begin this section of the book by focusing on the nature, forms and dynamics of deployment which I have seen in my clinical work with individuals, and then go on to use the deploymental perspective to discuss the social phenomena of grievance, violence, terrorism and fundamentalism – all of which are related to the inability or the refusal to mourn.

In my clinical work with narcissistic patients over the years, I have been struck by a specific configuration that I eventually conceptualised as *deployment*. In my definition, deployment entails a rigid self-organisation into a system of attitudes, roles and behaviours aimed at protecting one's self-esteem and dignity, at consoling or compensating oneself for what one has experienced in the past as unfair, painful, and humiliating; and, all this rather than deal with the hardships involved, mourn the losses and disappointments experienced and adopt adaptive and self-realising patterns.

The Characteristics of Deployed Individuals

All of us tend to utilise deployment in specific situations. When we are under pressure, we may act like soldiers, carrying out the duties assigned to us – even if these orders run contrary to what our conscience tells us. Often without noticing it, we live as if we were in a war situation, when we must do whatever is necessary to survive, without leaving any space for what we and others feel. At such times of pressure, trifling incidents take on the proportions of life-or-death matters, especially when we feel that our honour is at stake.

When we experience serious threats, any one of us might find ourselves rigidly entering into roles or positions aimed at protecting ourselves, and remaining there automatically and unconsciously. However, most of those who adopt such roles and positions are able to keep them within bounds, to use them flexibly and for a limited time, which allow us to function in our everyday lives in a more or less balanced manner.

Any deployment becomes pathological when too much weight is placed on one aspect that drives a person's life. In cases of pathological deployment, the loss of self is not only more conspicuous but almost chronic, to the point where growth and development are blocked. The deployment has no boundaries in such individuals. This is what occurs when corrective programmes are triggered automatically, as a sacred rule, without any attempt to stop and explore what the programme is (unconsciously) designed to correct and at the expense of what this might be. When individuals deploy themselves into grievance over real or imagined past injustices, this leads them to present themselves belligerently at all times, as they constantly feel they must be on guard to ward off and fight against similar injustices.

Deployed people are tense individuals who find it difficult to relax. They must always be ready to prove their special cause, as well as to prevent themselves from being discovered and caught in their weakness. Many of them lead a double life. Even when they function well or excellently at the professional level, their private lives are still devoted to blindly correcting self-injuries from the past. These people enact their exhausting programmes for instance by becoming workaholics at the expense of living a more fully satisfying and creative life. Indeed, one of the signs that may indicate deployment, is an all-consuming devotion to professional, religious, ideological or other commitments which narrows down into one-dimensional thinking or doing, and becomes locked into a deep perceptual and behavioural structure.

In effect, deployed individuals are driven to a frenzy of activity, as if by using their muscles and closing their feeling antennae they can immunise themselves from painful feelings, torturing thoughts and inner contradictions which would paralyse them if they allowed themselves to come in emotional contact with them. Cooper (1984) describes such people as difficult patients, and Steiner as 'stuck' patients (1993). In fact, most of my deployed patients had been in dynamic treatment before they came to me, but claimed that they had not been 'touched' emotionally or helped.

One of the major difficulties in treating 'deployers' relates to the nature of their motivation, which is not so much the desire to reach an understanding of their suffering, problems and conflicts, which might lead them to invest in inner work and change; but in many cases rather a compulsive need to repeat past behaviour and justify it until the 'others' or their representatives will accept their portion of responsibility for the deployer's grievance, will understand how they have wronged the deployer or at least acknowledge that they are sorry for their suffering.

Once they enter into deployment, these people are unable to leave the bunkers that they entered when they began their lifelong battle against the 'enemies' who have oppressed, humiliated or wronged them. Even though the war may have ended, they unwittingly continue to wrestle with the past through people in the present with whom they unconsciously relive their past injuries. They refuse to go back and relive the stressful situations in which they are stuck for fear of being overwhelmed by the strong and chaotic feelings which they have tried so hard not to feel; for fear of suffering again from an unbearable fall once they start to trust; and for fear of sinking even deeper into depression. Reliving the stressful situations would mean not only having to re-experience the unbearable pain they were trying to evade by the deployment, but also exposing themselves once again to the danger of being misjudged by the others who see them as troublemakers, jealous, greedy, demanding or otherwise 'guilty'. Thus, they are not able to mourn their losses and injuries and get on with their present lives. Instead, they cling to the 'just cause' that has become their *raison d'être*.

Admitting their share in the responsibility for the perceived injustices against them, even to themselves in the therapeutic process, would constitute defeat in that it would give credence to the claim that it is their problem alone. They therefore unconsciously devote their lives to proving that the fault, negligence, injustice or failure is of others and not their own. Gaining superiority and justifying themselves to themselves and to others, is one of the forces that unconsciously drives their continuing grievance and interferes with their ability to deal satisfactorily with their present personal goals and life.

Another kind of unconscious motivation that drives deployed patients often into self-defeating behaviour relates to the exaggerated sense of mission, such as fighting for the rights of a victim when the personal motives remain disavowed. As one of my patients who was compulsively driven by such a mission put it, after all the years of suffering and being a humiliated victim, all he can do to survive in dignity, without too much pain, is to demonstrate the wrongs inflicted on himself and the other children, and to protest against them. This becomes a kind of political mission for them. Then, at least following generations may escape his fate.

It is not only the need to be corrected, acknowledged and at times compensated that makes it difficult for them to give up their claim and shift the emphasis on their parts. People who devote their lives to such a mission are certain that humanity is much too forgiving to abusers, oppressors, rapists and murderers. And, understanding, they say, often means forgiving.

By stubbornly and resolutely clinging to their own misery, or one with which they identify and through which they unconsciously live their own lives, deployed individuals seek to shift and more fairly divide the heavy burden of responsibility they have been loaded with and finally achieve justice. Only then will their disrupted tranquillity be restored. Only then will they be able to reconcile themselves with their important others, deal with their own parts and reach psychic harmony and interpersonal agreement. Their lifelong battles thereby take on the coloration of a holy war which provides them with a channel for feeling honourable and dignified.

It is only after I had gained a fuller understanding of the unconscious motivations of deployed patients and their power dynamics, as well as more insight into the counter-transference reactions these evoked within me, that there was a significant change in my therapeutic approach to them (Moses-Hrushovski 1994).

Much has been written about anxiety as the central motive behind the defence mechanisms of the ego. But I regard shame, to which less importance has been given in the professional literature, and humiliation as the major force behind deployment.

Shame comprises a family of emotions that ranges from mild embarrassment to severe feelings of humiliation. Shame often expresses itself in a sense of shrinking, of feeling small and helpless. According to Lazare (1987), the autonomic reaction to shame includes blushing, fainting, sweating, the sensation of burning or freezing and a feeling of weakness. The cognitive aspect of shame, Lazare continues, is a painful awareness of oneself as defeated, deficient or exposed, as being inadequate or a failure – indeed, as 'feeling wrong' in the very essence of oneself.

Since shame inherently entails avoidance – the turning away of one's face, the breaking of contact – it is not surprising that it often remains hidden from the individual who experiences it. It must be uncovered if that individual is to be freed from its automatic constructions (Stone 1992). Another injurious result of shame is the non-communication of their real affects, to protect their self-esteem, as well as to provoke affective response in the other who should have guessed what they feel. In the treatment situation, the tendency not to communicate what they privately feel and think is not usually a conscious attempt to mislead, but an unconscious strategy to elicit an affective response in the therapist which will be reflected back to the patient – who otherwise feels empty and dead (Modell 1983).

Grunberger discusses the relationship between shame and narcissism. He describes a feeling that seems relevant to groups as well as individuals: 'Each time the child is confronted by an instinctual impulse that has not been narcissistically enhanced and integrated, this want of narcissistic confirmation will renew the pain of his narcissistic wound. He is reminded of his paradise lost, and in contrast to his earlier narcissistic omnipotence he has a searing sense of inadequacy and insignificance that can be compared with shame. Shame that the ego falls before its ego ideal' (Grunberger 1971:224).

Shame may be felt – and immediately disavowed – for being awkward, for some feature of one's appearance, about one or both of one's parents, around multiple behaviours, and even about feeling ashamed. It may be felt for having had fantasies, feelings, thoughts and wishes which one has had to keep hidden from others, and also for hiding that shame. Indeed, shame may be felt for anything that might be interpreted by oneself or others as indicating that one is weak, 'dirty', evil or a failure (Levin 1971; Lewis 1987; Morrison 1986; Stone 1992; Wurmser 1981, 1986).

These feeling states restrict the person who feels this shame both consciously and unconsciously to the point where major aspects of their lives are determined by shame or, really, by the need to avoid or counteract this shame, instead of being determined by the self and what they experience, wish and think, or about what one might be capable of, were one free to live one's life in the present.

One of the states that contributes to shame is an unfair imbalance of power or what is perceived as such. This includes feeling that one is not being treated as an equal, is being looked down on or made fun of, and especially that one is or has been forced or dominated. The world is then divided into two kinds of people: those who rule others and those who are the victims of rule; those who rape and those who are the raper's victims. Rape often becomes a conscious or unconscious symbol for a variety of states of oppression and pressure, from invasions of privacy to actual sexual or power abuse. It is thus not only the experience of being dominated, forced or raped, but also a symbol against which one is constantly deployed – cognitively, emotionally and conatively.

In their attempt to protect themselves from the paralysing threats of shame, humiliation and defeat, deployers utilise counter-shame strategies which often lead them to hurt, to offend or wish to paralyse or intimidate others. They constantly attempt to turn the tables on the real or fantasised shamer to keep from being blamed and shamed themselves. In other words, they humiliate others not only to get even but to keep from feeling offended, intimidated or hurt. These strategies are often viewed as unchangeable character traits, as givens, by both themselves and others.

Often it is difficult to tease out the specific mixture of shame, guilt and vulnerability that lies behind deployment. Since these deployments are usually enacted in such a rapid, powerful or automatic way, they often remain unnoticed by patients unaware of what they are really feeling and why they do what they do.

Being prepared or constantly on guard is a feature of deployment that usually accompanies whatever other form the deployment takes. This may mean being constantly in control to prevent exposing any weakness, failures, mistakes, or whatever may be interpreted as such. But being prepared for catastrophes to come, often turns into a self-fulfilling prophecy. It may also mean avoiding sudden shock or shame by being prepared for the worst, even though the individual knows deep down that worries are exaggerated. However, while this may calm deployed individuals, it at the same time preserves and enhances their state of tension.

A further refuge from feelings of humiliation, shame and guilt derives from the activation of inner rules which are piously observed as the providers of security against chaotic states that are threatening from within. This, for instance, can be seen in the person who will always be on time, and usually before, no matter what the circumstances, needs and wishes are. In some such cases this rigid rule has been unconsciously created out of the fear to be ashamed when some accident would occur. It related to incidents when they were not on time and wanted to bury themselves out of shame. Or another rule rigidly followed by some was 'never to gossip'. Through this behaviour they felt superiority over those who did gossip, by whom they felt offended.

Another function was to assuage their guilt and shame when they had gossiped and were rebuked. These rules are actively cut off from the stressful situations in which they were originally adopted, as well as from the functions they exert. These may be 'corrective' functions, to behave in a manner directly opposite to that of the manner of the 'offender', as a way to treat others as they would have liked to be treated.

Dissociation is a major feature of deployment. This mechanism, like the use of denial, helps the individual in certain circumstances to function in stressful states. Marks (1987) quotes a statement by Moshe Dayan in *Newsweek* (1981) to underline the fear-reducing (counterphobic) usefulness of dissociative manoeuvres, when by denial or detachment everyday life is made easier. Thus it helped Moshe Dayan to weather criticism when the opposition screamed abuse at him while he was speaking in the Israeli Knesset. 'Though it was not pleasant, I went on with my speech and felt no psychological stress. I withdrew myself, a sensation familiar to me from the battlefield, when I would cut myself off emotionally from reality. It was happening in a fog and was unreal to me, like the burst of shells, when crossing a field of fire' (Marks 1987:477). Heavily deployed individuals dissociate by employing their power in the direction of isolating painful moments from the past in order to sustain the pseudo-security they feel they have achieved. Their strenuous efforts to sever complex connections from their original context entails following rigid laws they impose on themselves in order to maintain the status quo.

Forms of Deployment

In addition to the characteristics displayed by such persons, their deployment many take many forms. One of the forms that I view as a major obstacle to self-development and change is the assuming of roles and the fulfilment of these roles either in reality or in fantasy. Some deployed individuals adopt the role of consoler, in which they feel responsible for compensating a loss suffered by the parent. In such cases, they play the role of saviour or parent to the parent who lost a significant other and is unable to mourn and thereby separate from the mourning situation. This sometimes involves 'becoming' a part of the denied part or carrying out a task that the parent has disavowed, because he or she has denied the appropriate feelings, for example, mourning *instead* of the parent or becoming depressed instead of the parent.

The invitation to enter such roles arises from thwarted needs of the parent. Indeed, many children respond to such needs almost automatically. A similar situation arises in treatment when analysts or therapists who are under heavy pressure to fulfil the expectations of their patients enter the role ascribed by the force of projective identification (Klein 1946) or otherwise.

The child's choice to accept such a role relates to the wish to please the parent and the need to relieve the unbearable tensions created by a parent or parents who are stuck in pathological mourning. Fulfilling this role may also be a way of unconsciously expiating disavowed guilt feelings, which often relate to unconscious fantasies of having somehow caused the loss, or of competing with one's siblings by becoming the perceived or wished-for favourite.

Many deployed patients who were victims of abuse automatically and unconsciously retain the role of a victim long after circumstances have changed. The abuse has left them unable or unwilling to view themselves as free agents who have choices and can determine and take responsibility for their lives. Deployment into the role of 'the good child', who automatically gives up what he feels and thinks and now wants to appease the other, often leads to a state of self-effacement in which this 'good child' ceases to know what he or she is, feels and wants. Later in life, these 'well-behaved, reliable, understanding and convenient children' often feel that they were exploited. In contradistinction to the role of the good child is that of the 'black sheep', which some deployed individuals assume in unconscious protest against what they perceive as arrogance and hypocrisy on the part of their parents or siblings. Enacting the role of the black sheep is a way of getting even with the parents they feel have wronged them. But this role does more than gain for them the satisfaction of 'sweet revenge'; it is also an attempt to gain more space for the hurt feelings which parents or other significant others have not recognised.

Those who adopt roles feel that it is safer than bursting into rage at those who have injured them or failed to protect them. But, like those who adopt strict rules which become their master instead of their servant, people who adopt roles aimed at keeping themselves calm and providing a sense of self-esteem when the tranquillity of continuity and routine due to a trauma has been lost run the risk of losing themselves in their roles. It is easier to 'become' a role than to shift from one role to another in accordance with changing needs and circumstances. Transforming these roles back into the erased feeling states and encapsulated situations in which they were formed is one of the channels through which analysts can help deployed patients find their lost selves and come closer to their real and complex personalities.

Deployment often takes the form of the assumption of attitudes and positions that are automatically, rigidly and often unwittingly activated, to the point where they largely determine the individual's functioning and ability to feel. An enormous amount of psychic energy is unconsciously invested in maintaining a self-image that was formed during a traumatic event and in 'living' through this self-concept in the present, despite the changes that have taken place in the interim.

Among the positions adopted is that of one who is being forced, as is the victim of an abuser or rapist who turns them into persons with no will of their own. These 'victims' cannot develop the tools to achieve what they might like to have or be, if they were in a position to want or even to know what that might be. Thus, they cannot rely on themselves to decide anything about their lives without becoming overly complicated and regretting what they had decided. They feel that they lack the power of judgement to know what is right or wrong. It takes a long time in therapy before they can come to realise that they are caught up in this position, to understand which conflicts and frustrations the position solved, and to see how it affects their lives. Only then can they begin to change their self-concept to that of a free agent who chooses and determines the life they actually wish to live.

Another position that helps maintain self-esteem and hope, although often at the expense of keeping its adopter from dealing adequately with the problems of life, is that of 'Peter Pan'. Peter Pans live imaginatively, as if time is standing still and there is no need to change and grow up, as if they will remain young and free forever. This position is often adopted after a traumatic event has occurred to which they are unable to adjust, and therefore unable to invest power in facing and overcoming it. It is also an indication of disapproval of the adults around, who they are reluctant to resemble. Pride is thus invested in remaining childlike and young to correct what they feel to be boring, base and unattractive in becoming grown-ups.

The 'Sleeping Beauty', is another common position. He or she is waiting for the fantasy prince or princess who will actualise all their expectations. They sit on the fence, unable to give up their fantasy wishes, unable or unwilling to decide between options. Men and women who adopt this position tend to be in a sort of war against order, planning and organising in accordance with the needs of the situation. It is often a rebellion against those perceived as pressuring them to the extent of choking them; it may become libidinised, thus obtaining satisfaction from postponement and pressure.

Another position frequently adopted as both weapon and defence is that of the arrogant and contemptuous person, who continues to enact this contempt through tones and gestures, as well as words. This contempt often indicates a split-off weakness and helplessness which is projected onto the other. Not giving importance to the thoughts, feelings and experiences of others, and despising uncertainty and impotence in oneself and others, is a variant of the contemptuous position. In such cases the contempt that has been enacted to ward off feeling insults maintains its existence in the form of assuming righteousness and superiority over others, to the point where it disrupts intra- and interpersonal communications, and perpetuates the loneliness of the child-in-oneself.

A position often encountered in the treatment situation, which presents a barrier to real change in individuals who have felt deeply offended, is that of the sullen person who remains unreconcilable no matter how much understanding is achieved in treatment. As well-known as this position is, it is often enacted in such subtle ways that it remains unnoticed by the analyst and by those with whom the patient comes into contact in daily life. Identifying these positions and roles, and helping patients who adopt them automatically to identify their pain and from where it has come, will often help them abandon the positions and explore other ways of dealing with tensions, pressures and distress.

Rather than considering the roles and positions adopted by deployers as unchangeable character traits, analysts who are able to identify them in all their subtleties can help their patients use them as a lever for reaching the painful and disruptive areas they have been helplessly caught in trying to escape at all costs. Once it is understood that the adherence to deployments may once have served as a means of survival but now presents a major obstacle to change, deployed patients are then more motivated to search and identify the emotional elements that have caused them to remain in the bunker long after the war has ended.

Being stuck in deployment is sometimes related to the tendency to libidinise the affects, to remain locked into roles and positions, like those who are addicted to the enactment of soothing behaviour or to masturbation fantasies. Indeed, most of my deployed patients remember having masturbated compulsively since early childhood and being unable to give it up despite enormous efforts in this direction. There seems to be some similarity between the tendency to yield to the regressive pull of masturbatory fantasies in childhood or adolescence, and remaining locked into roles and positions adopted long ago, even though they are interfering with constructive adaptation and development.

As I think about the power of being drawn into one's fantasy life or into an ideological world which subsumes one's entire personality, I am reminded of a Jewish joke told me by the late Uriel Weinreich. A group of people were taking a leisurely cruise on a ship when a terrible storm broke out. Soon the boat began to sink. Two were so engrossed in a talmudic debate, while the other passengers were hurrying to the lifeboats, that when someone shouted to them that the ship was sinking and they should hurry to the lifeboats, they looked at him in surprise, and asked: 'How is this relevant?' and continued their scholarly argument.

A form of deployment which connects us with the political aspect of deployment, which will be discussed in the following chapter, is what I call 'terroristic deployment'. Patients who enact this form of deployment are caught up in a sadomasochistic relationship both in treatment and in life. Such individuals attack immediately and fiercely whenever they feel offended by what they view as disregard, insult or abuse. At the same time, they disconnect themselves from the therapist, who becomes a stranger to them at such moments. Their violence is sometimes verbal, loud, abusive, harassing and cursing, sometimes characterised by the instant emotional disconnection illustrated in the above joke, and sometimes expressed in fantasy ruminations of revenge, such as murdering the perceived enemy.

The transference of patients with this form of deployment is often extremely intense, resembling a psychotic transference. Whenever they are asked to do something which they feel opposes their will (for example to free associate, which to them means to weaken their control), they attack fiercely, to the point where everything that has been slowly and painfully built up in the analytic work collapses.

It is extremely difficult for the therapist to rebuild the bridge to these patients, who often identify ideologically with terrorists. It is their conviction that only through power – whether in the form of active or passive resistance – can they bring about change in this world.

In those cases in which I have succeeded in re-establishing emotional connection with such individuals, by surviving all the tests they require me to stand up to, it has been a great relief to realise that what I sometimes took to be psychotic or psychopathic behaviour was a deploymental device in their lifelong battle; that a person who seemed to be totally closed to feelings was, in fact, soft and sensitive. But that only happened after having fought a long uphill battle in which we have jointly discovered the unique configuration of injustice as they have experienced it in the context of their developmental and social matrix; and after having uncovered their grief over losses and analysed the parts of cognitive dissonance, child mentality and fantasy that have been contributing to the despair. Only then have they become amenable to relinquishing their grievances and taking fuller responsibility for their feelings, actions and lives.

It was especially while working with these patients, and establishing contact with the psychic reality they have found so unbearable, that I began to pay more attention to the political aspects interwoven in the clinical work. Being alert to the deployments and using them as signs helped me reach the bunker in which these individuals had helplessly, stubbornly and unconsciously entrenched themselves.

The Family Background of Deployed Patients

In reviewing the backgrounds of the deployed patients I have treated, I found several common etiological factors that shed light on the dynamics specific to such patients. They tended to suffer from a failure of empathy in early care-giving, since at least one parent has had a narcissistic personality. All of them felt exploited – that they were expected to gratify their parents' needs and were not related to as separate and autonomous persons.

Another common factor was the experience of excessive shaming on the part of one or both parents, whether directly, through unfavourable comparisons of the child with another, or by having such ridiculously high, often unconscious, expectations of the child that he or she could never fulfil. At the same time, there was often a tendency to admire the special talents that many of these deployed individuals enjoy. These act to increase the children's feeling of grandiosity, their tendency to tyranny, and depression, especially when they feel disappointed and shamed at failing to meet their parents' inflated expectations and their own infantile fantasy wishes.

All my deployed patients suffered a traumatic event in their pre- or post-oedipal phase; for example, a death in the family, the serious illness of a family member or of the person himself or herself, a move from one country to another. The parents were generally so absorbed in their own tragedy or adjustment to the new environment that they were not open to signs of stress in their children, which added to the children's loneliness and feelings of desertion. Often these children found it impossible to reach the parents who were disconnected emotionally, and they felt that nothing they could do would ever be good enough and appreciated. They therefore tended to remain in a position of despair, and expected despair even after their circumstances and resources had changed, and even when they were extremely successful in many respects.

Many of the deployed patients I encountered also experienced childhood physical or sexual abuse by a member of their immediate family, a relative or a parent's friend or neighbour. They have a strong feeling that they must hide this whether out of guilt for not having objected to the abuse, out of fear of betraying the adult – who is also often liked by the child – or because of the stain of shame they feel they secretly carry. Much of the psychic energy they invest in deployments is directed at preventing being humiliated once more.

The Formation of Deployment as Uncovered in the Case of Ilana

Ilana was sixteen years old when she began treatment with me. She and her family had lived in Germany for a year when she was in kindergarten, and in Spain for two years when she was between nine and eleven. She was referred to me by the police after she had smashed a shop window in the main street of her town.

During the course of her twice-a-week therapy it gradually became clear that this act had been an expression of the fury she felt towards the arrogance of her older brothers and her teachers, all of whom she felt frequently dominated and humiliated her. Ilana had dropped out of high school because she felt that it was beyond her ability to do the required homework or to maintain the high standards she had been achieving in school before going abroad.

In treatment, Ilana talked about the fears and difficulties she had experienced in school. These had begun in the first grade, when she was diagnosed as dyslectic and sent for special remedial sessions as well as psychotherapy. To be singled out as requiring special treatment had humiliated her – as if she were retarded – as did the one-up position of her therapist, which brought her to stop treatment after several weeks. From Ilana's descriptions of what had particularly hurt her at the time, it seemed to be a combination of her vulnerability which related to the inequality she felt vis-à-vis her older brothers, who often mocked her, and some of the therapist's attitudes which had had an unwittingly humiliating element. In addition, Ilana felt that her parents had not explained to her why her teacher had suggested therapy, as if they, too, had felt ashamed of it.

Since Ilana was quite talented in non-verbal subjects like arithmetic and painting, her learning disturbance had been barely noticeable in the first years of the elementary school.

What had added to her difficulty in learning had been her family's move to Spain. Not knowing the language, and being different in dress and behaviour had added to her feeling of being shamed and ashamed. This reminded her of the year in Germany when she was five, where she also had not known the language.

She had a very vivid memory of how her inability to communicate had led to her being blamed for something she had not done, and humiliated.

As Ilana continued to share her feelings about school in Israel, it became clear that she still achieved high grades in maths and in art, but was weak in all subjects based on reading. It was after she received a failing grade in one exam, along with a denigrating remark from the teacher, that she decided she could no longer remain in school.

Though she had suffered particularly from that one teacher, she said that all her teachers turned out to be enemies. She talked about her feelings towards the species of teachers, and how she moved gradually from hating one particular teacher to hating them all. She saw them as non-humans, as if they were of a different kind. She knew that was an unfair generalisation, but that was how she felt.

As Ilana talked about these phenomena, I had the strong feeling that what she had experienced was one of the roots of dehumanisation in groups and nations as well as in individuals.

Ilana became a punk in appearance to demonstrate provocatively that she was neither a piece of furniture nor a mere grain of dust, without any unique qualities, that is there only to be trampled upon and shoved around like an object. After leaving school she made friends with a group of Basque terrorists who came to Israel to work.

Ilana identified with their rebellion and talked a great deal about them. What came up frequently was her powerful experience of leaving school. In her daydreams she frequently returned to the moment she had stood up in class proudly, said 'Goodbye' and left. She felt that this was probably the first time that she had stood up for herself after years of having felt that she did not really exist; as if she had not cared for her 'self' in all the humiliating environments she had been thrown into in her life. At last she had mobilised her strength and taken up her own space. Now she could breathe freely.

From the moment that she decided to leave school and stopped caring so much about what the others might think of her, she felt that she could begin life anew.

I have presented the details of Ilana's case because it is my experience that the effects of humiliation suffered in school situations, and those which accompany the move to a foreign environment – especially when there is not enough empathy to the emotional difficulties of helplessness and humiliation involved in the move – are a major force behind the formation of deployments.

In this respect, I believe that the entire school experience is generally not given enough attention vis-à-vis the formation of personality disorders.

Ilana's deep resentment of the injustices she suffered at the hands of her older brothers came up repeatedly in her treatment. While she, the girl, was expected to do chores, the boys were always exempt. In order to gain the love of her parents, she accepted her role but kept complaining about it. When her father took the boys to football games and she – who was no less interested in sports than they – was never invited to come along, her decision to rebel built up within her. What increased her pain was that she could never count on her parents' help when her brothers teased and abused her, since the parents thought that children should be able to manage these things on their own. But, being five and seven years younger than her brothers, she often felt oppressed and helpless.

One of the ways Ilana tried to deal with her resentment at being wronged, with humiliations, helplessness and with her great envy, was to adopt a masculine deployment. She recalled how she would march along with her Walkman, listening to music while she fantasised dreams of glory in which she was like famous actors she admired, strong both physically and in character. She made every effort to be hard and resolute, to talk like a man she admired. This was partly in identification with her successful father and disidentification with her mother, who she perceived as weak and miserable. Yet it was also a way of warding off her own feelings of helplessness and inferiority. In short, it was an attempt to correct the injustice she perceived as having being wreaked upon her in her upbringing.

In the course of discussing and uncovering fears, insults and shame from different phases of Ilana's life, of realising how she gradually deployed herself into a position of war, Ilana recalled a terrifying and humiliating experience from the first grade that she had never related to anybody. Boys had run after her during school recess, removed her underpants by force and then made fun of her. She remembered that her decision was never again to wear a skirt, a rule she never broke until she worked through her masculine deployment.

In the what follows I shall discuss deployment in a group, in the light of what I have learned in my clinical experience about how grief, grievance and the failure to mourn adequately can lead to social violence.

Deployment in a Small Group Setting

I shall end this chapter with deployment as experienced and observed in an intensive workshop for group analysts where I worked as a consultant. I was struck from the first meeting by the high quality of their work and the atmosphere created by its members. They, the co-therapist, I and the observer all contributed to the growth process that all of us experienced during its course. Although it is difficult to convey the uniqueness of the climate that prevailed in the group I might characterise it as the presence of unconscious active responsibility (Rangell 1992) as its members struggled from compulsive doing towards the mode of being – from being cautiously on guard while they still concealed their real feelings, thoughts and selves towards opening themselves to self-expression and identifying the deployments that were interfering with their development and change.

One of the members, Mr L, commented in the closing session that prior to this group, he could never have imagined how much shame he would have to overcome before he dared to tell the group about his origins in a broken family and the feelings of humiliation, falseness and inferiority which he had had to counteract throughout his life by numerous strategies. This brought another member to reveal that only now, after many years of silence, had she been able to write a letter to her parents in which she opened the door to renewed attempts at communication.

Mr M followed Mr L by sharing with the group his most significant experience from the workshop. As long as he remembered, what had distressed him most was the fear that some catastrophe would happen. He always felt that he had to be prepared for it and was never able to relax.

During the course of the workshop he found the inner strength and daring to reveal a traumatic experience of sexual abuse he had never mentioned before out of shame and guilt. To his great surprise and relief not only did the world not collapse around him, but the group did not reject him and he remained alive. Indeed, having shared his secret shame experience he felt much more accepted by the group which had evinced its empathic understanding and care. Now he no longer felt it necessary to be on constant guard not to be caught. Now he no longer had to torture himself about the possibility of the worst eventuality out of fear of being punished. His deployment into concealing his secrets had limited his ability to communicate freely, to be as creative as he might be and to be able to love another person.

Mr Z had behaved quite aggressively towards anyone who took the floor during the fourteen intensive group meetings that took place in eight days. When group members tried to link his domineering position in the present to the constant fights he had described with his domineering brother, he became contemptuous, the position he frequently assumed in the group, and insisted arrogantly that there was no connection whatsoever. He stated instead that it was his mission to save this and other groups from monopolisers; he withdrew sulkily into the position of one who has been offended through being wronged and is now misunderstood.

Fulfilling a mission was a way to protect himself from the shame of being competitive, jealous and domineering. It was also a corrective motivation to gain self-esteem by doing something he had wished his father had done for him when his brother was domineering. In his mind, he was in the role of a saviour – which consoled him from unresolved distress.

Nonetheless, at the next group meeting there was a different quality to his voice when he began to speak, and the group listened intently to what he had to say.

Mr Z related that he had had trouble falling asleep the night before as he was riddled by doubts and confusion because he no longer seemed able to distinguish when he was being genuine and when false. Once he had fallen asleep he had dreamed that he was floating over the streets, sliding on the snow. The police came after him to arrest him. He invented stories and lies to get them off his back. When he woke up, he suddenly realised how long he had been behaving as though the police were after him; how much of his verbal behaviour in all situations had been aimed at battering or warding off unknown enemies; and how he had been acting out the role of the innocent victim, abused and oppressed ever since losing his childhood battles with his brother.

What had particularly moved him in this workshop was that the group had neither retaliated nor given up on him. True, they had not let him get away with his obnoxious behaviour, but this had been because they really cared. This had helped him soften his deployment and come nearer to his inner truth so that he felt less driven to hide in falseness. Perhaps he would now be able, he said, to place more reliance on his real genuine self. The group was quite moved by this vivid illustration of how one of its members had turned from his deployment in the direction of development. They also felt that now they could better communicate with him and trust him more.

Miss O commented that she was upset. She wondered whether she would be able to find company she could enjoy after the group had concluded the course. When another group member asked whether Miss O felt that she had been hurt by the group, she responded that she had felt abandoned the night before when several members had gone in her car and had not returned when the play was over. It turned out that several group members had gone to see a play and that since Miss O had a big car they had been happy to go in it. Once Mrs L had brought up the subject, one of her riders after another had begun to describe the dreadful experience of driving with her.

Although she had driven quite dangerously, nobody had dared to say this openly, feeling how anxious and defensive she was and fearing that anything they might say would only make her drive even more recklessly. The loud laughter that filled the room as each of her riders had described the fantasies and fears they had experienced had been met by the utter surprise of the driver, who had thought she had been driving more carefully than usual.

As Miss O began to explore her behaviour it became clear that, by unconsciously deploying herself into the position of driving dangerously, she had been enacting feeling states and buried feelings from the past, for example her deep resentment over her parents' fears about her driving. She felt that her parents had been unconsciously living out their own insecurity through her. Sensing it, she had not driven for many years after she had received her driving licence since fears instilled in herself by the attitude of her parents, together with her own fears, had made her feel quite impotent and afraid.

She had worked on her own fears in her individual therapy and had begun to drive again. But her resentment was still active. Now she realised that she was saying through her behaviour: so, you don't trust me! I will therefore show you that, indeed, you cannot trust me! It is like a self-fulfilling prophecy. This opened a door for Miss O to work on other feelings and meanings which she could now sense and which had not been touched upon in her individual therapy.

The last speaker in this concluding session was Mrs W who headed a department in the hospital where she worked. She entered right from the beginning of the meetings into the role of the leader in the small group. Her conscious aim was to be helpful and constructive in her interventions. But, in fact, she filled the space with endless attempts to find quick solutions to problems that were brought up. Another member's interpretation that her interventions represented both an attempt to compete with the group leader, and the need to act in order to keep from becoming aware of what she herself was feeling, had the effect of toning her down so that she spoke less and listened more. But it did not stop her from continuing compulsively to explain away her own feelings and those of others.

It was therefore very surprising when in our last meeting she spoke for the first time in a gentle and authentic voice, and even sobbed. She was no longer as resolute and well-organised as before, she said. Now she smiled with one eye and wept with the other. She had felt burdened all her life, and had never stopped to unpack all the luggage she carried with her, to lessen the weight on her shoulders by removing what was not relevant to her present. Mrs W could now realise that here and in other parts of her life she had been enacting the rigid role of the 'good guy' who was trying to help others almost without listening to what the other felt or thought.

True, to be a physician in charge of a hospital department places a very heavy load on a person, but that is a different kind of load, she said. Perhaps she adopted her role much earlier, in childhood, when she grew up with a physically ill father and a depressive mother, and all expectations had been turned onto her though she was still a child. Because she had not been able to be a carefree child then, she felt that she could never be, as some of the other group members had dared to be, when they could share their experiences more freely and told their fantasies in a more playful way. She hoped that when she got home from the workshop she would not automatically re-enter her role as the expert adult who must help and impress everyone.

Once having broken the mould of the person who could handle anything, Mrs W mentioned another of her deployments: doing everything possible to win, as if she were in a courtroom. This was a position she had adopted vis-à-vis her self-righteous sister. Now that she felt she could also be the child who cries, how she looked to others was no longer what mattered most. Thus, whereas she had never exposed her weaknesses or allowed tears to smudge her make-up, she now felt that what counts more is what is inside her instead of wearing the mask against shame that strangles.

As she spoke, tears filled the eyes of many group members, therapists and observers. It was extremely moving to feel and see how someone who had been so powerfully deployed in her positions that most group members – and me the leader and co-leader – had almost given up trying to reach her, how she allowed her deployment to melt.

In the following chapter I shall discuss deployment in groups and in our nation in the light of what I have learned in my clinical experience about how grief, grievance and the failure to mourn adequately can lead to social violence.

Chapter IV
SOME ASPECTS OF DEPLOYMENT IN THE SOCIAL AND POLITICAL ARENA: FROM GRIEVANCE TO GRIEF, MOURNING AND CHANGE

In this chapter I shall discuss aspects of deployment as it is experienced and observed in and between groups with shared histories, symbols and perceptions. For it is my belief that the same denied and therefore unresolved tensions and grievances that predispose individuals to adopt deployments which prevent them from living freely and at peace with themselves and others, form at least part of the background of the social violence and fanatic terrorism that led to the assassination of Prime Minister Yitzhak Rabin. Whether in individuals or groups, grievances that remain denied or unexpressed, and therefore unmourned, are the basis of deployments which hinder the process of seeking productive ways to solve problems and of creating the dialogue among real or imagined adversaries which leads to integration, reconciliation and peace with oneself and others.

The dynamics of power are particularly important with regard to deployment as it appears in groups. The social and political grievances, pathological prejudices and unexpressed griefs that I have chosen to examine through the psychoanalytic lens are:

1. the phenomenon of male chauvinism in the Israeli society and the grief related to it;
2. ethnically related grief and grievances of immigrants to Israel;
3. deployments in the political arena.

I shall endeavour to explore the dynamics of these tensions and grievances and to point out what they have in common with the deployment in the individual in the clinical setting.

Many years ago, I was struck by one of Rollo May's clinical vignettes, in his book *Man's Search for Himself* (1953). May portrayed the behaviour of a bus driver who had driven the same route for forty years. One day, this driver suddenly drove his passengers along a different route in a different direction. After forty years, he simply could no longer stand going along the same way. This story symbolises the automatisation we all tend to become stuck in if we don't stop from time to time to ask ourselves whether the lives we are living are the one we want, whether there are other directions and options that we might choose if we had the freedom to seek them out.

Rollo May's book moved me in many ways. So many of us feel that we are caught up in hardships and frustrations. But these difficulties are not related only to circumstances and their limitations; they also relate to our being stuck, which is one characteristic of pathological deployments. We fail then to invest ourselves in reassessing who we are and what we feel and wish, and then to redeploy our forces in a direction that will enable us to reach more appropriate goals. This is true for each individual. And this is probably also true for groups and nations.

MALE CHAUVINISM AND THE GENDER ISSUE

I have chosen to discuss the phenomenon of male chauvinism as a form of social deployment. Even though it is not generally considered clinically pathological, it is abusive and malignant. Male chauvinism, or the macho attitude, presents a configuration in which personal motives and drives intermix with cultural values, a partly learned repertoire of behaviour, thinking styles and attitudes. The question is whether and how change can occur in the basic attitudes that underlie this phenomenon.

Professor Galia Golan, founder of Israel's first Women's Studies Program at the Hebrew University of Jerusalem (1995), argues that the myth that such changes have already taken place is one of the factors that maintains the barrier to bring about equality. One example of inequality is that out of twenty-five teachers in the Department of Jewish History there is only one woman.

As much as the masculine myth has changed over the course of time, it still is a source of much pressure for the women who feel victimised, and for many men who often feel that they do not live up to the expectations.

The myth of the 'real man' is that of a person who is tough, 'objective', and ambitious, who can dominate and control, and who has the capacity to take risks and the will to prove his courage and superiority. These traits, which are often experienced by others as offensive and arrogant, may be more pronounced in Israeli society, where they are also expected to display military traits, such as heroism, force, bravery and aggressiveness as our defenders.

Living in accordance with the myth of the 'real man' means that many Israeli men must deny their weaknesses and vulnerabilities and avoid any expression of softness or feelings, which are considered feminine qualities. Many Israeli men feel that if they relinquish this pose of power, they will forego their right to be viewed as real men. Although the efforts they must invest to maintain this role often distresses them, their self-esteem demands that they hide their distress and shame from themselves and others.

Virginia Woolf speaks about differences between kinds of mentalities:

> Perhaps a mind that is purely masculine cannot create anymore than a mind that is purely feminine... very able they were, acute and full of learning, but the trouble was that Mr B's mind seemed separated into different chambers, not a sound carried from one to the other. Thus, when one takes a sentence of Mr B into the mind it falls plump to the ground – dead; but when one takes a sentence of Coleridge into the mind, it explodes and gives birth to all kinds of ideas: some marriage of opposites has to be consummated (Woolf 1929:102).

Woolf outlines a plan of the soul in which there is a male and a female power in every individual. 'It is when this fusion takes place that the mind is more fully fertilised and uses all its faculties,' she wrote, 'that some collaboration has to take place in the mind between the woman and man before the act of creation is accomplished' (Woolf 1929:106). What Woolf implies here is the crucial importance of building a productive relationship between the male and the female within ourselves.

With such a set in mind I am discussing the dilemma of grief and grievances between men and women.

In their book, *Men in Change* (1992), Israeli authors Chen Nardi and Rivka Nardi describe the dynamics of male chauvinism which they found in many of their friends, colleagues and patients. The Nardis openly state that they could not have written this book if they had not witnessed the impact of the male myth on their own family life and that of many other families in Israel. Though movements towards women's liberation have fostered a climate in which Israeli women (except women from ultra-Orthodox families in which change is abhorred) are freer to develop new and different lifestyles and more appropriate social roles which have altered the traditional balance between the sexes, many women still are unfairly treated at home as well as in the workplace and in political life. Their grievances relate to the unfair division of labour and responsibility in the family, even though a high percentage of Israeli women work outside the home.

Whether the values that lead to this dissatisfaction are conscious or unconscious, they often lead to a lack of a feeling of self-fulfilment on the part of the woman, which in turn may result in the family's disintegration.

Chen and Rivka Nardi decided to explore the dynamics of male chauvinism as it affected the personal and interpersonal relationships between themselves as well as the married couples with whom they worked.

Their goal was to find ways to free themselves from definitions that pushed them into positions that no longer suited them. For example: (1) to be able to renounce the male precept of superiority and the consequent exhausting striving for maximum control; (2) to reach a better balance between work and family elements; (3) to develop more awareness of the feelings and multiple needs of each partner, as well as of the obstacles that were hindering change; (4) to invest in trying to find creative solutions for the problems which inevitably emerge when people leave the security of their old ways and enter unknown situations.

I shall describe some of the issues the Nardis arrived at in their exploration of the roots of male chauvinism, and the grief that resulted, and then I shall try to identify the grief they were unconsciously carrying within themselves behind expressed or unexpressed grievances.

In most of the couples studied by the Nardis, including themselves, there was a directing thought that women are primarily responsible for the well-being of the family and that what Gilligan (1995) terms 'the other voice', a form of thinking which is contextual and narrative, more creative, not formal and abstract is not sufficiently acknowledged and considered in the family constellation.

Like many men, Chen Nardi entered marriage with conscious and unconscious assumptions. One of them was that, as a man, he was expected to function as the head of the family and demonstrate his superiority in important family matters. Though Rivka Nardi works, it was taken for granted that taking care of their home and rearing their children would be mainly her responsibility. Should Chen decide to participate in these functions it would be regarded as an act of goodwill, perhaps with a hidden expectation on his part that he was to be thanked, or at least appreciated for it. There was usually no question as to who would take a sick child to the doctor and therefore be late for work, or who would remain home with a sick child or be responsible for finding a babysitter. These were usually the functions of the mother, whether or not she worked.

Researchers into gender conflicts claim that while couples often agree in principle that there should be equality, this is not the case in actuality – whether due to power motives, myths or styles of thinking, or due to circumstances such as requirements from the workplace.

The open or hidden power struggles caused by the grievances and rivalry entailed in this style of living had a great influence on the intimacy and spontaneity that Chen felt he could exhibit in his relationship within the family. The dynamics of inequality blocked not only his own emotional involvement but his ability to be sensitive to the emotional situation of his family. The style of life they thought they were capable of attaining when they were first married was not developing. They lacked the flexibility to build the life they really wanted because they could not give themselves enough opportunities for spontaneous emotional expressions of their dissatisfied, resentful and disappointed state.

Whenever conflicts arose, Chen and the other men studied tended to distance themselves emotionally. This led the women to keep their grievances to themselves and to not voice their multiple complex feelings since they felt that there was nobody 'there' to hear what they were saying. But, as Ethel Person (1988) points out, it is 'through sharing deep confidences with the beloved that we master our shame over past and present foibles, humiliations and weaknesses.'

Like most men, Chen was absorbed in the race to achieve his professional goals at the expense of what was going on within himself and his family. How had this come about? What impact has it had on his and other Israeli families? How can one change the macho patterns of living?

Chen and Rivka Nardi set out to uncover the role of power as a defence against narcissistic injuries developmentally experienced by men. When Nardi's working group first began meeting, the men found it difficult to voice their feelings out of a fear of social mockery. 'To fail at anything was awful!' most men felt, and said. From early childhood their parents and society had conveyed the message that, especially as future defenders of the state of Israel, they must avoid exposing weakness, or failure, and demonstrate success.

The constant pressure to achieve, to be superior and to be in control of themselves and others was personally exhausting. Now it had contributed to their tendency to dominate those they loved. These men tended to interpret mutuality as dependency, and they were defending themselves against such dependency, which they viewed as surrender. As Person puts it, the male's inhibited capacity for surrender damages him because it tends to preclude the possibility of the liberation that comes with surrender (Person 1988:266).

After a time, the men who participated in Nardi's male

support groups were able to relate shame-events of their past, when they had failed to behave in accordance with what they were led to believe was expected from them as 'men'. They recalled their satisfaction at succeeding to develop the armour of hardness, the 'thick skin' that helped them immunise themselves against feelings of pain and humiliation, and which sometimes involved detaching themselves from feeling in general. By restraining themselves from showing their psychic pain, they gradually became more closed to all their feelings. I dwelled on the findings of the Nardis since I think that they represent more universal dynamics behind deployments in men.

Karen Horney (in Person 1988) calls this 'the dread of being rejected and derided', and identifies it as 'a typical ingredient in the analysis of every man, no matter what his mentality or the structure of neurosis.' And Person comments that this 'dread of rejection is, for men, connected with anxiety about inadequate endowment and performing – whether sexual, emotional, or economic.' She goes on to suggest that the typical male fantasy entails the protagonist's journey either to recover or validate his masculine prowess.

It is my conviction that attitudes formed on the basis of personal dynamics, identifications with meaningful others and – of no less significance – by the pressures of the expectations of the environment, can be changed once there is a realisation that something is wrong and that people are prepared to identify the factors that are blocking them, by opening themselves to the complex interactive influences that have contributed to their deployment. And as Wheelis puts it: 'Values determine goals and goals define identity. It is founded, specifically, on those values which are at the top of the hierarchy – the beliefs, faiths and ideals which integrate and determine subordinate values' (Wheelis 1958:200). These values do not exist in a void, but must be worked through in the context of conscious and unconscious emotional motivations.

The macho attitude can be found everywhere. Thus physicians too often expect themselves to show no feelings, to act completely rationally no matter how they feel, and end up by becoming oblivious to their patients' feelings as well.

The rate of road accidents in Israel is thirty per cent higher than in Western Europe. Most of these accidents are due to the 'human factor' (Tzalal, 11 April 1995). The machoism expressed by many male drivers in Israel, who exhibit their rivalry by aggressively shouting or cursing at their 'rival' drivers indiscriminately, is seen as an opportunity for them to let off the steam related to the above-mentioned tensions, to the political situation and terrorism. This aggression leads to violence and deaths on the roads of Israel in numbers that exceed the deaths from terrorism and wars. It is a plague in Israel whose name is road-terror.

It is suggested that drivers live out the unconscious conflicts from their past and present as described by Nemiroff, Sugarman and Robbins (1968). The aggression and violence lived through road accidents may give them a temporary sense of power and manhood which corrects their underlying feelings of helplessness. It may also represent a deployment against falling into despair, resignation or deadly apathy.

The same urge that leads people to dominate their rivals on the road may sometimes merge into sadism. Person posits that individuals whose early experiences or, perhaps, their natures, render them unable to transcend ambivalent relationships, find rage an intimate and necessary part of their relationships. And this rage may emerge in the form of sadism. Whereas the dominating lover is motivated to secure his beloved's dependency, the sadistic lover has the additional need to humiliate his beloved or to deny his own humiliation and vent his aggression. Sadism, Person concludes, serves to inflate the self through the degradation of the other.

The final form of pathological male chauvinistic behaviour I shall discuss relates to the sadism that results in domestic violence.

According to the media, 200,000 women are battered in Israel every year. Seven thousand of them turn to Naamat's Centre for the Prevention of Violence in the Family for help. Many more suffer silently, whether out of fear of being punished or killed by their partners, or out of shame. Many of these women still regard their situation as a stain of shame-to-be-concealed rather than as an act to be avoided. The abuse is so traumatic that many of them not only find it hard to admit, but even refuse to remember it.

Criminologist, Ronit Lev-Arie, established the first Naamat Centre in 1983 and still heads it. She and social worker Dalya Yairi have carried on a long-term study of the sad social reality of Israel's thousands of battered women, from all ethnic, religious and social backgrounds. Lev-Arie and Yairi define a battered woman as one who lives with a man who controls her through terror, often emotional, economic, social and sexual terror, in addition to physical abuse. They have tried to utilise their findings to seek out ways to empower battered women so they can leave the circle of violence they have become stuck in. The title of their book, *Don't Just Raise Your Hands* is a message to both men and women: to men, not to use violence, and to women, not to give up their fight for freedom.

The study of Lev-Arie and Yairi (1996) shows that a firm and unequivocal demand on the part of women that the violence against them cease can be effective in putting an end to the destructive patterns of violence. Violence and 'muteness' are connected each with the other. To stop being silent and relate to the family terror is one of the conditions in trying to deal with the problem of terrorism. Threatening to leave their partners, and especially turning to the police, prove an efficient means of protecting themselves and warning the abusers that such behaviour will not be tolerated. There is also a need for abused women to look into their own behavioural patterns that unconsciously contribute to the violence; for example, the need or wish to fulfil the partner's expectations, to compensate them for their partner's childhood injuries by 'understanding' and forgiving them, as a kind of mission; or the desire to gain moral superiority over their abusers.

Many groups for violent men have been established in Israel since 1987. Most of the men who came to them see themselves as victims. 'It just happens to them'. These men do not begin to change until they can stop regarding themselves as victims of circumstances and take responsibility for their actions by examining their own lives to find why they have adopted the deployment into violence. Many of them have been emotionally or physically abused by a violent parent and adopt violence as a defence or to counter the shame connected with their own past. Only then can they become motivated to learn and practise self-restraint at a time when they are terrorised by feelings of shame and humiliation, and understand the dynamics of their pathological deployments which have been automatically used since childhood or adolescence as a defence when feeling helpless or in a blind identification with abusers.

Identifying macho or male sadistic patterns of behaviour based on individual and cultural dynamics, and identifying the kinds of deployments that lead women to accept or even collude with them may help bring a stop to the automatisation of destruction and self-defeating deployments and bring about change. This entails realising the damage of violence – and that of forgiving attitudes towards it – on all those involved, mourning the grief and investing oneself in the direction of new life values. For, 'Whether one conceives of culture as broader than society or personality as deeper, neither field can replace social analysis, but both can enrich it enormously, in part by suggesting certain long-range remedies for destructive patterns' (Sanford 1971:90).

GRIEVANCES ON THE PART OF ETHNIC GROUPS WHO HAVE IMMIGRATED TO ISRAEL SINCE THE ESTABLISHMENT OF THE STATE

The ongoing political stalemate concerning the peace process has been widely attributed to Israel's cultural divisions and ethnic tensions. The psychological problems of immigrants to Israel have not yet received an intensive and systematic examination from psychoanalysts. The Grinbergs (1984) described in their book unconscious processes activated in the individual as he or she faces the challenges of leaving one world behind and adapting to a new one, and the group processes activated by migration both in fantasy and reality. Volkan states that common elements underlie the psychology of all dislocated persons, and that these elements often lead to intrapsychic and interpersonal tensions.

Moving from one location to another involves loss – of country, of friends, of one's previous identity. Thus, all dislocation experiences may be examined in terms of whether or not immigrants are able to mourn these losses or resist entering the mourning process. The extent to which an individual is able to accept this loss determines the degree to which he or she will adjust to life in the new location (Volkan 1993:65).

In his book *Immigration and Identity* (1999) as well as in his paper, 'A Third Individuation: Immigration, Identity and the Psychoanalytic Process' (1995), the psychoanalyst Salman Akhtar highlights the factors that affect the psychological outcome of immigration in general; for example, issues of idealisation and devaluation, closeness and distance, hope and nostalgia, and superego modifications. According to Akhtar, immigration from one country to another involves a complex emotional process that has lasting effects on an individual's identity. I would add to this that it also has a great impact on our national psyche. All that is described by Volkan, Grinberg and Akhtar is relevant to problems of immigrants in Israel.

Like the United States, Israel is a country of immigrants. Since its establishment as a state, Israel has absorbed people with widely diverse ethnic backgrounds. This means that most of those living in Israel today have experienced not only the dislocation and loss connected with the move – or flight – from one country to another, but also problems related to employment, housing, schooling for their children and, above all, learning to function and seek answers to these problems in a new language. This usually involves, as well, a loss of status; for example, where professionals from Western countries or the former USSR cannot work in their fields because they lack the necessary language proficiency, or simply because there are not enough jobs in that field in a small country like Israel; or when a *kess* from Ethiopia, who had the status of chief rabbi of an area in that country, finds himself illiterate and unemployable, probably for the rest of his life.

Despite a lessening in the 'melting pot' ideology (sometimes referred to as a pressure cooker) and a move towards the new and politically correct pluralism and multiculturalism, newcomers still feel – and are – pressured to become 'absorbed' into the 'one Israel' through assimilation (Ben-Ezer 1992).

One of the main results of this pressure, a factor that in turn affects the ability of new immigrants to adjust, is the shame involved in being different from and feeling rejected by the very society they have come to in order to be accepted. In this regard, I can still recall how I felt as a new immigrant from Germany some fifty-five years ago, when hearing groups of other German immigrants speaking in public. It was the same feeling of shame that clinical psychologist Hannah Biran (1994), daughter of Eastern Jews, described, saying that the sound of the Arabic language of her parents always made her ashamed when she was a child.

What may be most insulting and ultimately painful for many of the waves of immigration to Israel is the paternalism on the part of veteran Israelis and the establishment's obtuse patronising attitude about which many complain. 'The Jewish-Israeli society,' writes Hannah Biran 'is made up in all its layers of immigrants who were torn from their roots and had to start afresh. In this society the terminology associated with those who came first took upon itself a mythical dimension. The first to come, the pioneers and the veterans are the Israeli aristocracy' (Biran 1995:46). Biran says that this phenomenon has so deeply pervaded our society that many immigrants who arrived after the 1948 establishment of the state never lose their feeling of inferiority vis-à-vis the old-timers, never come to feel that they are true Israelis. This attitude, which still characterises Israeli society today, has contributed to the arrogance and superiority towards immigrants, especially those from less developed countries.

Another factor that continues to influence the establishment attitude towards new immigrants is the Israeli myth of heroism nostalgically attached to Israel's founders.

Hanna Biran summarises some of the reasons why the true uniting, merging and integrating of Jewish Israeli society has failed to occur: 'It is a society which is suffering from the failure of its attempts at integration, repeated from generation to generation. The reasons for the failure to integrate diverse elements of the population living in Israel are psychohistorical and deeply rooted.'

Biran hypothesises that the split between Ashkenazi (Western) and Sephardi (Eastern) Jews is so deeply embedded in Israeli society that Eastern Jews who immigrated after the state's establishment never had a chance to be an organic part of the new culture. Even today, many of them still suffer an arrogant and separative attitude on the part of the Ashkenazi population that influences their social mentality. 'The people of the Second Aliya (wave of immigration, 1904–1914) who came from Russia to settle in Palestine left an indelible mark on Jewish-Israeli society for generations to come. Their values were deemed pre-eminent: settlement on the land and manual labour... The central idea was to give birth to a new sort of Jew, the forerunner of the proud Sabra [native-born Israeli]' (Biran 1994:44).

And as Volkan writes:

> The area of migration... is one in which the interplay between the external and internal worlds is prominent. The nature of external factors, the age of the newcomer and internal factors of the anxiety tolerance level, the level of ego strength (in order to deal with separation from the past) will determine the individual's ability to mourn and to adjust to the new environment (Volkan 1993:68).

Biran also hypothesises that the failure of Israel's capacity to integrate Jews from Arab and North African countries in the 1950s was, in part, the unconscious threat they posed to the emerging society. 'In the first years of the life of the state it was a society which determined clear values for itself and held onto them. In addition, there was the trauma of the Holocaust which led to the placing of emphasis upon military security. The slogan was: 'we will no longer go like sheep to the slaughter.' The national identity had to be both uniform and clear' (Biran 1994:45). In this context, she suggests, it was more natural for Israelis to emphasise 'the conquering hero' than to expend energy on trying to achieve a cohesive society. After decades of being perceived as 'blacks' in contrast to the 'white' Ashkenazim, the Jews from Arab countries internalised their so-called inferiority and began to identify with these processes, and became ashamed of their origin.

Forty years after the mass immigration of Sephardi Jews, the same process automatically went into effect when the Beta Israel Jews of Ethiopia were brought to Israel. Treated as uncultured when, in fact, they had been rendered discultured by the move from their agrarian lives to urban Israel, the black Beta Israel community suffered the same paternalistic and patronising treatment that their Sephardi brethren had suffered so many years previously.

They suffered in silence until 28 January 1996, when about 10,000 Ethiopian immigrants converged on the Prime Minister's office to protest the latest insult – an insult to their blood, which is one of the main symbols of Beta Israel society. It turns out that Israel's blood bank, fearful that the blood of people from Africa might contribute to the spread of the Aids virus, had a secret policy of destroying blood donated by Ethiopian Israelis. The insult to their blood – which the Beta Israel viewed as an insult to their community and a violation of their physical identity – led to a violent demonstration on the part of the mainly docile and silent Ethiopian Israelis, in which more than seventy people were hurt. 'Today the anger which has built up during all the years of being lied to and expected to remain quiet is being expressed,' said Addisu Messala, head of the Unified Ethiopian Immigrant's Organisation.

Prime Minister Shimon Peres then accepted the demonstrators' demand that a commission of inquiry be set up, and appointed Israel's fifth President, the beloved and revered Yitzhak Navon of 'old' Sephardi heritage, as its chairman. At the same time, Peres issued an apology to the Beta Israelis on behalf of the government for the slight to the community. At the time, it was the feeling that the policy of silence had to stop and the reasons for the discarding of Ethiopian blood – that members of the community are fifty times more likely to be HIV positive than other Israelis – be explained as having nothing to do with racism.

The fact that the blood policy had been kept secret was part and parcel of the paternal and patronising attitude towards the Beta Israelis. And no less important a factor in this mishap was the fear of bringing about hurt and humiliation. Dr Amnon Ben David, the MDA (Red Shield of David) official who continued to carry out the policy of his predecessor, did so in order not to 'embarrass' Ethiopians by refusing to accept their blood. The decision not to inform them that their blood was being destroyed was related to difficulties in communication and the lack of sensitivity that contributes to ethnic insult.

Once there was more readiness to listen to them, the Beta Israelis were more able to express their feelings of grief over the insult to their persons and their blood. What was particularly painful, they said, was that the establishment had lied to them because it felt they could not rely on them to understand the situation, that it had seemed to view Ethiopians as people without responsibility. The Ethiopian leader, Addis Messala, refused to accept the Blood Bank's explanation and requested that Peres extend the commission's mandate to include all major problems facing his community, including religious and educational issues, and the high rate of suicide of Ethiopians in the army. Said Messala: 'In Ethiopia, we suffered because we were Jews, but not because of our skin colour. We never dreamt that after all our suffering to reach Israel we would still have problems related to our Jewishness and, in addition, problems with our colour.'

An expert on Ethiopian Jewry, Micha Feldman, relates that there is an Amharic proverb that 'A large stomach can contain almost the entire world.' But, continues Feldman, 'There is no room in an Ethiopian's stomach for wounded pride. There is no Amharic equivalent for "I'll swallow my pride!" At that point, the stomach bursts' (Fishkoff, 6 August 1996).

The experts agree that it was the insult to the Beta Israel community which released the Ethiopians' rage. 'It seems that all cruelty, violence and crude behaviour are projected onto the stranger. In this way one can preserve the goodness and purity of one's own identity' (Biran 1994:50). And as Feldman put it: 'Respect is cardinal to Ethiopians. When Prime Minister Shimon Peres apologised for the blood fiasco, he hit the nail on the head. He helped restore the loss of honour felt by the community. I hope that the rest of the Israeli public will realise how sensitive the community is, how it was hurt and how important to them it is to be part of Israeli society, so that we can continue to build this fine fabric of integration between two societies which are such worlds apart.'

Maya, a young member of the Beta Israel community, read a poem she had written to the members of the Absorption Committee:

> Neither day nor night do I have anywhere to be.
> I stretched out my hand and you turned it away.
> I gave of my blood and you poured it out.

In agreeing to broaden the commission's mandate, Shimon Peres told a joint meeting of coalition factions in the Knesset that 'This is not a political subject. It is one that touches on the very roots of Jewish history.' It is this attitude of Peres and many other Israelis, in combination with the ability to take responsibility for what Israeli society has been doing to hurt and humiliate the Ethiopians, that may help their grievances from turning into rigid deployments.

It is not only an issue of solving problems with housing, education, religion and work that the Ethiopian immigrants have. It is not only the disintegration of their families and their familiar world that they have to mourn. It is of no less importance to deal with their set of grievances and their deployments against feeling the underlying grief. We can learn a great deal from our clinical work about the pain of feeling rejected and how people contribute to the feeling of being excluded. For the question always remains: what part do the new immigrant's personal strengths or weaknesses, their real or emotional difficulties, defences and deployments vis-à-vis frustrations, pressures and tensions play in the obviously difficult absorption situation?

'We do not mean that a group is like a flesh and blood organism,' writes Vamik Volkan (Volkan 1996:8), 'but its members will share reactions to drastic events.' The Israeli government's immediate and many-pronged reaction to the grievances expressed in the Ethiopians' violent demonstration should help prevent them from turning the 'Blood Libel' (Bartholet, 2 December 1996) into a 'chosen trauma' (Volkan 1988) that will be condensed into similar traumas from the past.

Volkan uses the term chosen trauma to refer to an event that makes a large group feel helpless and victimised by another large group and thus shares a humiliating injury. It reflects a group's unconscious choice to add a previous generation's mental representation of the event with its associated change of function to its own identity.

When the group draws the emotional meanings of the traumatic event and the defences against emotional hurts into its sense of identity, these mental representations of hurt and deployments against hurt, shame and humiliation are passed on from generation to generation and are transformed into severe obstacles to growth and change. Whereas when society provides means to perform a shared week of mourning and takes responsibility for their parts, while acknowledging unfairness and suffering, creative outcomes rather than pathological developmental tendencies might be entailed (Volkan 1988).

Understanding the complex group of factors involved in group deployments may be one step in bringing about the transition from pathological prejudices on the part of the establishment which result in aggressive encounters that perpetuate hatred, humiliation and fear, to a dialogue, that would facilitate rapprochement, development and integration based on respect for the identity of all the groups that make up our society.

DEPLOYMENTS IN THE POLITICAL ARENA

I shall open this section with a description of how psychological factors due to interpersonal dynamics affected the political actions of right-wing Prime Minister Menachem Begin, who was believed by all to be stuck in his refusal to sign a peace agreement with Egypt. Vamik Volkan (1990) described how after months of shuttle diplomacy, in September 1978, US President Jimmy Carter summoned Egyptian President Anwar Sadat and Begin to his retreat at Camp David.

In twelve days of intense negotiations, the two agreements known as the Camp David Accords were attained. The first contained the framework for a peace treaty between Israel and Egypt, in which Israel would relinquish all of the Sinai Peninsula. The second agreement laid out a framework for a comprehensive peace in the Middle East.

The moving story about how Begin, the tough politician, agreed to sign these agreements has been related in President Carter's book, *Keeping Faith: Memoirs of a President* (1982). On the final day of the peace talks, Begin was still refusing to sign any agreement. Morale was very low. Then a group photograph of Carter, Sadat and Begin was snapped and the Israeli Prime Minister asked to have three copies signed by his co-negotiators. He wanted them for his grandchildren. Sadat signed the photos, as did Carter, who wrote personalised inscriptions to each child. Carter describes what happened when he brought the signed photographs to Begin's cabin:

> I handed him the photographs. He took them and thanked me. Then he happened to look down and saw that his granddaughter's name was on the top one. He said the name aloud and then looked at each photograph individually, repeating the name of the grandchild I had written on it. His lips trembled and tears welled up in his eyes. He told me a little about each child and especially about one who seemed to be his favourite. We were both emotional as we talked quietly for a few moments about grandchildren and about war (Carter 1982:399).

It seems that this superficially insignificant incident led Begin to have a change of heart about the peace agreement. Soon after this interchange, he decided to sign the Camp David Accords.

Dynamics that take place in the person to person interchange exist also in groups. Once we spot the deployments into being hard-hearted and opaque towards the other's feelings and needs due to old myths and accounts, ways can be found to build bridges for reaching understanding, reconciliation and a better capacity for solving problems.

The same political deployment exemplified by Menachem Begin can be seen in Yesha, the political organisation of Israelis who settled in the territories occupied by Israel in 1967. Following the June 1967 victory, a political climate hitherto almost unknown emerged in the country. Rabbis claimed that the hand of God could be seen in this victory, and the previously secular state began to become increasingly impregnated with religious overtones. The fusion between religion and ultra-nationalism that was created moulded a new Israeli consciousness of deeply religious individuals, who were ready to give their own lives and take the lives of others in the holy war over the Whole Land of Israel which the Almighty had promised to 'his people' (Zayyad and Ciegelman 1995).

Many of these settlers and those who followed them are convinced that Israel will be overrun by Arabs from neighbouring lands if it gives up even an inch of territory for what they feel is a peace that cannot be trusted. The settlers are deployed never to forget the mass suicide at Massada in 70 CE, the conversion and torture of Iberian Jews during the Inquisition, the massacre in 1929 in Hebron and the murder of millions of Jews in the Holocaust.

These memories, certainly important to the history and future survival of the Jewish people, are also an obstacle to negotiations that might facilitate a peace that can be trusted.

In his study of the attitudes of members of Gush Emunim (the main Israeli settler's organisation) towards their Arab neighbours (1988), Israeli author and journalist David Grossman describes the use of what I call deployments to ward off the conflicts and feelings of uncertainty and confusion. They are analogous to the power ploys that people use when they are involved in a struggle with their important others.

While conducting the research for his book, *The Yellow Wind* (1988), Grossman spoke with many Gush Emunim members, who view Israeli rule over the Greater Land of Israel as of supreme importance to the Jewish people. At one of his discussions with people at a West Bank settlement, Grossman asked those present to describe how they think the neighbouring Arabs perceived and experienced the Israeli occupation. One settler immediately responded that they, Gush Emunim, are not to blame for the situation. The fact that he felt constrained to make this statement so precipitously, and that the others present nodded to indicate their agreement evinces the group's need to push aside their unconscious feelings of guilt. Then Grossman asked: 'Let us suppose that your view is one hundred per cent correct, and that history will confirm this when the time comes. But now I ask for a little flexibility in your thoughts. What do you think the Arab feels now, in his everyday life, in his very personal thoughts, together with his children? How does he perceive your presence here at this place which he has been used to viewing as his land?' (Grossman 1988:37)

Although Grossman continued to ask the same question in different forms over a period of forty minutes, those present could not or would not allow themselves even a fleeting moment of empathy, sympathy or understanding towards the people whose fate was so intimately intertwined with their own.

Seemingly frozen in this respect, the settlers could not break the bonds they could not admit existed. In this connection, another member proclaimed that he was not willing to spend even one moment thinking about the situation of the Arabs around him because, after all, he was involved in a fight with them. His statement that if he allowed himself to identify with or feel sorry for them, even fleetingly, it would weaken him and thereby endanger not only him but the whole group, was met with a murmur of agreement. Such closing off of empathy to others, not only to victims in general but even more so to victims of one's own actions, is a deploymental mechanism that is rigidly preserved as a self-survival strategy.

Some months after the assassination of Prime Minister Rabin, the Israeli public learned that a series of secret dialogues between leading figures in the Council of Yesha and representatives of the Palestinian Authority had been going on for the past two years (Herb Keinon and Jon Immanuel, 4 August 1996). The meetings had been initiated by Dr Joseph Alpher, Director of the Israel–Middle East Office of the American Jewish Committee, in 1994.

The first meeting had taken place in Alpher's garden, with himself and one person from each side. Subsequent meetings, with an increasing number of participants, were held in Jerusalem and at the Foundation for International Security in London. Alpher says that, although the intention was not to reach a political solution, these talks did have political consequences. He told *Jerusalem Post* reporters Keinon and Immanuel that:

> This was the best way to break down the very rigid stereotypes they had of one another. There was no aspiration to get them to agree. But both sides wanted to avoid bloodshed and they got to know each other as human beings. ...Most of the Palestinian leadership which came from abroad had very strong notions of what the others were about. They thought the settlements were fortresses where few people actually worked. The settlers had very fixed stereotypes of Palestinians. Their views corresponded to the ways people generally saw the PLO twenty years ago.

The decision to avoid political discussion was made to prevent the meetings from getting 'into ideologies which are pretty close to a zero-sum-game.' Settlers wanted to know if they could travel through Palestinian towns. Palestinians wanted to ensure that settlers would not disrupt Palestinian elections. Despite the decision to stick to the problems of everyday life on both sides, a crack in the deployments of both political groups took place during the meetings. More about the positions of the settlers and their deployments will be portrayed in Chapter 5.

But not every member of the Council was in favour of these meetings once they were discovered. Yesha spokesman Yehiel Leiter said they did more harm than good because the Council was already at a crossroads that threatened its future. While some felt that the talks merely allow a coming to grips with reality, the majority viewed these meetings as affording Palestinians the recognition that would ultimately injure Eretz Israel (the Land of Israel). Keinon (4 August 1996) pointed out that this might force the Council to decide on a direction sooner rather than later.

The same deploymental closing off of themselves and of their empathy to others out of fear of allowing themselves to feel shame or guilt that might weaken, break or even disintegrate them, came up at a meeting of Palestinian and Jewish teachers with whom I worked several years ago. Here the right-wing Jews would declaim against Arab ingratitude for the benefits they had been provided by the Israeli government, and against continued acts of Arab terrorism. Here, too, the aggression of the Jewish members was employed in the service of defending themselves against their guilt and shame. When I suggested this to the group, I was amazed that it took quite some time before any of the Jews present expressed any notion of what Israeli Jews had to feel guilty about.

Similar mechanisms of deployment, of returning over and over again to the wrongs of the past instead of working for the potential of the present and the future, have been experienced on both sides of the fence. Thus Israeli journalist Yair Horowitz (1993) cites an anonymous Palestinian journalist at a meeting in Spain as saying: 'One could not expect that everything would fall into place just by putting the two peoples, or their representatives together. What the Palestinians need more than anything is freedom and the development of their independence, while the Israelis need recognition and psychological acknowledgement to overcome their fears.' When a number of Palestinians looked askance at this remark, the journalist added: 'It is difficult for us Palestinians to believe that the Jews are really afraid. We do not understand how Israel, strong as it is, with a strong army and so many resources, could be afraid of Arabs. But it is true. They are afraid and do need help in overcoming these fears.'

Many Palestinians fail to understand Israeli fears of another Massada, another Inquisition, another Holocaust – which would erase the gains the Jewish people have made towards maintaining themselves as a viable nation and religion. These Palestinians see Israel as their occupiers and as the strongest military power in the region. Their deployment into victims does not allow them to understand how acts of terror operationalise the Israeli deployment into 'Never Again'. This Palestinian journalist seemed to understand that group deployments exist on both sides.

This exchange reminded me of how moved Yitzhak Rabin was when Anwar Sadat stood before the Knesset on 20 November 1977 and told those assembled that he understood the Israeli need for security. 'The mere fact that an Arab leader who had waged war against Israel came forth and stated that he understood our need for security and that a way must be found to meet our legitimate concern was absolutely revolutionary' (Slater 1996:368). Becoming aware of the deploymental aspects that affect both sides' ability to come to an accommodation may be a major step on the road towards reconciliation. If it goes together with the needed policy of the peace process, it might even diminish terrorist acts.

Israeli journalist Gideon Levi (1993) wrote about a group of Jews and Arabs who met with a rabbi and an imam in an effort to present a unified front against fundamentalism on both sides. This small group attempted to deal with fanaticism and the individual correlates of fundamentalism, two stances which function similarly vis-à-vis warding off signs of weakness in deployed individuals and groups as will be discussed in the following chapters. With the encouragement of the imam and the rabbi, and under the influence of individuals from both communities who constituted a positive and constructive core, this group began their efforts to reach national rapprochement by first meeting each other and trying to break their own stereotypical views of 'the other'. The fact that they entered this mutual effort regretting the sorry state of affairs that still exists between their two peoples, and wishing to do whatever is possible to improve what is improvable, indicates that they are able to mourn what is tragic instead of clinging to pathological grief and grievances. But even though it is a far cry from these steps towards mutual recognition and dialogue to real reconciliation on a national level, it is still my belief that such encounters may in the long run contribute to such reconciliation.

One of the major obstacles to reconciliation on the part of many Palestinians is their claim that Israelis must recognise the injustice of the occupation before there can be any reconciliation. This is typical for those deployed into grievance. They add that, even if it is true that if the Palestinian leadership had not rejected the UN partition plan in 1948 and not preferred war to continued negotiations, the question today is what can and should be done to solve problems of the present and to restore the rights and honour of the Palestinian refugees. What appears so crucial for both groups is the capacity to identify the feelings of grief related to loss which underlie the grievance, to mourn and be more liberated for the present and future, rather than remain in positions of grievance and bring about self-defeat.

At the other pole of consciousness are those Israelis for whom the establishment of Israel was the fulfilment of an age-old dream and a means of national survival. Before these people are prepared to seek reconciliation with the Palestinians, much less agreeing to a Palestinian state, they insist that the Palestinians give up any idea of restitution for damages they brought upon themselves, stop all acts of terror and violence, change their covenant finally and publicly – in short, begin implementing the concept of peace in their speeches, actions and education.

Although these Israelis emphasise full symmetry in the mutual fostering of peace, they do not necessarily recognise the Palestinian need for recognition of what they continue to view as injustices and as their condition for reconciliation.

A major task for both sides is to mourn our dreams so we can get on with our lives (Gideon Levi, 14 January 1996). David Grossman (1988) asks whether we Israelis are all reacting as if we are still in a situation where nothing can save us unless we concentrate all our power on defence, whether we are so fixated in our state of stress that we are incapable of giving 'even an inch' out of fear that we will lose everything once again, and be humiliated anew as a nation. How did this trauma stop us from seeing reality and set us unconsciously in the direction of closing ourselves to the only chance to live peacefully with the other?

A central question for both sides is how to remember the tragedies of the past, and to do whatever is possible to prevent them from happening again, without allowing traumatic events from the past to prevent us from living in the present, investing in and hoping for a better and more creative future. Despite the difficulties that deployed individuals and groups have in giving up what they have owned and dreamed about for so many years, and what has served as both consolation and a strengthening device, once there is some kind of breakthrough in the direction of mourning losses, working through deployments, ceasing to function automatically and to become open to present needs and possibilities, there is a glimmer of hope for a better future.

To summarise the elements of deployment that are common to individuals and groups, I would like to spell out the following aspects: feelings of grievance that endeavour to justify the real and perceived complaints against unjust acts; an emphasis on the sense of entitlement (Moses and Moses-Hrushovski 1990), one of the defences against humiliation and shame, as an endeavour to retrieve what is felt to have been lost or denied; the exertion of excessive power to achieve goals, which constitute an unconscious obstacle to change and growth; dissociation between feelings and their motives, between feelings and actions, between self-experiences of the past and present memories thereof, between intellectual parts and emotional ones, with coexistent alternative ego states in which several selves seem to function at the same time, one not aware of the other; the strong wish for and investment of psychic energy in reparative correction aimed at correcting unfair and humiliating treatment from the past in fantasy or real life in order to re-establish the lost state of psychic equilibrium; there is a strong sense of mission, of a drive to be of special service to humanity mixed with the child's grandiose thinking related unconsciously to narcissistic injuries from the past. This sets the stage for the next chapter which takes up the topic of terrorism.

Chapter V
GRIEVANCE, FANATICISM AND TERRORISM

The assassination of Israeli Prime Minister Yitzhak Rabin shocked the Israeli people and the world. Israelis in particular were stunned that this man, the first national leader to approach a comprehensive settlement with the Palestinians and Israel's Arab neighbours, had placed his political life on the line in an effort to put an end to violence and terrorism, and had now been cut down in the midst of this attempt by a Jewish terrorist, by one of their own fellow citizens.

At first, people sought comfort in the hope that Yigal Amir, the Bar Ilan University law student who had carried out the assassination 'in the name of the Jewish people', was mentally deranged. But almost immediately it became clear that Amir could not be described as psychotic, as a psychopath, or even as emotionally disturbed in accordance with the classic textbook definitions of these terms. Nonetheless, it is clear that Yigal Amir was emotionally unhinged by his obsession, which ties in with pathological deployment.

After his apprehension and arrest, he spent much time telling whoever would listen that his act had not been the act of a criminal but rather of someone who was ready to sacrifice his life – at least his freedom – to preserve the ideals and the love of his people for their land. That he sacrificed the life of a man who felt the same way, but for diametrically opposed reasons, never bothered him. He insisted that he felt no remorse! In short, Yigal Amir would seem to belong to the group of true-believer terrorists who view their acts against those who disagree with them as a holy mission (Dror 1996).

Terrorism has been defined as a form of political violence

evolving out of social, economic, psychological and political problems. It is designed to influence the attitudes of those whose reactions will determine the political outcome (Weinberg 1992). These acts of violence 'from below' are intended to express rage against, to disrupt or to topple the existing political order (Volkan 1993). Each terrorist and his or her act of terrorism must therefore be studied in the context of the national culture and history that shaped them. I shall thus outline some of the psychopolitical and historical phenomena which may have contributed to the ideology that motivated Yigal Amir to try to change the course of Middle Eastern history with the three shots he fired.

The Six Day War was a major event in the transformation of Religious Zionism. For many of the factions of the Orthodox community, the Israel Defence Forces' miraculous victory over the combined Arab armies that were threatening to destroy the Jewish state, the consequent liberation of the sanctified parts of the Land of Israel, including the Temple Mount and the Western Wall, and the unification of Jerusalem were seen as heavenly signs that the age of the Messiah was nearing.

Religious Jews viewed events in 1967 as a turning point, as a fulfilment of the prophecy that Israel would control and settle the full biblical extent of the Jewish land. This fusion of nationalism and messianic prophecy produced a movement of settlers who were reclaiming the eternal right of all Jews to the biblical Land of Israel. These religious Zionists, who believe that all this land was given to them by God, and that no political leader could give the land away again, adopted the Zionist credo of creating a territorial base for the Jewish people with zeal. Aided by the government, they established settlements throughout the West Bank and the Gaza Strip which Israel had occupied after the 1967 war. For them, the dismantling of these settlements, which now began to be considered, constituted a blow to the national interest as well as to the Word of God.

One manifestation of the attempt of the National Religious party to reconcile their religious and national orientations was by establishing *Yeshivot Hesder*, or places of learning, that combined Talmudic studies with military service, in the vicinity of the new settlements. Hesder soldier-students were encouraged by their rabbis and youth movement leaders to be the best in both military service and religious studies, two seemingly incompatible areas. The *Hesder Yeshivot* produced a group of highly motivated young men with a strong national identity, committed to both Jewish and Zionist core values. But the inherent contradiction between these two values caused many of them to suffer divided loyalties between their rabbis and their commanding officers. In addition, these young men who, we must not forget, are between the ages of eighteen and twenty-one, often felt that their status was being challenged by both the secular and the ultra-Orthodox communities.

In the subsequent search for an ideal that would demonstrate their validity and uniqueness to both themselves and to others, they began to focus on Eretz Israel, or the biblical Land of Israel. Eretz Israel and its settlement provided the *raison d'être* both for their nationalistic and their religious dedication.

During the Six Day War of June 1967, Israel occupied the entire Sinai Peninsula up to the Suez Canal, a region that had been under Egyptian sovereignty since 1922. Jewish settlers began to move into the Sinai shortly after its occupation by Israel. The major planned settlement effort was established in the 1970s in the Yamit region.

In the atmosphere of doubt that followed the Yom Kippur War when we had not been prepared and had almost lost, this group, who had had to evacuate their settlements in the Sinai, provided the core of those in the National Religious camp who considered themselves the vanguard of Zionist resolution. Calling themselves Gush Emunim, or the Block of the Faithful, they broadened religious Zionist ideology to include active redemption of the Holy Land. The revisionist nationalist tradition, identified with Rabbi Avraham Yitzhak Kook and his son Rabbi Zvi Yehudah Kook, had left its impact on the ideological discourse of religious Zionism, and it was with this strain of religious Zionism that Gush Emunim identified and after which it sought to model itself.

The basic idea was the holiness of the entire Land of Israel. In accord with the Kabbalistic tradition, sparks of Holiness are spread throughout the universe, including the Jewish people, the Land of

Israel and, by extension, the Jewish state. Therefore, every inch of the original Land of Israel, particularly the land recaptured in the 1967 war, is holy and must be retained in preparation for the appearance of the Messiah.

It is out of the hard core of Gush Emunim that the Jewish underground and modern Jewish terrorism grew. The aim of the Jewish terrorists is to maintain Jewish rule over the territories 'regained' and to avoid the establishment of a Palestinian state which would remove the holiness from the land.

Gush Emunim and the Jewish underground found inspiration not only in Rabbi Kook and his son but in contemporary rabbis who preached the doctrines of the Kooks. The nationalist–religious movement that formed the backbone of Gush Emunim and its offshoots was bound to lead to disturbances in the stability and democracy of the Jewish state. As Naomi Gal-Or pointed out in *The Jewish Underground: Our Terrorism* (1990), the Israeli people and government had to treat Jewish terrorism in the same way as Arab terrorism. For both spring from the same well of nationalist–religious fanaticism, and both are fuelled by the clergy. But this was not done, and until now there has been a tendency on the part of the police not to deal with them as harshly.

Before the establishment of Gush Emunim and its adoption of the ideas of Rabbi Kook, religious Zionists had a pragmatic language through which they could communicate with secular Zionists. But once those of a super-nationalistic bent adopted the messianic views of Rabbi Kook, values closer to those of the ultra-Orthodox than, for example, to those who formed the religious kibbutzim in an effort to advance the union between the secular-material and holy-spiritual worlds, dialogue became difficult to the point of impossibility. Extreme religious Zionists began to view those who did not talk their language as moving away from the 'truth', and then to consider them as villains.

The battle between the ideology of a pluralistic democratic society in the land handed to the Jewish state by the United Nations versus that of the closed God-given Land of Israel that had the potential of encompassing all the biblical territories became more acute, as political leaders in Israel signed agreements involving the handing over of 'Jewish Land'. To the genuine surprise and profound shock of most Israeli settlers in Sinai, the peace treaty contained a clause stipulating the return of the entire peninsula to Egypt and the removal of all Jewish settlements by April 1982. The Yamit area began to be penetrated by new 'settlers' under the leadership of Gush Emunim who were devoted to preventing the retreat and removal of the settlements at almost any cost. The violent Yamit confrontation between Jews and Jews became a peak which ended in the last days of the removal in April 1982; already with a view to the future of settlements in the West Bank.

Erik Cohen, Professor of Sociology and Social Anthropology at the Hebrew University of Jerusalem, discusses the nature and meaning of the removal of Israeli settlements from Sinai as required by the Egyptian–Israeli peace treaty. Cohen considers the removal an ambiguous resolution of a basic existential conflict over whether Israel is a secular 'legal–rational' state versus a religious, traditional one, the key issues being the relative importance of two Zionist values: territorial expansion versus peace. He predicts that a bitter struggle will occur when peace negotiations involving the West Bank begin (Cohen 1987:140).

The first serious indication of the deep split came in 1982, when Yamit in Sinai – which had originally been settled by government edict and with much government support – had to be handed back to Egypt as part of Menahem Begin's agreement with Anwar Sadat. Israelis sat glued to their television sets as Hesder Yeshiva students battled Israel Defence Force soldiers in an effort to prevent the hand over. The split deepened, and dialogue became even more strained eleven years later, as the Rabin government began to implement the Oslo II Accords.

While a large part of the Israeli public accepted the necessity to give up territory on the West Bank and Gaza in return for the promise of peace, the religious settlers and their adherents claimed that no person in this generation was permitted to reach an agreement based on giving up territories since this went against God's command. It is not difficult to see how this position led to the one that views any person who attempts to give back territory as a destroyer of the Jewish faith and an enemy of the Jewish state.

Yitzhak Rabin's attitude towards the settlers and their achievements, in what had essentially been barren land, shook them to their core. For more than twenty-five years they had believed that they represented a new type of Zionist pioneer that was settling the land in preparation for the messianic age. Now Yitzhak Rabin had not only signed the Oslo Accords, but had made it clear that he viewed settlements in the occupied territories as an anachronistic failure of his first government. However, while the Prime Minister was ready to admit his mistakes and forsake conventions that blocked the implementation of peace, his pragmatic approach, and the impatient and insensitive manner in which he dealt with the insecurities of the settlers, led the latter to respond by doing everything in their power to bring as much of the Israeli public as possible to join them in creating difficulties for the peace process. They experienced Rabin's policy as a wrong done to them, as a failure and a defeat, in addition to a danger to Israel's security through handing over land to Yassir Arafat's Palestinian Authority. Unfortunately, the Hamas bombings in 1996 played a large role in helping the settlers win adherents to their point of view.

For now the settlers and their rabbis, joined by other extreme right-wing rabbis and politicians, stepped up their inflammatory rhetoric. It was at this point that their propaganda began to include denunciations of Yitzhak Rabin as a traitor and murderer of Jews, once as a Nazi or as Yassir Arafat, and that banners proclaiming these denunciations began to appear at demonstrations against implementation of the Oslo Accords – where they were not denounced by less radical opponents of the peace process. As Diamond (1971) puts it, such propaganda is an integral ingredient of terrorism.

This history was part of the ideological background of Yigal Amir's crime. A graduate of Hesder Yeshiva and a zealous supporter of the Jewish Settlement in Judea and Samaria before he entered the Law School of Bar Ilan University, Amir participated in many legal and illegal demonstrations and helped organise ideological weekend trips to Hebron and to extremist Jews who had moved to Eastern Jerusalem in solidarity with the settlers. He came to the decision to murder Yitzhak Rabin as the only way to prevent implementation of the Oslo II Accords, and was much influenced by Dr Baruch Goldstein's massacre of Muslims at prayer time in the mosque at the Tomb of the Patriarchs in Hebron. Here was a man who stood up for what he believed, thought Amir, one he could respect – indeed, one who seemed to be a hero to the many extremist people who attended his funeral and continue to applaud his act even now. As Amir put it, Goldstein understood that the government and the media wanted to put the people to sleep by concealing the truth from them (Melman, 17 January 1996).

If the Goldstein massacre was the catalyst, Amir's plan to assassinate Rabin in order 'to save the Jewish people' was bolstered by two rabbinical precepts which he had learned in his yeshiva studies: (1) that of *din rodef* (indictment of the pursuer), which states that one who is witness to an attempt on the part of one Jew to kill another, is called upon to kill the potential assassin. This rule, set forth by the twelfth-century codifier Moses Maimonides, was now applied by some rabbis in Israel to Rabin. The same was true of: (2) the precept of the *mosser* which warrants the killing of any Jew or Jews who attempt to turn a fellow Jew or his property over to a non-Jewish oppressor.

Respected talmudic authorities have made it clear, before Amir's act, that the interpretation of such precepts is permitted only to Jewish scholars versed in the relevant Halakhic law, and that secular government policy must not be judged in the light of such precepts. Ashkenazi Chief Rabbi Israel Lau said that the prohibition against shedding blood is one of the seven laws stemming from Noah (from the Ark) and therefore predates even the giving of the Torah.

Nonetheless, Amir told those at his court hearing that he was obligated to murder Rabin by Halakhah and that at least one Rabbi had told him that Rabin deserved to die, although Amir later claimed that he alone had decided to commit the act, perhaps with the support of God.

When the Israeli police and General Security Service tried to determine whether any of the rabbis allegedly involved with Amir had handed down a halakhic ruling that Rabin must be murdered – thinking that Amir's assassination scheme would never have got off the ground without such endorsement – they were unsuccessful in obtaining any such admission despite lengthy questioning.

In what follows, I shall attempt to disentangle the ideological from the personal pathological roots of Yigal Amir's act of terrorism. But I want to begin this section by stating that I found myself so conflicted when I tried to understand Amir's motives and their background, that it took me several months to be able to utter his name, much less to think or write about him. It was too painful to deal with Amir who had been the cause of such a loss and so much damage to the state, and who had no sensitivity whatsoever to the enormity of what he had done. I was shocked that he did not show the slightest remorse over the death he had caused. After all, even if Halakhah did command one to murder someone to save the Jewish people, did that mean that one must exult over the act? And I was revolted by Amir's rhetoric, driven by his grandiosity and by feelings he was totally unaware of. I felt as if any attempt on my part to understand what lay behind his act could be misperceived as excusing him; that trying to understand might be confused with being understanding. And the last thing I wanted – or now want – to do is to condone Amir's terrorism in any way.

Amir's act was so terrible that for some time I distanced myself emotionally from Amir and ignored him, regarding him as subhuman. But I gradually came to the realisation that refusing to try and understand and analyse the personal, social, cultural and political elements that had contributed to this act of terrorism reflected an escapist attitude on my part. For true concern and vigilance cannot be obtained without understanding. I tried to disconnect myself from my personal feelings and become more neutral, which was not always achieved. Finally, I came to view exploring the tragedy through my psychoanalytic lens and from the perspective of what I had learned from my clinical experience as something that might add to the body of knowledge and understanding, which might perhaps some day help prevent repetitions.

Another obstacle to understanding the complex motives that lie behind such a crime is related to the fact that real understanding of the inner conscious and unconscious dynamics of the criminal can only be achieved through exploring the deep and subterranean currents of that person's psyche. But it is difficult to have access to the terrorist mind since terrorists rarely entertain the sort of doubts and conflicts that lead them to enter psychoanalysis or psychotherapy, where motives can be explored. The in-depth clinical interviews required to reach the personal wounds and unconscious motivations that are intermixed with the ideological motivations behind a political murder, which Amir claimed it to be, were not available to me. For, perhaps in order to keep him from becoming the famous – or infamous – public figure which Amir desired to become, whatever was uncovered by the psychiatrists and psychologists who interviewed him in prison has not been publicised in detail.

I have had to rely on the scant and not always reliable information given to us by the media to achieve my understanding of this tragic terrorist act and the issues related to it. The study that follows cannot, therefore, be considered a clinical case study. It is instead an attempt to learn more about the dangers that an obsession with an ideology may involve.

Unresolved Conflict, Obsessive Belief, Fanaticism as a Way of Life

I find much of what André Haynal (1983) has written about fanaticism and fanatics applicable to Yigal Amir. Fanaticism is a concept, a perspective, a state of mind, as well as a megalomanic condition. Fanaticism is found whenever a cause takes precedence over human life, whenever blind devotion to that cause takes precedence over free will, whenever obsession takes precedence over discernment.

The etymology of the word 'fanatic' links it to excessive religious enthusiasm. The origin of fanaticism is found in excessive religious zeal and faith.

While he had operated alone, Amir said at his court hearing, 'it was not only my finger that pulled the trigger, but the finger of this people, which had yearned for the Land of Israel for 2000 years.' Amir spoke at length about his having acted only through his intellect; that, if the Torah and the 613 commandments are viewed as a way of life, they enable a person to be in total control of his instincts. In his view of Judaism, if one acts according to one's feelings, one acts like an animal, not a human being. He therefore strove to overcome the body's drives. For one of the lessons of Judaism, he continued in a calm and assured tone, is to allow the intellect (the Torah) to overcome the emotions. Thus, if the Torah tells you to do something that goes against your emotions, it must be done. For example, stopping smoking may be difficult, but it can be done.

In describing how he taught himself to suppress his feelings, Amir said that every aspect and question that arises in a person's life is like a computer program, determined in accordance with the battle to suppress drives and let the intellect reign supreme.

All this fits in with Haynal's suggestion that 'salvation of the soul' becomes the ultimate psychological force that powers the fanatic's behaviour, and that any means available is justified to attain this supreme goal. To Amir, saving the soul overrides the commandment not to murder. In one of his speeches Amir explained that in war, too, the act is negative, but the aim is divine! Therefore one is allowed do it!

Haynal writes that in his illusion of having found the absolute and superhuman, the fanatic believes himself to be in possession of the truth which confers upon him omniscience, invulnerability and omnipotence, all superhuman qualities. His feeling of omnipotence is accompanied by a narcissistic thrill at the idea of being among those chosen by God or history. Haynal conceives of the elation as protecting the fanatic from anxiety by providing structures of security, characterised by the externalisation and negation of the intrapsychological conflict.

I think that these phrases describe the emotional qualities that Amir transmits through his verbal and non-verbal behaviour very well. In the animistic phase, Haynal continues, man believes himself to be all-powerful; in the religious phase he yields to the gods; in the scientific conception he recognises man's weakness and limits. Most often the fanatic exhibits a mixture of animistic and religious thought.

Some fanatics are visionaries with charismatic personalities, whose emotional vibrations exercise a fascination over others, especially over those suffering from weak and unintegrated selves and who rely on absolutes to calm their chaotic inner lives. As became clearer after the election – and more will be written about this in Chapter 6 – Amir had such an impact on certain types of people. Others belong to the obsessional type, whose cold manipulative streak and strong need for control, accompanied by the conviction that their cause is 'just', partially silences their feelings of anxiety, shame and guilt. It is in the obsessive fanatics that we often see their deep hatred concealed; often based on dissociated personal injuries lurking behind the façade of being one of the 'just men'.

It seems that Amir used religion as a means of curbing impulses which, if given a free reign, would expose the evil aspect of what he believes in. It is likely that his becoming absorbed in the intellectual and mystic areas was part of the dissociative mechanism he used.

Haynal describes the obsessive fanatic as one who 'has a narcissistic egocentric way of thinking (he alone is right), a belief in the omnipotence of his thought (thanks to which he will be able magically to change the world, to bring forth paradise) and finally a projective mechanism which rids him of any trace of weakness and human flaw' (Haynal 1990:41). In individuals with ego weakness, splitting and other related mechanisms, such as primitive types of projection (particularly projective identification), denial, omnipotence and devaluation, protect the ego from conflicts through dissociating or actively keeping apart contradictory experiences of the self and of significant others. These defences reduce the adaptive effectiveness and flexibility of the individual's ego functioning (Kernberg 1994).

In attempting to overcome his sense of weakness, Amir presented himself as strong and hard-headed, projecting onto others that which he could not admit to existing in himself. Apparently, he became so preoccupied with dominance and submission and so absorbed in fantasy power-games that the boundary between these games and reality gradually faded. 'I never felt I would go after Rabin,' he told his interrogators. 'I always thought that I was only talking, that I would not really have the power to do it, even though I knew that it had to be done. I would tell myself that it was necessary to kill him, but I would smile as I said it. Nobody believed that such a nice and logical guy would actually kill someone. Even I did not know that I would kill him.' And, indeed, this did make it difficult for others to know what he really had in mind. None of those to whom he voiced his thoughts, believed Amir would really shoot Rabin.

The capacity to carry out the murder – besides fulfilling the mission dictated by ideologies – seems to have been a self-power test, a private game of courage. Since Amir viewed weakness as contemptible, I think that he could not admit it to himself and projected it onto others. Then, when he thought he perceived this weakness in others, it may have unconsciously reminded him of his own weakness and he turned violent and began to delegitimise his prey. Amir felt the need to delegitimise our Prime Minister, he said, when Rabin shook the hand of Arafat, the greatest murderer of Jews, when he freed terrorist infiltrators who would later murder Jews. And when Rabin continued his contacts with international figures about the peace process, Amir viewed this as 'grovelling before the nations.'

'The spine of the government is very weak,' Amir told the commission set up to investigate his crime on 12 December 1995. 'This is why they are prepared to give everything up for the sake of peace. Everyone is shocked by the killing of this prime minister who grovelled before the nations. But he had no national honour! The nation was paralysed, and someone had to act!' In his mind, the only way to galvanise the nation back into action was to assassinate the Prime Minister.

In accordance with the fanatic's narcissistic and egocentric way of thinking, Amir perceived those around him as being of lesser value than himself and he viewed the world through the lens of his own eyes alone – always seeing himself as the only one with the correct solution. Anyone who differed with his views or his solutions became in his eyes part of the contemptible masses. Kernberg (1993) writes that the grandiose self of the malignant narcissist identifies with the representation of an idealised object, so that the idealised aggressive internalised object finds an echo in the external world, and is 'drugged' to perform sadistic acts.

Personal Pathology: the Mixture of Ideology and Deployment

The political nature of the assassination stems from the fanatic-religious background. The question is whether this combination – the one that led Amir to perpetrate his terrorist act – has personal pathological roots. Weinberg writes that, in general, 'no striking psychopathology' has been found in the study of captured terrorists and that many experts on terrorism have implied that terrorists are 'normal'. Gabi Weil, chief clinical psychologist at a Health Ministry mental health centre, a member of the team which examined Yigal Amir in prison, confirmed the confessed assassin was sane when he murdered Prime Minister Yitzhak Rabin; that he can distinguish between 'the permitted and the forbidden' and is in no way psychopathic (Raine, 13 March 1996). Weil describes Amir as an individualist, acting alone without consulting anyone He had no problem forming rational or intellectual relationships but he was practically incapable to do so emotionally or intimately. A committee concluded that he was sane and capable of standing trial, and that nothing suggested that he was not in full possession of his faculties when he shot Rabin. He planned the murder over a long period of time and freely admitted his intent to eliminate Rabin. If Amir is capable of standing trial, does this mean he is sane? Can anyone who commits such a heinous crime be considered entirely 'sane'?

A close look at Amir's rhetoric, arrogance and contempt for others, at the eerie smile that so many would have liked to wipe off his face – all this gives one a sense of the emotional failures that must lie behind his ideological zeal and his resort to terrorism.

Volkan (1994) writes that certain patterns seem to emerge from the study of the psychology of the individual terrorist: one usually finds evidence of identity problems caused by early psychological traumas or narcissistic injuries. Dr Arthur Hyatt, a psychoanalyst who has worked in the prison system for many years with those sentenced for life, sees traumatic childhood experiences and unexpressed childhood feelings as the determining factors behind murderous acts. In the case of Yigal

Amir, early narcissistic wounding may explain his use of splitting, projection and externalisation, as well as the rage reactions that could easily be detected in his speeches and reactions both in and out of court.

Weil said that Amir suffers from narcissistic and schizoid tendencies. And as Volkan writes in a chapter about malignant narcissism, 'To slaughter others in order to feel superior or to maintain one's self-concept is the most vicious form of the malignant narcissism' (Volkan 1994:92).

The smile of Amir relates to his narcissistic features. Amir was pleased and proud of his act. There was no sign of guilt feelings. This is the arrogance and sense of mission he felt when he murdered. He believed that he was something special, Weil said, and believed he acted as God's emissary, and that he did what he did for the good of mankind (Raine, 13 March 1996). He had the conviction that the people were in danger of a coming holocaust. Weil said that he acted out of a strong religious belief. It was not psychotic since it relates to the religious culture in which he grew up (Harel, 13 March 1996).

Mortimer Ostow (1986) demonstrated that classical apocalyptic texts reflect a psychodynamic pattern that prevails among many individuals beset with rage; from the dynamic point of view the apocalyptic syndrome is likely to be elicited by difficulties in the management of rage as we could detect in Amir's behaviour. The murder that Amir committed reflects the dangers when apocalyptic moods – which abounded in his mind – are taken not as a means of providing pseudo-comfort but as programmes for activism.

Volkan (1993) suggests that the political authority under attack by terrorists may represent a despotic father or those who were humiliated by a weak father. But we know very little about what was in Amir's unconscious mind when he shot Yitzhak Rabin, much less about his childhood and family life.

Amir's mother is a nursery schoolteacher. From what the media has reported, she appears much more dominant than her silent husband. It has been reported that she considered Yigal as the brightest and most promising of her children. Amir's father, Shlomo Amir, is a scribe, who has spent his life making copies of the scriptures. He dresses in the clothing typical of the ultra-Orthodox and appears to be an introverted man, sunk in his prayers. He is a member of the Independent Agudat Yisrael, a not so extreme religious party.

Amir studied in an elementary school of the Haredi Independent Agudat Yisrael. Then in a *yeshiva* called Yishuv Chadash (New Community), a very Orthodox, elitist religious school whose students wear black *kippot* (skull caps). Most of them were Ashkenazic. In the evenings, he studied for the matriculation. He was an excellent student, but problematic (Kapeliouk, 1996).

Shlomo Amir wanted his son to continue learning in this type of *yeshiva* and stay out of the army, but Yigal rebelled and registered in a Hesder Yeshiva. It was said that his mother supported him in this wish. His father is convinced that it was militarism that destroyed his son – that if Yigal had continued in the original *yeshiva* setting, it never would have entered his head to commit an extremist act. Amir described the Hesder Yeshiva in which he studied as a highly disciplined place that requires its students to strive for excellence, high achievement and to renounce material pleasures.

In my clinical experience, when high expectations to excel, on the part of parents who unconsciously live their thwarted ambitions through their children, come together with rigid values on the part of the educational system, this may lead to unbearable pressures on the child. One of the ways of dealing with such pressures is to develop overly high ambitions to be a special person, which goes together with deployments against the fear of losing self-esteem and the dread of being humiliated should one fail to fulfil the high expectations.

Gevirtz (1996) interprets Amir's murder of Yitzhak Rabin as a megalomanic attempt to stretch his limits and gain the recognition for superiority that he had been seeking throughout his life at home, the *yeshiva*, the army and at the university, as well as in the anti-peace demonstrations he had organised. It would seem that much of this drive is designed to correct narcissistic self-injuries that Amir suffered in his childhood.

Over-evaluation of the intellect at the expense of empathic attention to feelings, regarding emotional needs and bodily sensations as inferior or evil, or feeling shamed when one does indulge in any of these, may have contributed to the individual unconscious choice of dissociative processes which lead to splits, disavowals, denials, projection and seclusion. Splitting constitutes the dominant mental operations of people with unintegrated selves and contradictory functions. Persons with this personality constellation idealise their grandiose self, split and project onto others all the hatred and devalued weakness. People who rely strongly on splitting and externalisation look outward for the source of their difficulties. And once they find the needed outside enemy to blame, they tend to find the absolutist polarising rhetoric of terrorism extremely attractive. The statement, 'It's not us, it's them. They are the cause of our problems,' provides a psychologically satisfying explanation for what has gone wrong with their lives.

Another piece of information may throw light on Amir's personal problems: Amir's friends have reported that several months before the terrorist act he was crushed when his girlfriend dropped him and married a friend of his. His mother is said to have added that his spirits were low, he lost his appetite, he lost weight; he began to lose his hair and he tended to seclude himself at home. Amir attributed his depression to political despair. His depression and his feeling of seclusion deepened, he said, as the peace process accelerated and his friends seemed less willing than they had been before, to join him in his anti-government activities – participate in demonstrations. Dr Gabi Weil, the clinical psychologist who examined Amir, suggests that his political fanaticism served to accelerate the potential eruption of Amir's depressive personality structure.

Another factor that may have contributed to Yigal Amir's narcissistic wounds and the formation of his defence mechanisms and deployment is related to ethnic factors. The ultra-Orthodox *yeshivas* such as the one in which he learned as a youth, usually have a predominance of Ashkenazi students, who often adopt an arrogant attitude towards Sephardi students. This can lead to feelings of resentment and humiliation, which feed the deployment into grievance. His Yemenite origin also could have added to Amir's grievances. In fact, many Yemenites bear a long-held grudge against Israeli society, in recent years stemming from the issue of Yemenite children who are said to have disappeared in the wave of immigration during the 1950s: the government claims they died while being processed as new immigrants, but their fate, in fact, is still uncertain, in spite of commissions of inquiry. This issue has become a *cause célèbre* in recent years. While there is no evidence that this issue affected Amir's grievance, it cannot be discounted as a possible factor in aggravating it. For, as I have mentioned in the previous chapter, a growing feeling of injustice and tension among groups that feel wronged, abused or dominated, constitutes a seedbed for resorting to deployments, which may lead to explosion and political tension.

In what follows, I shall discuss the pathological aspects of Yigal Amir from the deploymental perspective.

Grievance

A major characteristic of the pathologically deployed individual is grievance. The phenomenon of grievance has intrigued me for many years (Moses-Hrushovski 1993). A grievance is a 'wrong', real or fancied, which someone considers grounds for complaint against persons seen as responsible for an unjust act or circumstance. When people become pathologically deployed into grievance, it becomes their mission to seek out the faults and injustices committed by others. Grievance represents a relentless attack on the object in a situation where it is difficult to identify what, if anything, would release the object from an implacable grip (Feldman 1993). Much of the psychic energy of individuals deployed into grievance is invested in achieving a correction for what they view as unfair treatment, humiliation or lack of care on the part of an important other; in other words, in the endeavour to retrieve what they feel has been lost and to re-establish their lost state of psychic equilibrium.

Behind the phenomena of grievance lies a combination of the need to prove that one's claims are legitimate grievances, to retaliate against the others who perpetrated the injustices against them and to induce these others, or those in the present who represent them, to correct and 'make good' whatever they allegedly did to bring about the state of grievance. Partially, this is intended to make the others at long last feel what they themselves had felt, and to understand, rather than condemn them, for their grievances.

There is a mixture of social commitment with grandiose and fanatic thinking in deployed individuals, who are driven obsessively by such a need for a reparative correction and a strong tendency to cut off whatever connects with their personal grievances, experiences and motives. Grievance – rather than grieving – serves as a defensive organisation against acknowledging the role of pain, loss and envy.

The mental state dominated by grievance is repeatedly played out in fantasy, sometimes consciously, but often unconsciously. The sense of entitlement characteristic of grievance (Feldman 1993; Moses-Hrushovski 1993; Moses and Moses-Hrushovski 1990) causes those deployed into it to seek justice, and to feel the call to duty and the devotion to a cause that is accompanied by a quest for vengeance (Steiner 1996:434). This sense of 'right' is easily transformed into an assumption of righteousness, so that what begins as a demand for justice is often taken over by a more malignant destructiveness.

Amir became locked onto Yitzhak Rabin after the Prime Minister signed the Oslo II Accords, 'knowing' that this would endanger the land, the Jewish state and its people. Once Amir decided that the only way to keep the Accords from being carried out was to kill the major person responsible for doing so, there was nothing that would have prevented him from executing his plan. And he did so in a manner typical for heavily deployed individuals by first targeting his object and then approaching his goal stage by stage. Indeed, throughout his trial he stressed that it was not Rabin the person, but Rabin the symbol that he had in mind.

In a letter to Noa Ben Arzi (Rabin's granddaughter), Amir wrote the following: 'You wrote that what we have in common are three bullets. But there is much more... It's possible that your grandfather was the most fascinating person for you; but I did not kill your grandfather. I killed the person who filled the role... that endangered our people... I looked into myself so many times from your point of view, trying to face your feelings but I still feel that I am right in what I did…'

To me, these words and the attempt to demonstrate empathy with the granddaughter of his victim are evidence of the sickness of Amir's mind and the extent to which his deployment has clouded his thinking. It seems to indicate that his allegedly ideological grievance concealed an essentially narcissistic delusional system which he used to shield himself from any awareness of whatever was so unconsciously painful for him. By relegating his victim to the status of something to be destroyed in the fulfilment of his mission, Yigal Amir did not and cannot relate emotionally to the fact that he took a human life.

Police Chief Superintendent Motti Naftali, an investigator in Rabin's murder has described his amazement at how composed and cold Amir was during the preliminary investigation; also, how he had dared to ask the police interrogating him for cookies right after committing the murder. In my view, Amir behaved with the ruthless and dehumanised detachment of a sociopath who dehumanises others in the name of religious and nationalistic ideology (Diamond 1981; Moses 1990).

The strongest sense of unfairness connected with grievance often leads those deployed into it to become so absorbed in the mission designed to alleviate it that their perceptions become narrowed to a point where they are unable to consider complexities. They become obsessed by a series of representations that eventually take over their entire mind. The resultant closed system seems to them to provide all the answers at a cognitive level; to them they cannot be falsified and promise omnipotence at an emotional level. To possess the absolute truth is to have a net of familiarity spread over everything, for eternity. Then there can be no surprises and nothing unknown. This state can often be addictive, the perverse gratification gained thereby adding to the hold that the grievance has on the personality.

In Bott-Spillius's (1993) terms, individuals deployed into grievance are impenitent and justify their hatred in a number of ways. In the case of Yigal Amir, his impenitence, arrogance and presumption could be seen when he was trying to justify his actions to Judge Edmond Levy by claiming that if the legal system in Israel had been operating correctly over the past three years, there would have been no need for him to kill Rabin (Marcus 1997).

Amir's deployment was also evinced by the way in which he blindly persisted in carrying out his mission. He spoke like a prophet who foresees future catastrophes and sees it as his mission to warn the people and be their saviour. I wondered whether his name Yigal which 'means the one who will redeem', in Hebrew, might indicate the presence of such unconscious expectations on the part of his parents. It was as if he was recruited by God to fulfil his role, as if he were one of God's soldiers and his person, his self, was completely lost in the role. In my view, the 'idealised good object' of Amir, which has been abducted against its will (Steiner 1996: 435) is the 'Land of Israel'.

I have no way of knowing for certain whether his idealisation of the 'motherland' relates only to this myth, which is zealfully adhered to by so many religious and extreme right-wing Israelis, or whether it is also related to unconscious feelings towards and identification with his own mother. When he was describing the emotional and mystical drives that led him to kill Rabin, Amir said: 'My emotions have been drained these past three years. I felt something like a mother who sees someone about to kill her children and shoots without feeling.'

As we have seen, Yigal Amir tends to alienate himself from others and to numb his feelings by isolating himself from emotional and sensory experience. Such dissociation is another feature of deployment. It spreads along a broad continuum with coexistent alternative ego states, as if several selves are functioning at the same time, each one unaware of the others – similar to 'multiple personalities'. Dissociation may occur between feelings and their motives, between feelings and actions, between the emotional and intellectual parts of one's self. Amir appeared to be frozen into a state of emotional death, as if all his feelings had been transformed by his religious and ideological zeal.

Thus, he has repeatedly insisted that he has no regrets over what he did and does not even seem to understand or relate emotionally to the fact that his act involved the taking of a human life. In his discussion of the dynamics of sociopaths, Diamond

(1971) writes that 'more prevalent and more dangerous to society are those who are not psychopaths or schizophrenics, but those who under certain circumstances can behave with the ruthless, dehumanised detachment of the sociopath.'

The personal pathology of Amir, who regards his criminal act as a political murder, reminds me of the deployment into terrorism which I have discussed when I described forms of deployment elsewhere (Moses-Hrushovski 1994). Patients deployed into terrorism act in a violent manner because of accumulated malignant aggression following physical, sexual or emotional abuse, or because of disavowed feelings of guilt, shame or rejection. But they commit murder only in the domain of fantasy, unlike Yigal Amir who crossed the border between fantasy and reality.

It is yet difficult to understand what exactly causes a person to perform an act in contrast to those who have the same fantasies and wishes, yet do not act on them. I think that a further study of the distinctions between petrified, pathological narcissism and normal, flexible narcissism as did Solan (1997; 1998) may help us to gain better understanding of these issues.

Chapter VI
THE ASSASSINATION IN THE SHADOW OF OBLIVION: THE FAILURE TO ADEQUATELY MOURN THE DEATH OF YITZHAK RABIN AND THE INCREASE IN JEWISH FUNDAMENTALISM

The assassination of Yitzhak Rabin is a national trauma that has been mourned insufficiently. Although the outpouring of grief was enormous and deep, 'was' is the operative word. For the period of grieving and mourning, with a few notable exceptions, was too brief. Many of us felt that there was a failure to really come to terms with the trauma, what lay behind it or to learn about what it meant and means to us as individuals and as a society.

In part, this was because Shimon Peres and the Labour Party advanced Israeli elections by five months in order to capitalise on the sympathy for Rabin and his battle for the peace process, but this came together with the party's decision to refrain from exploiting the Prime Minister's death in its campaign advertisements and speeches. This seemed to have cut off the expression of grieving and mourning. The result was that the period allotted to this necessary function, especially after a national tragedy of this dimension, was not long enough for the Israeli people to really come to terms with the trauma and with what lay behind it; or to grapple with what it means to us as individuals and as a democratic society. This failure to mourn adequately has prevented us also from delving into the reasons why someone like Yigal Amir could commit his crime convinced that he was doing so to save the Jewish state, and why some extremists supported his heinous act.

On 18 June 1996, the day on which Netanyahu's government was sworn in, David Moshevitz, a businessman published in the name of the 'We Shall Not Forget' activist group an advertisement in the nation's most influential daily newspaper, *Ha'aretz*, citing a passage from I Kings 21:19 which reads: 'Hast thou killed and also taken possession?' This chapter of the Bible relates the story of how King Ahab obtained the vineyard of Naboth, the Jezreelite who had refused to sell it, with the help of his wife Jezebel; it describes how Jezebel wrote letters in Ahab's name calling for Naboth to be stoned to death because he had allegedly 'cursed God and the King.' It was after Naboth was killed by 'two base fellows' and Ahab had taken possession of the vineyard that the prophet Elijah was commanded by God to say to the King, 'Have you killed and also taken possession?'

It was noted at the end of this advertisement that it had been placed as a painful reminder to the public and to all those who take God's name in vain upon the swearing in of a new government in Israel 230 days after the murder of Yitzhak Rabin (Gordon, 9 September 1996; Palgi, 7 February 1996).

This famous passage from the Bible has many possible interpretations and connotations, one of them that those who had incited against Rabin and the peace process were reaping the benefits of their abhorrent zeal. But also implicit in the advert was the rest of the verse: 'In the place where dogs licked up the blood of Naboth, dogs shall lick your own blood.'

In other words, those who placed the advert in *Ha'aretz* were accusing the right and the National Religious camp of benefiting from the rabble-rousing against Yitzhak Rabin which they had done nothing to prevent, and for creating the super-heated political atmosphere that made the assassination possible.

Some months later, Moshevitz said that until those who took part in the incitement which led to Rabin's murder owned up and asked for forgiveness, the government did not deserve to be in power. Moshevitz expressed the feelings of many Israelis that if Prime Minister Binyamin Netanyahu were to acknowledge his part and say the words which would lead to national reconciliation, a different atmosphere could be created in which a more sincere soul-searching could be achieved: each searching his own soul rather than the other's. Such a decision would also make more people understand the significance of political murder in a democratic state (Yudelman, 8 November 1996).

In the immediate aftermath of the assassination, millions of Israelis, including those who opposed Rabin's policies, were touched by the tragedy and began to think about how they might have contributed to it. A large part of the National Religious camp also took up the issue in public as well as in private. This process stopped to some extent when the Orthodox and right camps defended themselves against feeling guilty about their part; especially when they were indiscriminately attacked by the non-religious and left. Their guilt – and indeed the guilt of Israelis from all parts of the political spectrum – for having contributed to, or having done nothing to prevent the outrageous libels hurled against Yitzhak Rabin caused many Israelis to forget, repress or at least not think enough about the tragic event itself. Hatred and accusation took the place of real mourning, which would have had to involve the examining of the problems surrounding the murder, the admission of direct or indirect responsibility for what had happened and the commitment to deal courageously with lessons learned from the tragedy.

Whatever healing might have grown out of that terrible event was lost – for example, clarification of the relationship between the messianic ideas of the religious right and the nationalist camp versus the democratic values and ideals of the majority of Israelis; and between the moderate right versus the fanatical right and fundamentalistic religious values.

In what follows I shall inquire into the deploymental factors that have served as obstacles to adequate grieving and mourning and which, according to my thinking, continue to serve as obstacles to national reconciliation and integration, and to peace in the Middle East.

Yitzhak Rabin sacrificed his life for the peace that Israelis most seek (even if there are deep differences of opinion as to how this peace is to be attained). He fought to instil the belief that peace is achievable, and that any Israeli government would have to follow the path of the peace process in order to open a new era for Israel itself as well as for the entire Middle East. Amir murdered Rabin thinking that he was speeding the biblically prophesied apocalypse that is to herald the Final Redemption. He thought he was thus derailing the Oslo process that he considered a march down the road of unilateral surrender.

He did not derail the process , but many difficulties have been heaped on it since, especially after the May 1996 elections. We now know how Rabin's legacy for peace and against violence was followed by the Likud government led by Binyamin Netanyahu, especially because he was forced to include in his coalition a wide variety of smaller parties with differing ideas on how or whether to proceed with the peace. Thus, one could not know from Netanyahu's public pronouncements whether it reflects what his government plans or if his latest statement was made in response to demands from one or the other parties in his coalition.

In attempting to analyse the reasons for Netanyahu's victory over Shimon Peres in May 1996, in what was the first direct election of an Israeli Prime Minister, it should first of all be pointed out that he won by less than one per cent of the popular vote. So the question should really be why he succeeded in attracting the parties that represent minority ethnic, political and cultural groups to his government, and why such a large portion of the Israeli public voted for these parties despite the fact that many or most of them long for the peace for which Rabin had fought. This involves an investigation into the grievances of these people and how they led to deployments designed to alleviate these grievances. I believe that such group deployments not only obstruct the possibility of change, growth and integration but, as long as they are left unchecked, they contribute to the intensification of fundamentalism – as happened in Israel.

There was a general feeling that the establishment did not pay enough attention to the feelings of a number of ethnic groups, who had never felt treated in an egalitarian way, and that their physical, economic, social and emotional needs were not acknowledged or met. Labour had no crystallised social policy, because it had insufficient empathy and direct contact with weaker social minority groups, such as residents of development towns or disadvantaged neighbourhoods. Also, Labour did not succeed in developing a definition of a secular Jewish identity which could have brought parts of the moderate religious camp nearer.

Being deployed into expecting the others to change, rather than for themselves to do so, was one of the factors for the deadlock we then suffered from. The settlers could not forgive Rabin and Peres for the almost offhand dismissal of their despair at the prospect of being evicted from the territories that the Labour Party was prepared to hand over to the Palestinians. Their feeling of helplessness at having to sacrifice the way of life they had fought to build for themselves for a supposedly better future was exacerbated when all they could see was increased terrorist activity in the present, which added to their insecurity and their need to be strengthened against the dangers to their existence. Also, after years of believing that problems with the Palestinians could only be solved through unity within Israel against a hostile world, and after having built their strong deployments against empathising with the enemy, it was extremely difficult for them to change their conception and accept Yitzhak Rabin's view that the problems can indeed be solved by compromising with them.

As I have suggested in Chapter 4, the biggest mistakes of the Labour government were in the psychological sphere, in its paternalistic attitude and its imperviousness towards ethnic groups such as Jews of Middle Eastern or North African origin (Sephardic Jews), or new immigrants from Russia and Ethiopia, who felt ignored and wronged. People who voted against Labour and the left-leaning Meretz were protesting the insult to their way of life more than opposing the Labour government's peace efforts or other policies.

It appears that half the Israeli nation had deployed itself against emotional injuries that might have been avoided had the Labour government changed its arrogant and elitist attitude and had shown more sensitivity to their feelings and emotional needs. Such a responsive change that requires the relinquishing of old elitist attitudes could, so it seems, have contributed to realistic mourning, to reconciliation and change.

As Meron Benvenisti wrote right after the elections (14 June 1996), 'Elections in Israel are like an ultrasound film of the inner limbs of the body politic: a weakened spinal column [the central parties] results in a splintering of the vertebrae [the ethnic and cultural groups] which are dependent on it. The last election made it clearer than ever that Israel is a mosaic of minorities among which there is only loose contact. The weaker groups joined together against those… they saw as patronising and who made them feel alienated.'

Benvenisti asks whether the loss of the old myth of the melting pot ideology constructed to suit the secular Ashkenazi pioneer ethos is something to mourn, or whether this loss is to be welcomed because it allows each group to give expression to its own, discrete inclinations. If the latter is the case, Benvenisti said, it may mean that these groups no longer feel too weak and humiliated to sound their voices in the framework of the commonality. This is, then, one step in the direction of self-expression, negotiation and reconciliation, and as such works against deployment.

After Yitzhak Rabin's assassination, we saw a spate of letters, articles, opinion pieces and commentaries in the country's newspapers about our social, spiritual and national identity. The consensus was that, even if we and the Israeli government have never intended to negate the rights of existence of every Israeli in our pluralistic society – indeed, had in general based our way of life on democratic values – we have tended to maintain minimal or no contact with those who are different or whose ideas differ from ours under the often mistaken, or too quickly arrived at, assumption that 'there is nobody there to talk with.' It was felt that one of our mourning tasks should be a change in such attitudes that hinder reconciliation and integration.

Many Israelis on both the left and right felt that another reason for the political shake up was the shutting off of grief and mourning about Yitzhak Rabin's assassination, and particularly what it symbolised. 'Forgive us, Rabin. They have murdered you again,' read a note at Kikar Rabin. The right wing kept the murder in the background because Rabin's killer came from its camp. It seems that this was a deploymental strategy to free them from disavowed guilt. And the left was reluctant to mourn and grieve in public during the election campaign for fear they would be accused of capitalising on the tragedy to gain votes, and of ascribing collective guilt to the whole religious and right sectors.

As trauma became taboo, it was gradually even more difficult to mourn and internalise the meanings that Rabin's murder has had for our lives and our values. And, in the shadow of this oblivion, the extremists exploited the situation to further their position, to the point of justifying the murder as they had justified Baruch Goldstein's massacre of innocent Arabs in the middle of their prayers. Further, we witnessed the admiration of the 'Yigal Amir Fanclub,' that will be discussed later on. Thus fanaticism and fundamentalism gained in power.

There are many reasons why people find it impossible or difficult to mourn. Despite the obvious differences between them, I am reminded here of the trauma of the Holocaust, which for so many years in the past was not dealt with in Israel in any real emotional and cognitive way. Rabin's assassination was so unanticipated, so sudden and so disorienting that it could not be digested and integrated as an historical memory. The Holocaust was too traumatic for those who were directly affected (Moses 1993) – and few in Israel were not. Both traumas induced shame and guilt at having let it happen or at having survived. And in both instances we felt that our helplessness to prevent what happened was unforgivable.

Another reason for not allowing ourselves to grieve and mourn in a more complete manner might be related to the fear of betraying those who died, as if the reinvestment of mental energy in the world due to a successful act of mourning were tantamount to the abandonment of those who were killed. Thus loss has to be kept alive and incompletion of mourning results (Kravitz 1995:414).

Pathological grief entails a holding onto the lost objects. Roth suggests that one nonadaptive result of this tenaciousness is that an individual's or a group's (nation's) energies are anchored partially in the past, where it is unavailable for the current tasks of ongoing and progressive life. To Roth's way of thinking, tens of centuries of persecution, pogroms and threats of annihilation have resulted in the Jewish people atavistically transmitting a heavy heritage of unresolved guilt from one generation to the next. He claims that the Jews' psychological propensity towards unresolved grief may link specific Holocaust experiences with matching individual psychodynamics to induce an intense state of mind that he terms 'contagious mourning' (Roth 1993:49). I think that this phenomenon does exist in Israel and may have limited our ability to get on with carrying out the necessary mourning tasks as they were discussed in Chapter 2, and invest the best of our powers to reach reconciliation and integration. Powers to bring about change are thus locked in the catastrophes of the past and in our being deployed into preparedness for their repetition.

The Israeli novelist, David Grossman (1995), writes that the terrible fears that the Holocaust has imprinted on his and so many others' psyches has brought suffering to at least two generations of Jews, especially in Israel, and caused the entire nation to unconsciously live in preparation to defend themselves against a new Holocaust. And as Volkan suggests, 'the group draws the emotional meanings of the traumatic event and mental defences against emotional hurt into its very identity, assiduously passing these mental representations of hurt, guilt, shame and defence against them from generation to generation. It becomes a 'chosen trauma' that acquires renewed emotional power whenever it becomes condensed with new traumas (Volkan 1994:7). When inordinate emotional investment in the mental representation of the loss persists, it becomes difficult to bring mourning to its resolution.

It may be that the extremely intense collective mourning that followed the murder of Rabin had an arresting effect on the individual work of mourning, because it was built on an accumulation of previously unmourned traumas. The last trauma, added onto the previous ones, became so overpowering that the individual became part of the group, and possibly lost for a while his or her separateness and individual mourning. And perhaps this failure of individuals to carry out the complete work of mourning in turn helped bring national mourning to a premature closure. Another obstacle relates to another sombre phenomenon: the need of certain Holocaust survivors to idealise those born after theHolocaust down to the third generation, to somehow protect them from having to experience the grief and pain of mourning, and to use the younger generations as linking objects (Volkan 1981) or memorial candles (Vardi 1992) to replace those who were lost in the Holocaust. Other individuals and groups choose an inanimate linking object like the concept of the Land of Israel – to serve as a symbolic bridge to representations of the dead. They view this bridge in a magical way, thereby gaining the illusion of absolute control over the psychological meeting ground of the past with the present presented to them by the linking object.

The combination of the narcissistic grandiosity that has prevailed in Israel at least since the establishment of the Jewish state stemming from a variety of sources, including the revitalisation of the idea of the 'chosen people', especially after 1967 (see Moses 1982), with that of having been wronged created an attitude of entitlement. This attitude entails the strong need for these injuries to be acknowledged and for us to be forgiven for our misdeeds because there is a special history that justifies them (Moses and Moses-Hrushovski 1990). Such feelings of entitlement together with our chosen traumas and chosen glories, have no doubt contributed to the Israeli nation's difficulties in mourning Yitzhak Rabin. 'Chosen traumas are linked to the group's inability to mourn, mourning being an obligatory response to change or loss in the normal course of events (Volkan 1996:271).

The failure to complete mourning involves the blurring of the multiple meanings of the murder, refusing to look deeply enough into all of the contributing factors, and refraining from owning direct or indirect parts of responsibility. This state of affairs has set the scene for the growth of extremism at both ends of the political and religious spectrum. Being caught in deployments due to disavowed feelings of guilt and shame means putting off the emotional work that is considered necessary to fulfil the mourning tasks and learn the lessons of the assassination.

As Palgi (1996) puts it, we in Israel must arrive at a clear and unequivocal understanding of our current social, political and religious life and how these factors can work together to maintain the existence of our democracy. This cannot be accomplished without a real and thorough struggle with Yigal Amir's crime on the emotional, cognitive and behavioural levels, or without the admission of our direct and indirect responsibility for contributing to or not doing enough to counter the atmosphere that made it possible.

According to Yirmiyahu Yovel of the Hebrew University, 'The issue is whether Israel will shape a life according to the Western democratic concepts or one infected by Middle Eastern fundamentalism' which is defined as the insistence that all aspects of life, including the social and the political, must conform to a set of sacred scriptures believed to be inherent and immutable (Munson 1988).

The justices of Israel's Supreme Court contend that our legal system has begun to open the door to greater religious pluralism. But the Orthodox and ultra-Orthodox whose parties captured twenty-three of the 120 Knesset seats in 1996 and twenty-nine seats in 1999 respond that the laws of the secular Supreme Court cannot compete with Halakha, Jewish religious law, which they place above the laws of the state. Whereas most of the West has avoided this problem by disconnecting the relationship between church and state, the three main religious parties in Israel whose goal it is to place the state under the law of God have striking parallels with Islamic fundamentalism.

What depresses so many Israelis in Israel today is not only the dramatic increase in votes for the religious parties, but also that these parties seem to have gained their votes by appealing to the fundamentalist element with which moderates find it difficult to reach common ground; and that this type of religious fundamentalism has turned into a political movement interested in acquiring power to further its religious goals; as now do the NRP (National Religious Party) who had previously been more moderate.

To illustrate the difficulty, or the impossibility of communication between the ultra-religious and the moderate groups around problems of ideology and with respect to their part in the responsibility for the political murder, I shall bring parts of an interview of the journalist Amnon Barzilay with Rabbi Druckman of the NRP, an important Rabbi on the religious right.

When Barzilay remarked that there are those in the National Religious camp who were not sorry that Rabin was assassinated, Rabbi Druckman responded with a sharp retort that taking the life of another Jew is one of the most terrible crimes according to

Halakha. He went on to attack left-wing author Amoz Oz for the latter's statement that the 'Jewish Jihad' represents a danger to democracy in Israel. There is no fundamentalist current in Judaism, Rabbi Druckman insisted, when Barzilay asked him about the growing number of people in his camp who feel that the laws of the Torah should overrule those of the state if and when secular law fails to preserve the Land of Israel.

Dismayed at Rabbi Druckman's refusal to consider that he and his colleagues should perhaps do some deep soul-searching about the phenomenon of religious-political fundamentalism, Barzilay continued to press the rabbi on the issue of religious versus democratic values. Asked whether he also placed Halakha above democracy, Druckman replied, 'Yes, but that is not a reason for there to be any contest between the two.' In his view, 'Nobody regards democracy as a prime value. It is only a means [while] Halakha is eternal! Halakha has existed for thousands of years, even if only a minority espouses it today.'

Still trying to find some common ground, Barzilay asked Rabbi Druckman if he saw any connection between the ideology of Baruch Goldstein, who slaughtered Arabs at prayer, and that of Yigal Amir, who is said to have abused Arabs and bragged about it when he was a soldier, before he murdered the Prime Minister at the peace rally. Rabbi Druckman could see no connection.

In other words, Rabbi Druckman did not accept any responsibility for the fact that extremists like Yigal Amir and his like were a product of the educational system which he represented, and he did not show any readiness to enter into a soul-searching process. What is distressing is also that there was no awareness or willingness to admit the existence of problems involved in fundamentalism. It is simply ignored and denied.

Michael Sassar, an old friend of Rabbi Druckman, wrote him the following open letter:

Chaimke,
I am writing you these lines with the blood of my heart. I blame you and your educator friends for creating the spiritual climate that contributed to the legitimisation of [Rabin's] murder... You have long preached in the name

> of the Halakhah that one is commanded to disobey the laws of the state if they call for the settlements to be removed! And even after the murder you did not hesitate to compare giving up parts of the Land of Israel with desecrating the Sabbath – as if Jewish law is unequivocal. The certitude in your sermons on hagiography is based on a superficial and almost fundamentalist way of thinking, as if there were not many possible interpretations of Halakhah. Is there never even a small question mark in your mind as you interpret these events? Would you be willing to give some space to those who oppose your opinions? You are not educating for independent thinking, but instead for blind obedience, and for an absolute certitude that precludes humility.

Sassar speaks also from the 'blood of the hearts' of many of us who feel helpless vis-à-vis this certitude and closure that is typical of both the fanatics and fundamentalists. Deployment into certitude and closure are serious obstacles to mourning: one is so fundamentally protected from feelings of grief, conflicts and fear from loss – through the 'fortress-mentality' that nothing can be grieved and changed.

One glaring indication that Michael Sassar was correct in his charge is the formation of a 'Yigal Amir Fanclub'. This phenomenon was brought to the attention of the Israeli public on 9 August 1996, less than a year after the Rabin murder, when three seventeen-year-old girls from the state religious girls' school in Kiryat Gat, interviewed on Israel Television, expressed their admiration for Yigal Amir and called him a hero. These young students of a moderate school system told the interviewer that they had attended the court sessions at which Amir had testified after his arrest and were sending letters of encouragement and admiration to him in prison. They said what they claimed was true of a much larger number of Amir groupies at the Gross School who were collecting every bit of press information on their idol in scrapbooks.

The reports on this group of teenage religious girls sent shock waves across the religious and political spectrum and raised a public storm, especially after Israel Radio reported that the walls of the Gross School were covered with pro-Amir graffiti calling for 'Death to the Arabs' and warnings that 'Peres is Next.'

Ashkenazi Chief Rabbi Yisrael Lau, who is known for his moderate views, yet is unable to control phenomena of religious extremism, decried the behaviour of these girls as utter madness. He called for the teachers who knowingly or unwittingly permitted the proliferation of such attitudes and who related to the assassination with forgiveness or even support, to be jailed! Members of the left-wing Meretz Party held a protest vigil outside the school. The Labour faction not only denounced the teenage adoration of Rabin's assassin at the Gross School, but demanded an investigation into the scope of the phenomenon, which it called a national disaster.

Israeli President Ezer Weizman expressed his disgust of the Fanclub and those who allowed it to continue functioning at the school, asking it be attacked at the root level. But when there was a total denial on the part of the educational staff of having known about it – let alone supported it – it was difficult for many teachers at religious schools in Israel to enter into a meaningful dialogue with the students about the factors that contributed not only to the lack of mourning but also to the identification with the assassin.

Abraham Infelt, Director of Melitz, a non-profit organisation made up of educators from across the religious spectrum and specialising in informal education to promote pluralism, or at least more understanding between those of different religious orientations, warned religious Zionists to see the Fanclub as a call to deal with the fanatic impulses in their midst. Another Melitz executive, Shalom Orzach said that the teachers in many of the state religious schools tended to inculcate their views among the students, implying that only they know the real truth and that their way is the only way to reach truth. Orzach called for an open debate on these and related issues.

Abraham Stern from the religious Kibbutz Hanatziv said that, although Yigal Amir is a murderer and may be emotionally disturbed, the religious population must come to terms with the fact that 'He is one of ours. He grew up among us.' Bar Ilan is the university of the Zionist National Religious community, Stern continued, and that community must treat Amir's continued descent into fundamentalism and fanaticism while attending its law school 'as a source of worry.'

But, in an interview with Israel Army Radio, then Education Minister Zevulun Hammer of the National Religious Party called it a blood libel to say that fundamentalism is an integral ingredient of religious education. He was responding to the sharp criticism of the state religious education system for isolating its students from pluralistic and democratic influences and to the call for an end to the separation between religious and secular students. He stated that the National Religious School system had condemned right-wing extremism from the outset and had combated these trends with programmes and courses on coexistence and religious tolerance. However, it is not clear whether the steps taken in this direction, or the days that were devoted to the memory of Yitzhak Rabin, are enough to cut through the sense of certitude, domination and also defensiveness that still characterise the system.

It would seem not. For, in a yet unpublished survey of 249 students (135 girls and 114 boys) from five representative Jerusalem schools, it was found that twenty-five per cent of students in the state religious schools think that the murder of Yitzhak Rabin was necessary, as opposed to ten per cent of those in the regular state schools, and this includes the nationalist right-wing students, who are not necessarily religious. These figures make it imperative that we in Israel engage in a deep examination of who, why and how people become attracted to fundamentalist thinking and beliefs.

Two investigative journalists published articles about the results as well as the atmosphere in some of the schools studied. It appears that many students interviewed about the meanings of Yitzhak Rabin's assassination were anxious to share their thoughts, feelings and conflicts with them because they felt that they had not had enough opportunities to express or grapple with them; that the discussions were prematurely closed off.

Some of them said that although there had been much talk about Rabin's personality and about how terrible it was that he was killed by a Jew, there had not been enough public discussion about Amir's motives, about the meanings of a political murder, or about how minorities in the country who have been insulted and not related to might find solace in fundamentalist religions and political attitudes. True, there were some formal gatherings, but the atmosphere was such that in many of them people did not feel free to say what they really thought or felt. Not only were they inhibited by the principle (or fantasy) that school is not a place for political debate, but many had the feeling that other students and even some teachers, shied away from letting Rabin's murder really 'get to them'.

Whether this was due to the natural inclination to try and maintain stability in one's personal life, or due to the difficulty of grasping the horrendous implications of Amir's act, the fact remains that the meetings that did take place were conducive to not allowing people to look into themselves or those around them nor to discuss what they saw in an open, sincere and complex manner. Thus, many young people, like many of their elders, have remained alone with the implications of a political murder.

In addition, it is possible that the lack of frameworks in which people – and especially youngsters – can openly express whatever chaotic contents around the political murder of Yitzhak Rabin may come up, interfered with fulfilling one of the major tasks of mourning – to search the various aspects of responsibility rather than denying the complex problems of reality. People were locked in finger-pointing or continuing life as if everything were as before.

Willed into Existence

Despite protests to the contrary, the phenomenon of the Amir Fanclub and the survey of student responses to the political murder strengthen the belief that the assassin was not a lone gunman, merely acting out a personal fantasy. The sad fact is that it was willed into existence by a fanatic strain that has developed at the extreme margins of Israeli society. In fact, Professor Uriel Simon of Bar-Ilan University said in an interview with Israel Army Radio that the admiration for Rabin's assassin and the justification of his deed are not merely a marginal phenomenon.

Simon told his interviewer that religious Zionism did indeed undertake a process of soul-searching after the Rabin assassination, but the process was cut short prematurely after the victory of the right in the national elections. This means that the values absorbed at home and in school by the girls from Gross School have not been significantly examined by those responsible for National Religious education.

What became clear from many responses of the students who were interviewed was that many of them, also from the religious camp, were very sad and cried for Rabin. But when they recalled the subsequent series of terrorist bombings in which so many Israelis died, they paused to think, and worried. Many of those who had previously supported the Oslo Accords now began to fear that the Arabs could not be trusted and that the Oslo Accords would bring not peace but increased risks to our society. No less important was the conflict of loyalty that many of these students began to experience. It was as if by continuing to support Rabin's efforts they would be betraying the innocent victims of these and other terror acts, just as many people, especially those on the extreme right, continue to base much of their current thinking about Israel's security on their memory and similar feelings about the millions who died in the Holocaust. This is one form of the pathological deployment, when the conflict of loyalties and the guilt of the survivors operate unconsciously with the result that the dead from our past – and not so very far past – determine our present goals and cut off possibilities for our future.

A fantasy was expressed that Rabin had the power to put a stop to the terrorism, but did not do so. The longing for an omnipotent powerful figure and the fantasy wishes that he alone will save us is symptomatic of both fundamentalism and fanaticism and characterises many Israelis who tend to disavow responsibility for trying to deal with the complex set of phenomena involved in the effort to transform a history of war and strife into one of reconciliation and peace.

Several students who admired Yigal Amir said that it was his courage and power that impressed them. 'He did what we only talked about.' 'His action made him great in my eyes, although he should have chosen another way than murder to demonstrate his power.'

In reading these statements, I cannot help but feel that the students who identify with Yigal Amir's act were unconsciously trying to correct and repair a personal and perhaps also a national state of deep injury, which they perceived as due to their cowardliness, impotence and paralysis in terrifying situations. Through identifying with parts of Yigal Amir's courage, they wished unconsciously to correct their state of shame from when they had been inactive.

Although teachers in all the schools of Israel were asked to help students, to lead discussions on the severity of political murder and its implications for democracy in Israel, not many of them have the attitudes or skills necessary to facilitate sincere soul-searching. They do not have the attitudes of tolerance and pluralism needed to facilitate sincere and open thinking and communication. Some of the ways to promote such emotional and cognitive attitudes and skills in educational leaders, which might further the mourning tasks and reduce the fanatic and fundamentalist trends, will be discussed in the postscript.

Some Comments – a Year After

The Knesset unanimously passed the first reading of a bill which calls for the establishment of a centre in memory of Yitzhak Rabin. The proposed centre will include an archive, memorial sites and an educational institute. The anniversary is to be a day dedicated to teaching about democracy and tolerance in schools.

Multiple events took place on the anniversary, including special sessions in classrooms and army bases, a memorial service at Yitzhak Rabin's tombstone, speeches in Parliament, discussions on television and radio, and crowded rallies with those who grieved for Rabin and were missing him.

There were those who committed themselves to the lessons learned from the murder, and who mourned. But not all in Israel mourned their leader a year later. There was a lack of attention paid to the murder in quite a few schools, especially in religious ones. Hundreds of ultra-Orthodox schools have made it clear that they plan no special lessons and many more have made no secret of the fact that for them Rabin was not a hero. In none of the Torah study brochures prepared weekly by various religious institutions in Israel was there any link with the anniversary of Rabin's murder.

On the left, many thought that until the Labour Party learned to liberate itself from the alienation, arrogance and opacity towards those who are neither left nor secular; and until they gain more empathy with the emotional, spiritual and economic needs of broad social strata, of various ethnic groups, the polarisation will remain and nothing will change (A Golan, 4 June 1996; Galili, 8 November 1996; O Shohat, 21 May 1996).

The murder of Rabin has not exorcised violence from Israel: violence on the roads, violence in family life, even violence in schools – all are connected in a way and contribute to the acts of terror.

On the eve of the first anniversary of Yitzhak Rabin's death, a member of the Knesset, Yael Dayan, was attacked in the Jewish Quarter of Hebron by a Jewish terrorist from Jerusalem. He had served three years of a twenty-year sentence, having avenged the murder of an Israeli soldier by Arabs. Now he threw a cup of boiling tea in Dayan's face, causing second-degree burns.

The brutal physical attack on Member of the Knesset Yael Dayan was just one more in a series of violent acts, both physical and verbal, whose causes have not been sufficiently addressed during the past year. There is still a high level of silence which is being read as acquiescence, even sanction, not only by those on the fringe, but by their mainstream supporters of whom there are many (Goodman, 14 November 1996).

'A year has passed and nothing has changed,' said Yonatan Ben-Artzi, Rabin's grandson, speaking on behalf of the Rabin family at the state ceremony marking the first anniversary. 'We are swimming in a sea of confusion... looking for the way out; it seems that there is no end to it' (Tzur, 25 October 1996). There is chaos that creates turmoil, anxiety, shame and guilt. These harden into self-defeating deployments; but chaos may also become a source of growth through finding creative ways to mourn and reach reconciliation, peace and integration. There is a constant interactive relationship between the collective and the individual, between the political and the emotional.

Let us look a little more closely at Jewish fundamentalism and how it seems to affect the possibility of change.

Chapter VII
FUNDAMENTALISM AMONG ULTRA-ORTHODOX JEWS: DEPLOYMENTS AGAINST CHANGE

In this chapter, I shall focus on the Ashkenasic Haredim, the Israeli orthodox religious group, who – according to my thinking – represent Jewish fanaticism and fundamentalism in its extreme. Unlike the National Religious Zionists, this group is not Zionist, nor nationalist nor democratic.

To give some background information: Heilman (1992) finds approximately 550,000 Jews in the United States and in Israel who are Haredim, about half of them in Israel; there are different factions in the group and different points of emphasis; common to the ultra-Orthodox movement of the Haredim is a powerful belief based on strict adherence to certain tenets held to be fundamental to their faith. For instance, Abramov (1976) writes that according to Neturei Karta (a very small group, mostly ultra-Orthodox, who do not recognise the state of Israel and will not speak Hebrew because it is a sacred language) the world must be transformed to fit the Halakha (religious law); and this will come about in God's own time when the advent of the Messiah will create a new physical and spiritual reality adapted to the Halakha.

Another group, Agudat Israel, are concerned with preventing legislation that runs counter to the Halakha. The end justifies the means in their battle to change the system. The Haredi community is a very closed group that lives, in many respects, in the past. Heilman (1992) describes how on his first trip to Jerusalem he was fascinated by the living incarnation of the past, where people still held fast to every tradition and where nothing of substance can penetrate from the outside world.

In his book, *Defenders of the Faith: Inside Ultra-Orthodox Jews*, he writes that the term 'Haredim' was first used to denote all Jews who were religious, observant and pious. Later 'Haredim' became reserved for those who had not made accommodations to and compromises with modern lifestyles. One basic element is their emphasis on traditionalism. A second element of Haredi belief is to be one of those who tremble 'at His word'. This is where the term 'Haredi' comes from – Isaiah 66:5. It means to share an existential angst about the continuing survival of Judaism and Jewish ways of life, and about its capacity to withstand the cultural onslaught of modern secular society. Their education revolves and evolves around a narrow and parochial interpretation of Judaism in which it is considered sinful to study anything that contradicts this interpretation.

The position of the Haredi spiritual leaders who advocate this way of life is focused on two premises foreign to any liberal pluralistic society based on initiative and labour. The first premise is that the redemption will come only when all Jews spend all or most of their time studying the holy scriptures as interpreted by Haredi rabbis and adhere strictly to Halakha. The second is that since man cannot trust his own common sense, intelligence and integrity, he should not be able to think or decide for himself, to entertain thoughts and truths other than those deemed 'kosher' by the Haredi rabbis (Rolef 1996).

According to their belief, education for openness and democracy destroys respect for parents (Bakshi Doron, 21 November 1996, the Sephardic Chief Rabbi of Israel). There is no crack in their faith. They tend to raise barricades around themselves, as they are afraid of outside influence. They define themselves as a 'learning society': men seclude themselves in *yeshivot* in which they study the holy scriptures without maintaining contact with general culture and knowledge. 'Learning Torah is not a part-time occupation, but rather a full-time preoccupation, contiguous with life itself' (Heilman 1992:173).

According to Abramov (1976), it cannot be emphasised sufficiently that the Ashkenazic community of the old *yishuv* – which towards the end of the nineteenth century created the basic patterns of ultra-Orthodox Judaism in Palestine – was unique in that it did not have to concern itself with the primary object of all societies, making a living.

The old *yishuv* was largely free to ignore the outside world. It could turn its energies entirely towards the pursuit of the religious life. The Haredi community built into its basic patterns exclusiveness, resistance to change and a tendency towards militancy, all of which characterise them to this day.

The meticulously guarded isolation tended to breed an attitude of self-righteousness and superiority. Since the establishment of the state, they have been supported and financially maintained by donations from abroad and by the Israeli secular and religious working citizens upon whom the Haredim tend to look down with contempt and arrogance (Dankner 1996).

The Haredi community is not the only community that receives money from the state without giving anything in exchange. But it is the only one that turned this behaviour into an ideology and an accepted norm. 'What would be so bad about a religious sector that is able to stand on its own two feet? Why can't the kingdoms of David and Solomon be the model for our modern Haredim? Why does their model have to be that of *schnorr* and *haluka* (fund-raising and distribution) of Jewish history's less glorious days?' asks the political scientist Susan Hattis Rolef (2 October 1996), thus expressing the deep resentment that many Israelis feel towards the Haredim who live at the expense of the nation and do not share its duties, such as military service.

The Haredim are very certain of their superiority and 'purism', they are convinced that they represent the real Judaism. Many secular Jews tend to debate with them from an attitude of inferiority – as though they do not have a crystallised Jewish identity and the spiritual values that go with it – though they consider the Haredi community as an ossified, uncreative and prejudiced society with undemocratic attitudes and ways of living. This position increases the power of Israeli fundamentalism (Shohat 1996) and weakens the state in its fight for democracy and individual freedom as ultimate goals.

Though fifty-one per cent of Jerusalem first-graders were Haredim, as television channel 1 broadcast on 20 September 1996, in a report on the relationship between the Haredim and the secular Israeli, they are still a minority in the country. Nevertheless, they make no bones about using their political power to suppress the lifestyles of those who are not Haredi, be they secular, National Religious or even devout Sephardim who the Ashkenazic–Haredi disdain.

The Haredim see no value in democracy, the laws of the state and its rules. On the contrary, they fight them. Wherever the Haredi are dominant, they impose norms that suppress the ways of living of those who are not Haredi (Sheleg 1996).

Among their methods of making others obey their rules is the *herem* (excommunication order). Thus, for instance, huge posters are hanging in the Haredi neighbourhood issued by the Rabbinical Court warning all Jews not to come within four cubits (an ancient measure derived from the forearm, about eighteen to twenty-two inches in length) of an excommunicated person involved, not to have any dealings with him, talk to him or count him for a *minyan* (prayer group of at least ten persons) in the synagogue (Shapiro 1996).

To permit a look into customs that reflect their beliefs and ways of living, I shall briefly describe a mass public prayer to exorcise *dybbuks* (evil spirits that are said to seize a living person suffering from mental and emotional problems), as reported by Hecht (1996).

Professor Yoram Bilu of the Hebrew University's Department of Psychology and Sociology explained that the exorcism of *dybbuks* is an Ashkenazi phenomenon dating back to the sixteenth century. The *dybbuk* would appear in the womb of a woman and speak with a different voice, often that of a man. To make the *dybbuk* leave, the exorcist would bring the victims to the synagogue, tie them up if the spirit was violent and gag them if the spirit refused to be quiet. This mass public prayer to exorcise the *dybbuk* was performed in a somewhat different manner. It was a combination of a revivalist meeting, and prayers for the ill, peppered with requests for donations.

More than four hundred men and women crowded into the Ohel Rachel synagogue in Jerusalem's Mekor Baruch Quarter on 12 August 1996 for what was billed as a mass prayer to exorcise *dybbuks*. The rabbis who fasted that day blew *shofars* (the ritualistic horn of Judaism) in the ears of the victims, who suffered from mental, emotional, neurological or other physical illnesses, in order to heal them (Hecht 1996).

The most revolting aspect of their behaviour is the growing violence that reaches the dimension of terrorism as a political system. The attack on the centre for Jewish pluralism of the movement for Advanced (Reform) Judaism is one of the less well-known examples.

After the 1996 elections, the centre received hundreds of threats from important *yeshivot* in Jerusalem such as *Sphat Emet*, and *Beit Avraham* – threats to burn the centre, announcements about hidden bombs, messages praising the wisdom of Yigal Amir's murder of Rabin; suggesting that if he were free he would have liquidated all the reformists. Anat Galili, the spokesperson of the centre, claimed that the police did not hurry to investigate.

Terrorist tendencies were also demonstrated in their violent attacks against secular women who worked in the Ministry of Education, which is near the neighbourhood of the Haredim. The increased power of the Haredi parties led them to feel entitled to throw stones and dirty nappies at those who were perceived by them as sinners: women who were judged insufficiently modest in dress or appearance, or at the policemen who protected those attacked.

The perpetrators relied on the police not to deal with them harshly, or on the courts to mete out lenient sentences, and on the rabbinical authorities to refrain from condemnation (Abramov 1976:233). These forgiving attitudes on the part of the rabbinical educational and legal authorities served to encourage their power of terror and demagoguery.

The most dangerous development was the Haredi delegitimisation of the Supreme Court and the attack on its president, Aharon Barak. Haredi parties long ago indicated that they fear the judiciary might cancel religious laws that are in conflict with basic laws of the state. They have in the past accused the Supreme Court of pre-empting the Knesset, prior to legislation.

Less than a year after Yitzhak Rabin's assassination by a Jewish student stimulated by ultra-Orthodox fanatics, there was danger of a recurrence. This time, the target was a jurist, Professor Barak, President of the Supreme Court, the recipient of an Israel Prize for his many scholarly books. His crime was that the Supreme Court had recently ruled that a major Jerusalem thoroughfare, which borders on an ultra-Orthodox neighbourhood, should not be closed on the Jewish Shabbat, pending further proceedings. The Bar-Ilan thoroughfare has become both a symbol and a test case.

Throwing stones at the policemen guarding Bar-Ilan Street, delegitimising the Supreme Court and its president, sending threats to his life, attacks on the workers in the Ministry of Education and other acts of violence, constitute a dangerous series of terror acts which are neither stopped nor condemned by the Haredi leadership.

The uproar started when at least six ultra-Orthodox newspapers launched a vitriolic campaign against Supreme Court Chief Justice Aharon Barak (Gross 1996).

Two articles appeared on the 27 August 1996 in the Haredi papers, one in the *Hashavua* and the other in the *Yated Ne'eman* (Gordon 1996), the mouthpiece of the Agudat Yisrael Party. *Yated* attacked Supreme Court President Aharon Barak for being 'a dangerous enemy of Orthodox Jews,' dangerous to both Judaism and democracy (Gordon 1996).

'This dangerous enemy is called Aharon Barak,' said the piece in *Yated*. 'He is stronger than any government. He overshadows the police, the legislation and also the executive... He has arrogated to himself the right to decide for me and for you what we are permitted to think and what we have the right to fight for... ' Following this introduction most of the piece was devoted to an analysis of the source of Barak's power and how it could be undermined.

The key is very simple, the article said: 'A politician who is photographed at every opportunity and speaks into every microphone... sometimes receives great honour, but he is also exposed to criticism and contempt, a great deal of contempt.' The author, Haim Walder, then related a story he had heard from his grandfather 'of a rich Hungarian Jew, who despite being generally hated, was considered above everyone else, until one day, he slipped and fell in the mud. From then on, the people no longer considered him superior and treated him as his nastiness deserved', this is also the way to handle Barak, the report said. Having gotten involved in political matters, he is already in the mud.

The Haredi journalist Yisrael Eichler said that Haredi education teaches them to heap disgrace on a power that is cut off from Judaism. Eichler explained that the religious community felt as if Barak's power was superseding the influence they felt they had won fairly in the elections. But whatever their thinking is, we can see and feel how their criticism of the court's decisions was not aimed at the substance of the decisions, but at the judges themselves. And as Uriel Lynn notes, 'when the criticism is concentrated *ad hominem* on one judge and brands him as an enemy, it no longer constitutes judicial criticism, but is a declaration of war.'

The Haredim declared that 'we must not scatter our ammunition. The battle must be concentrated on that man who is extremely dangerous to democracy and freedom!' The phrase 'dangerous enemy' became a code word in the post-Rabin assassination era (Dershowitz 1996). The incitement against Rabin had started from Haredi articles. Not even a year had passed and the same incitement repeated itself.

The country is still feeling the assassination of Rabin, by a killer who seemed to many to have been influenced and inspired by rhetoric coming out of the extreme religious national right. Yigal Amir's act was followed by months of national soul-searching as to whether something could have been done; that if the verbal violence had been nipped in the bud, perhaps the murder could have been prevented. The extremist religious press has debated whether Rabin should die or not, and has repeatedly used terms like 'traitor', 'insane', and 'non-Jew'. And so, every word of the editorials which have appeared during 1996 and 1997 in Haredi newspapers vilifying Barak has been taken seriously (Sommer 1996).

The general feeling was that this was a lesson that we did learn from the awful incitement that preceded Rabin's murder. It was quite a common feeling that it was just this kind of hate speech which had stimulated Yigal Amir to believe that it was his religious duty to strike down the dangerous enemy; that now these attacks could not be interpreted anymore as anger from a fringe element who, for all their ferociousness, would do no harm (Sommer 1996).

Public condemnation of the articles from all sides of the political spectrum followed. 'If you say to people like these that Barak is Judaism's most dangerous enemy, it is like branding him as a traitor of Judaism as was done to Rabin,' said Moshe Negbi, an Israeli Radio legal expert, who felt that the articles against Barak, as well as the posters condemning Barak that appeared in Jerusalem neighbourhoods, all had the elements of incitement that appeared in the attacks on Rabin last year. The violent tone of the articles and the posters – he said – could almost be translated into violent acts, especially when directed at a public which considered religious values above the law. Negbi expressed his astonishment at how the justice system could have treated the incitements that preceded Rabin's assassination with such inexplicable passivity.

A public furore erupted over the attacks against Supreme Court President Aharon Barak; they were unequivocally denounced by both opposition and coalition members. Nearly every public figure from the Bar Association to President Ezer Weizman came strongly to the defence of Barak and the Supreme Court. 'The Supreme Court is the citadel that upholds the law and protects human rights in Israel,' said Science and Technology Minister Ze'ev Begin, son of former Prime Minister Menahem Begin. 'We must not impinge on its powers or reduce its sphere of activity.' Meretz leader Yossi Sarid compared the attacks on Barak to the incitement against Rabin. 'They had incited against Rabin, called him a traitor, and Rabin was murdered,' he said. 'That is a fact. All the rest is pretence, crocodile tears and saying it was not our hands which spilled this blood. But someone is responsible for what happened. And what happened once could happen again.'

Hashavua editor Asher Zuckerman said that the article in his publication expressed the dissatisfaction of much of the *Haredi* community with the method of appointing judges. Others argued that the Supreme Court is not above public criticism; that the court must take into account the values that are current in parts of the society and its legitimate feelings. There is a significant portion of the population who claim that the courts are no longer neutral mediators; that when the Supreme Court makes a decision in matters of values over which there are legitimate differences, it is hard to prevent the deterioration of its status.

Since the assassination of Yitzhak Rabin, and even more after the recent Haredi attacks on the President of the Supreme Court, one of the main questions which has occupied the public is the difference between freedom of expression and criminal incitement. 'There is freedom of expression but there is no freedom of incitement,' stressed Finance Minister Dan Meridor, who spoke of the attacks on Barak as a campaign of severe incitement, unprecedented in the state's history, aimed at damaging not only senior justices, but at undermining the basic values of society and the public's confidence in the system of justice. Meridor said that a torn society such as ours cannot survive without the restrictions laid down by the Supreme Court. He commended the Supreme Court justices, singling out Barak for his unique concept of democracy and Judaism in the state and his protection of the most basic interests of society.

The airwaves were full of calls from politicians with proposals to close down the Haredi newspapers, or to do something to stop their publications or take legal action against them. Attorney-General, Michael Ben-Yair decided not to open criminal investigation of Haredi journalists and rabbis who attacked the Supreme Court and its president. Ben-Yair noted that he is, in general, reluctant to prosecute people for what they say because of the importance of allowing freedom of expression. Taking legal action in such cases, he said, is likely to lead to one of two undesirable consequences: either it will put a gag on people who hold such views or it would focus even more attention on these views, giving the perpetrators a platform in court from which to expound their views. Legal action would also alienate the Haredi community even further (Gordon 1996).

Barak discussed the recent attacks on himself and on the Supreme Court with the Knesset Law Committee saying that they 'damaged the delicate fabric of Israeli democracy' (Gordon 1996). As to the claim that value judgements are unfairly mixed into the rulings, Barak explained that there is no court in the world that does not make value judgements; just as the law reflects values, so also the legal divisions reflect values. These value judgements must not, however, be subjective.

Barak suggested that the wave of anger would soon blow over and saner voices would prevail. He stressed the importance of free expression as long as there is no injury to the public order. He responded favourably to the suggestion of Rabbi Eliahu Bakshi Doron (Sephardic Chief Rabbi of Israel) to initiate a dialogue with the Haredi community regarding the High Court and the Supreme Court's decision.

Alan Dershowitz, Professor of Law at Harvard, was pained to see Barak, recipient of the Israel Prize, needing to be protected from Jews, he who had survived the Nazi Holocaust. He writes (1996) that the great enemy of democracy and of freedom in today's world is religious fundamentalism which believes it has the right to enforce what it believes to be God's command. There is no real difference, Dershowitz maintains, between Islamic fundamentalists who issue a death warrant against Salman Rushdie, a Christian fundamentalist who calls for the killing of abortion doctors and Jewish fundamentalists who call for the assassination of a Prime Minister who is seeking a controversial peace.

Haim Cohn, a former Supreme Court justice, who came out vocally in support of Barak, sounded his despair when he said that 'we are in the midst of an extremely cruel cultural war... There is no solution because there is not and there cannot be at this stage, a common language' (Gordon 1996).

When we look at these fundamentalist elements four years later, we witness a very striking phenomenon of similar tendencies in the reaction of the Shas Party and its spiritual leader, Rabbi Ovadiah Yossef, to the judgement of the Jerusalem District Court which indicted Aryeh Deri, head and leader of the Shas party, for corruption with no remorse, and sentenced him to six years in prison. The big party (now seventeen members of the 120 members of the Knesset) all rebelled against the judgement and pronounced Deri's innocence and justice in all communication media.

'Although only a small number of people take part in violence, thousands provide active support and millions remain silent and oblivious,' wrote Gerald Steinberg, a teacher of political studies at Bar-Ilan. 'The sobering reality is that in the long run it is our religious and cultural conflicts that pose the greatest threat of all to our society and to our people.'

I found myself writing and reading about the Haredi community, and suddenly I asked myself how I had become so involved in it. Was it because of a need to relate as a psychoanalyst not only to the individual self, but also to the group self (Moses 1982) and the national psyche which are all closely interwoven? Was it because from extreme situations, it is easier to learn about the normal? 'The extremism and the contrast are the key to understand the Haredi street,' wrote Amnon Levy (1981), a secular journalist who traced the Haredi life during four years. 'There is so much violence in their culture,' he wrote, 'they live so near to us and influence our ways of life. Yet so much about them remains unknown.'

It is only when we have mobilised an empathic attempt to really understand them and try to remove the 'blind spot' that interferes with our seeing the whole picture and reduce the sense of estrangement that exists towards the different parts of Israeli society that we will be able to avoid the black hole that might otherwise swallow all of us up (Kleinberg, 27 November 1996). Thus perhaps this drive of mine to look at the broader spectrum and become acquainted with the grievances of the various ethnic groups that contribute to the violence, and especially with such an extreme group as the Haredim, whose violence for hundreds of years has been denied even by historians (Rosen, 15 November 1996) is an attempt to do what Kleinberg suggested.

As the historian Ilan Assia writes (8 November 1996), the Haredi radicalism in which Yigal Amir grew up had a partial ideological influence on him, even if the contrasting nationalistic religious ideology had the main impact on him. Thus, interest in the Haredim was part of my exploring the meanings which the political murder of Yitzhak Rabin had for us. But, primarily, I feel that what motivated me to deal with the Haredim was the part they had in this chain of events, which so strongly reflect the strategies of deployment.

Fundamentalistic Religion and Deployment

Religion and faith can be spiritually nourishing and provide tranquillity, peace and solace. However, when religion turns into a political power conflict and into a battle in the name of God, it can easily become a source of hatred, bigotry, obscurantism and inhumanity. As Erik Erikson said: 'In the name of high moral principles all the vindictiveness of derision, of torture and of mass extinction can be employed' (Erikson 1964:224). Would people be more respectful of others and otherness, if they could realise the moral problem of persons feeling entitled to coerce others to live according to their version of truth, while ignoring the injustice this involves for others? There should be space for each to live peacefully according to his or her faith. But when power motives, that often operate unconsciously or partially unconsciously, are mobilised, when there is a strong sense of entitlement and a need to blame others for difficulties that exist; when the badness is projected onto others without any readiness to look into one's own part and inner world; and when fights against the others are fought in the name of holiness (Moses 1983) – then this is a sign of pathological deployment which needs to be dealt with firmly and completely.

The general feeling of many secular or more liberal religious Israelis is that leaders of the Haredi and the non-Haredi religious community should be more active and unequivocal in calling for an end to Haredi violence; that we need a strong unified and unifying voice, capable of rejecting violence and pressure from all sides, together with a rational determined policy, such as finding foci of solidarity and voluntary principles of mutuality, and, most importantly, the separation between religion and state. In addition, I feel that our alertness to the presence of deploymental aspects, and our attempts on a variety of emotional, cognitive and behavioural levels to deal with these aspects, would enable us to find new and creative ways of resolving the conflicts between Judaism and tolerance, Judaism and democracy, Judaism and universal culture.

Rabbi Mordechai Elon, a leading voice in the religious Zionist movement, notes that the population of Israel is behaving like adolescents, attaching too much weight to their ideology and world-view, without the maturity of seeing beyond it. Today one side views retaining the Land of Israel as *pikuah nefesh* (danger to a life that must be saved, something which overrides all other religious injunctions); the other side sees continuing the peace as *pikuah nefesh*. A political outlook should not be bloated into an existential question on which the country stands or falls.

'For Rabbi Mordechai Elon, the government's redeployment (of the Israeli army in Hebron) and move away from the Cave of the Patriarchs will be a private day of mourning, but it is not an existential threat to Israel... The Jewish people lived two thousand years without Hebron, but when we start shooting at each other we won't last a day!' (Tzalal, 18 October 1996).

I think that Rabbi Elon, who is active in the National Religious Party, relates to an essential aspect of deployment – the tendency to put too much weight on some selected elements at the expense of being with the whole; on narrowing down and then fighting for a narrow goal, while ignoring what matters most – the unity (of the nation). André Haynal's study of fanaticism shows how fluid the borders between the fanatic's state of mind and the psychological state of a person are, with no apparent signs of imbalance. 'A potential fanatic is hiding in each of us, albeit in different degrees, and fanaticism can be found in any camp.'

It is, therefore, crucially important to study in each of us the seeds of fanaticism and the enactments of deployments, which we unknowingly tend to carry out or be caught in; we must be alert to their existence and try our utmost to maintain control over them.

I want to conclude with a satire written by Ephraim Kishon, a well-known Israeli satirical dramatist. When Yossi Banai, an Israeli actor, read this satire on television, I felt that it beautifully demonstrated some major aspects of deployment.

The Trade Union Building has been Destroyed by Ephraim Kishon

The players: Fuchs, Stucks

The place: Stucks's bedroom. Stucks is sound asleep in his bed.

	It is early in the morning. Someone is knocking at the door.
STUCKS:	(*Wearing pyjamas, gets out of bed, grumbling to himself.*) Damn it all… Go to hell! Who would wake a man up at this hour? You can't even rest for a minute… Of all the— (*he opens the door*). Good morning Mr Fuchs, this is really a pleasure. What happened?
FUCHS:	(*Bursts into the room, very excited and breathless.*) Hello! I know, Mr Stucks, you're mad at me. Never mind, I'd be mad too if I were you. But when I tell you what all this is about, I bet that you will tell me: 'Fuchs! For a thing like that you just had to wake me up, even in the middle of the night!'
STUCKS:	Maybe you would be interested to know that I still want to sleep today?
FUCHS:	(*Somewhat taken aback.*) Please, I wanted to do you a favour. I've already stopped by all the residents on the first floor and I thought, really, that Stucks deserves a sensation like this… (*Slowly, emphasising each syllable.*) Tonight they blew up the Workers' Committee Building…
STUCKS:	The Trade Union?
FUCHS:	The Trade Union!
STUCKS:	Blew up?
FUCHS:	Blew up!
STUCKS:	Tonight?
FUCHS:	Tonight!
STUCKS:	I didn't hear any explosion.
FUCHS:	I didn't either. It seems that we were sleeping too soundly. But Konstadter almost went deaf. He immediately ran to consult me at half past two in the morning. After that he hurried to the neighbouring

	buildings, and here, in our building, I'm organising things. What do you say about that? An enormous building like that, really almost a skyscraper, destroyed all in one night right under our noses! That really is something, don't you think?
STUCKS:	Is this thing certain?
FUCHS:	(*Nearly howling.*) Well excuse me, it will be in all the newspapers!
STUCKS:	So why did you wake me up?
FUCHS:	What do you mean, *why*? Do you want to sleep when half the world is being destroyed? A sensation like that? In one night to blow up the whole Trade Union?
STUCKS:	Tell me, Mr Fuchs, why are you so happy that they blew up the Trade Union Building? What's so good about that?
FUCHS:	What's so good about that? It is a little strange, Mr Stucks, excuse me. In spite of it all we showed them—
STUCKS:	Showed whom?
FUCHS:	Them! At least not everybody gives in to them… There are still some real men around, as they say… All the world will know that in the middle of Tel Aviv, by the light of the moon, they destroyed an enormous building! Such a sensation! (*Stucks goes to the window and looks out.*) We fought in World War I, so we know how to appreciate what it means to blow up a building at night.
STUCKS:	Thank you. You can stop now, Fuchs. Come over here and look. Not a single word you said is true. The Trade Union Building is standing right here!
FUCHS:	(*Puts on a wounded expression and doesn't budge.*)
STUCKS:	(*Raising his voice.*) Mr Fuchs, the building stands just

	as it always has.
FUCHS:	(*Doesn't budge.*)
STUCKS:	Don't you hear?
FUCHS:	I hear. I'm not deaf.
STUCKS:	Maybe you want to look outside?
FUCHS:	This is a fantastic occurrence.
STUCKS:	Why don't you want to prove it to yourself with your own eyes?
FUCHS:	I don't want to.
STUCKS:	Why not?
FUCHS:	Tonight they blew up the Trade Union Building.
STUCKS:	But look outside!
FUCHS:	I'm not going to look.
STUCKS:	Why not?
FUCHS:	There's no need to look.
STUCKS:	But the building is standing there right in front of your eyes!
FUCHS:	It is not standing. Tonight they blew it up.
STUCKS:	(*Starting to get annoyed.*) How can you say a thing like that, when you can see it here with you very own eyes?
FUCHS:	I don't have to see anything. Konstadter told me, and that is enough for me.
STUCKS:	What the hell! So what if Konstadter said so?
FUCHS:	Aha! You're going to say that Konstadter is a liar? Have it your own way, I'll tell him. Do you have any idea what connections Konstadter has?
STUCKS:	Who is Konstadter, for God's sake?

FUCHS: You don't even know who he is? So how do you dare slander him?

STUCKS: (*Shouting.*) But when you can see Konstadter standing right here in his place all in one piece... Konstadter is standing right in his place.

FUCHS: Do you hear what you are saying? Konstadter is standing there? What, are you trying to mix me up? You are talking crazy, such nonsense.

STUCKS: (*A little subdued.*) Not Konstadter, but the Trade Union Building is standing in its place. I really would like you to come to the window and verify this fact before I completely lose control.

FUCHS: I'm not going to argue with you. Konstadter told me, and that is certainly enough for me.

STUCKS: But here, right in front of your eyes.

FUCHS: Don't be so stubborn, Stucks! You're hardly a boy any more. You're a grown man! I can bring you witnesses who heard with their own ears, when Konstadter told me, that tonight they completely destroyed the Workers' Committee Building!

STUCKS: Listen, sir, usually I am thought of as a man who thinks clearly. If I tell you that in a very short while I am going to lose my senses and start to go wild, you can be certain that that is what will happen. I ask you again: are you willing to come to the window or not?

FUCHS: Even the radio said it, if you want to know.

STUCKS: Which radio?

FUCHS: Konstadter's radio. A great receiver with five lights. It even picks up Hong Kong! And anyway – mister – don't push me! If I want to know if they destroyed the building or not, I can peep out from my window too. But I don't want to peep out from there either.

STUCKS:	(*Roaring.*) But here you will peep out, Fuchs! Get over to the window, Fuchs!
FUCHS:	(*Retreating.*) Maybe I'll come some other time?
STUCKS:	No! Now! Look, damn it, or this will be the death of you!
FUCHS:	(*Forced to the window, but avoiding to look out, even though Stucks is holding him by the neck.*) Under no circumstances!
STUCKS:	(*Struggling with Fuchs.*) Look, you bastard, look! Open your eyes, do you hear? Answer me! Answer me!
FUCHS:	(*Groaning.*) I'm near-sighted.
STUCKS:	So look close up, damn it all! Is it destroyed or not? Answer me! Answer me!
FUCHS:	(*Trembling.*) Don't torture me!
STUCKS:	What about the building? Did they blow it up or not? The devil take you! Is the building standing or not?
FUCHS:	What are you shouting about? Can't we settle things quietly?
STUCKS:	Look! Is the building standing or not?
FUCHS:	Now it is standing.
STUCKS:	What do you mean, now?
FUCHS:	At night it was destroyed, and by morning they built it again from scratch.
STUCKS:	They built it up again from scratch. You can't build a building like that in one night!

FUCHS: No? You just don't know what Solel Boneh[1] is capable of doing, at least where their buildings are concerned!

Why did I choose Kishon's play?

Kishon's poetic drama epitomises deployment through the deadlock created when one is locked in one's belief and when factual data cannot open a vision to clear evidence. The satire portrays those who blindly follow their beliefs or myths, which seem to fulfil certain conscious as well as unconscious wishes. Perhaps the vengeful destruction of the huge Trade Union Building symbolises the rebellion against a super power or unfair rule. I do not know the author's meaning, but to me it felt as if Fuchs was so furious at the trade union that he already saw it burning, rushing to celebrate the enemy's defeat, wishfully thinking that the feeling transmitted was a fanatic's enthusiasm and zeal, even though, as it turns out, the building still existed and stood as ever.

The satire illustrates how deployment pushes one into narrow one-track-mindedness, where reality does not count. One sees what one wants to see. One believes what one came to believe without letting oneself be disturbed by facts and without minding the inadequacy of one's behaviour and speeches. One thereby holds onto 'having a small head' – an Israeli colloquial phrase which describes entering the role of not wanting to see the whole picture, of narrowing one's focus and behaving accordingly, lest one be confused by the awesome complexity of the situation. Additionally, one cannot then be held responsible. It is a simple and resolute refusal to open one's eyes and use one's senses and mind to examine the reality around one. The certainty of conviction in one's version of the truth is then unshakeable. When Stucks raised doubts, they were considered to be irrelevant. How can one doubt the belief? There was no readiness whatsoever to check the validity of the proclamation – be it because of the insult of not being trusted, or because of the thirst for sensation and excitement which may help in the survival of depressive times; or

---

[1] The Israeli Trade Union Building Company.

in order to avoid the humiliation involved in realising that one is in error and admitting to it; or because one does not want to give up a fantasy wish.

Whatever his motivations, Fuchs reveals the repertoire of counter-shame strategies often used by persons who are deployed, both to prove their self-righteousness and to save face. When at last Fuchs agreed to look and admit the truth he immediately invented a new version: the building *was* destroyed at night, but by morning they had rebuilt it from scratch.

Through identifying with Stucks, we can feel how such a deployment, when seen in others, can cause us to lose control and explode or become despairing and feel that there is nobody to talk to.

The kinds of deployment that have been portrayed in this little play exist as a 'fortress mentality' in extremist groups such as the religious national Zionists or the Haredim, as well as in many situations of our everyday life. Individuals then are sure they know how it should be and what the whole truth is. They will stick to it rigidly; not only will they have no insight into their misplaced omniscience, but they will feel very hurt when others try to suggest different thoughts, perceptions and feelings. As long as such features of pathological deployment into one-track-mindedness, polarisation and extremism are not identified, owned and then transformed back into personal feelings and accounts, it is exceedingly difficult to establish a real dialogue, to achieve a mutual and meaningful encounter and to create lasting reconciliations.

Summary

There is a growing rift between the ultra-Orthodox, that include religious fundamentalists and fanatic nationalists, and those who are democratically oriented, including the moderate right and moderate religious as well as our Arab citizens.

The meaning of the assassination did not succeed in creating a common experience for the whole people; on the contrary, each camp became more entrenched in its positions. In the terms of Staub (1995), an 'ideology of antagonism' has been established between those groups which powerfully guides the groups' emotions, thoughts and actions. Staub proposes that in order to create a connection, positive relations and reconciliation in a situation of such deep hostility and antagonism between the groups – vision, imagination and action along a number of avenues to be pursued simultaneously are required.

People need to become aware of the values, beliefs, ways of thinking and emotional tendencies within themselves, many of which often create or maintain the antagonism and deployments automatically. From the debates that have been raging over the meaning and the legacy of the assassination of Rabin, I would like to point out the following.

In the ultra-religious groups the emphasis is on the holiness of the Land, whereas in the others it is the sanctity of the human being which is the supreme value; for the democratic group, the person is sovereign and the source of authority, whereas for the ultra-Orthodox God is sovereign and the source of authority: the individual is merely a tool to actualise God's will. One group is driven to form a halakhic state where Halakha determines the ways of living and beliefs of the individual; the other group espouses freedom of the individual, openness, pluralism and universalism.

Whereas the democratic values such as pragmatism, positivism and rationalism stress the present, the existence on earth here and now, as well as facing the future – the ultra-religious stress the life of the next world as the important vector, seeing present reality as a passing and minor corridor for it. They are solidly planted in the past. For instance, time stopped between the 1929 massacre in Hebron and now. Baruch Goldstein, who avenges their blood by killing innocent people who pray, may – according to this timeless perspective – become a Holy Man!

We are on a major crossroad: how shall we form our individual and national identity? Will it be a democratic society for which we will do everything to safeguard its rules and values? Or a society in which political militancy dominates, which negates laws, democratic structures and institutions? Will it be a modern, democratic, enlightened state that lives peacefully with its neighbours according to Rabin's vision, or will we adopt again the belief that 'all the world is against us', a prophecy that may be fulfilled if we act according to fascist beliefs and values? Is there no solution for us while we are in the midst of an extreme cultural civil war, because there is no common language – as Haim Cohen, the former Supreme Court justice said, when he expressed his despair? Are there signs of hope that more people find pride in our heritage, history and land without admixing it with messianic hatred, admiration of power and self-righteousness? More and more people are convinced of the essential need to investigate the basic components in the world-views of the fanatic groups that contributed to the growth of Yigal Amir and his supporters. More of this will be discussed in the postscript.

Chapter VIII
POSTSCRIPT

Learning to Live with Conflicts and Reducing the Forces of Fundamentalism and Fanaticism – within Us and among Us

Yitzhak Rabin's assassination has brought the majority of Israelis to the conviction that we must do everything in our power to provide an atmosphere in which 'wild weeds' like Amir will not be able to take root in our society.

On the first anniversary of the assassination, former Israeli president, Chaim Herzog, warned that as long as we do not uproot the cancer, namely the fanaticism that led zealots like Amir to commit their insane acts, we remain in danger of seeing this nightmare recur. For this purpose, it is necessary to concentrate our attention on all aspects of our lives that might lead to a worldview conducive to fanaticism, and for us to encourage any and all trends that oppose nationalistic extremism, orthodox monopoly and coercion. Only then might we achieve the type of reconciliation that will allow us to recognise our own conflicts and differences and go on to reach reconciliation with the Palestinians and our Arab neighbours.

But only two months after Herzog's talk, on 1 January 1997, Noam Friedman shot and killed innocent Arabs in the market of Hebron. Whatever the mental state of Noam Friedman was, he acted in an atmosphere of fanatical religious nationalism and he uttered the slogans of the movement. Friedman justified his act on ideological grounds similar to those of Yigal Amir. He, too, was motivated to kill 'the enemy' in order to preserve the Land of Israel, the Torah of Israel and the people of Israel. His smile, like

Amir's a year earlier, transmitted the feeling that he was a messenger of God. And he, too, insisted that he had no regrets, adopted an arrogant attitude towards his investigators and insisted that he would continue to murder as many Arabs as he could. He wanted to thwart the partial withdrawal from Hebron and exact revenge for those who to him were Jewish martyrs like Baruch Goldstein – a murderer like himself – but also Nachshon Wachsman – a victim of Palestinian fanatics. The sad fact, then, is that despite the general Israeli desire to oppose the fanatical religious nationalism that has led to the same kind of murders we have experienced on the part of Hamas fanatics on the other side, Noam Friedman was still able to claim backing for his act.

Friedman's shooting orgy in Hebron again demonstrates what many in Israel consider the greatest menace to our society: the dangerous mixture of religion and nationalism – of God and politics. It has become clear that the 'wild weeds' who commit such acts of terrorism do not act in isolation. They form a 'brotherhood' which is supported by extremist rabbis who continue to infect their followers with their perverted view of the Torah. These rabbis have made the grave of Baruch Goldstein a place of pilgrimage; they order religious soldiers to disobey orders that allegedly counteract what is written in the Bible; they either defend those who follow their injunctions to the bitter end or, when they do condemn such acts, blame them on the Labour government for having placed Israel in an unbearable position.

It is true that the rabbis who have forbidden soldiers to participate in the implementation of Israel's accords with the PLO are a small minority and include only three out of thirty heads of *hesder yeshivot*. But, if we are to embark on the road of eliminating the 'wild weeds' who are attempting to prevent reconciliation among ourselves or with our neighbours, whether in the Palestinian authority or neighbouring countries, we must somehow convince the world that we will not put up with political or spiritual leaders who legitimise or condone violence, no matter what the seemingly high-flying reasons allegedly behind it are.

Military correspondent Zeev Schiff (1997) has suggested that we can begin showing Jewish terrorists exactly how we regard them by extraditing them to the Palestinian Authority just as Israel has demanded (but not always succeeded in attaining) that Hamas and Islamic *jihad* terrorists be extradited to Israel.

An increasing number of religious leaders are coming to realise that the values they have been inculcating in religious youth distort the spirit of Zionism, Judaism and humanity in the same way as the Islamic mullahs who read the destruction of Israel into the Koran. Moderates on both sides widely accept the need to re-examine components of religious world-views that have been leading to what I call deployment into terrorism and the inability to see alternative paths to religious fulfilment.

According to the psychoanalyst Charles Hanley (1995), ideologies are characterised by a dangerous polarity that may sustain a high level of beneficial support and cohesiveness among those who share that ideology and way of life, together with an equal degree of self-righteous hostility towards those who don't. Much thought must be invested in how to perpetuate the need for values while making certain that the values being fostered include space for critical judgement, and tolerance for those with different values. Ideology may lead to perilous results when it is based on a consuming devotion that leads to narrowed thinking into unidimensionality, especially when that ideology is adopted by individuals like Yigal Amir who are excessively defended by the unconscious psychological defence mechanisms of splitting and dissociation.

The defence of disowning one's negative characteristics and projecting them onto others may help a person to maintain conscious self-esteem, but it also lays the groundwork for prejudice and racism (Firestone 1996:232) and plays a significant role in maintaining feelings of divine sanction and specialness, particularly within religious groups. I will say more about possible ways to reduce prejudice and racism in part four of this chapter.

Grinwald (22 November 1996) insists that the corrections and reparations that help break down pathological deployment have to start in one's own home. As a religious Jew, he criticises those who call themselves religious, yet who condone violence 'for the sake of religion'. He claims that a person who is religious in a spiritual and internalised sense cannot but be shocked by those who push the religion into dark corners and who use violence in a variety of ways which include seducing and brainwashing those who are lost or confused so that they turn to religion (Grinwald, 22 November 1996). This kind of behaviour has nothing to do with religion. On the contrary, it leads to a distancing of many Israelis who believe in tradition away from religion. It is not the religious who are 'no good' – it is the misuse of religion for the sake of political battles that is harmful.

When a person begins with the conviction that only he or she knows the truth, and that those who believe in any other truth are either ignorant or evil, that person leaves no room for a real debate among legitimate opinions within himself or herself and between himself and the others, a debate where dialogues could replace power struggles and violence. However, when the culture provides an opportunity for everyone to listen to the multiple voices within themselves, a much richer quality of existence results, involving the use of a diversity of personality layers instead of the one dimensional conviction offered by the certitude that there is only one truth for which we live or fight to the death. This is so since the polarisation and extremism that often follow one-dimensional thinking usually relate to previous states of crisis and trauma, to not being able to mourn and work through the tragic experiences of loss and to relinquish myths and fantasies that obstruct the process of liberalisation and reconciliation.

To mourn and work through such experiences is a prerequisite for achieving a sane, humane and tolerant society. 'Each piece of knowledge that does not lead to new questions,' writes Riselva Shimburska (24 January 1997), 'lacks the warmth that is essential for life and becomes dead.'

Shimburska goes on to say that such a rigid and dead mentality has proven dangerous to humanity. I am thinking of the racist way of thinking which brought about the Holocaust. This danger is often overlooked by those in the religious sector who hold fixed and ossified attitudes and preach against those who do not accept their interpretation of the Word of God. Professor of Philosophy at Bar Ilan University, Eliezer Goldman, is one of a growing number of Orthodox leaders who feel that the teachers of ultra-Orthodox students brutally impoverish their charges by 'shielding them from the works of great humanistic thinkers, artists and scientists as if this would defile them.'

'If the fundamentalist ultra-Orthodox will not allow education for pluralism, and towards exposure to the other and to what is different; and if they continue to view those who do not think like them as betraying the people and erring, more wild weeds will grow,' is the opinion of Rabbi Aharon Lichtenstein, head of the Gush Etzion Yeshiva. Simplistic religious education with its underlying fear of the new and the different, can become constricting, reductionistic and xenophobic, writes the psychoanalyst Bennet Simon (1996) speaking of religion (as well as of psychoanalysis) at its worst. Even though ambiguity and complexity are uncomfortable, he continues, we must not allow the fear of them to paralyse us into stasis.

According to journalist Yair Sheleg, himself a product of religious nationalistic education, one of the main problems with this education is that it calls for devotion to 'the greater Land of Israel' in complete dissociation from values such as the sanctity of the human being, morality and justice. The result of this type of education is seen in one of Yigal Amir's ideological speeches in which he claimed that he 'would have killed infants and children,' as is written in the Bible, 'in order to protect the Land of Israel,' and that he 'would have done it without problems of morality' since it is a commandment 'I have no problem with.'

Instead of attacking the senior rabbis who brought religious Zionism to the centre of the national platform, but who lack the flexibility to be open to some of its dangers when emphasised to the exclusion of other values, Sheleg suggests that the religious establishment concentrate on changing the attitudes of younger rabbis, whose norms and political views are much more complex. But this, too, will not be a simple matter.

Many of us have come to realise that to allow the small minority of fanatics, religious or political, to continue valuing the Land of Israel over human life, will only increase the polarity in Israeli society, as I will elaborate below.

As long as the ultra-Orthodox do not understand the depth of injury that their coercion causes for the rest of the population, the rift between secular and Haredi Israelis will deepen, with the moderate Orthodox population caught in the middle. 'It is an outrage to try and impose Haredi customs on Tel Aviv,' said a secular man in response to the demonstration of thousands of Haredim against the Supreme Court for not prohibiting what they view as a desecration of Sabbath in that city. If the ultra-Orthodox do not begin to change on their own, and there is little reason to suppose that they will, the government must be persuaded to take steps to bring the next generation of Haredim closer to the human values necessary in a democratic society. It can do this by insisting that the schools supported by the government teach the 'secular' subjects that will enable that generation to earn a living, outside of the government stipend they receive for studying in *yeshivot*. Some Haredim like Rabbi Adin Steinsaltz, who has established a school for boys in which both religious and secular subjects are taught, without playing down the emphasis on Torah study that lies at the heart of Haredi belief, have begun to reconsider their approach and are aware that they must change their economically self-destructive, culturally self-restrictive and reclusive social patterns.

Rabin's assassination has convinced many non-Orthodox Israelis of the need to break the Orthodox monopoly of Jewish sources of religion. Leaders of this empowerment movement report that thousands of people are turning to Jewish studies, learning and discussing Jewish texts in small groups, taught by anti-fanatic Orthodox as well as Reform and Conservative rabbis. The movement to empower non-Orthodox Israelis by repossessing traditional texts is one way to both establish an Israeli-Jewish identity and at the same time meet the religious sectors.

Uri Avneri, an avowed secularist, suggests to undo the myth that on a narrow bridge with room for only one cart, the secular cart which is supposedly empty should give way to the religious one. He regards the secular cart as loaded with a most valuable living content as it is open also to world culture. Together with many secular Israelis, he proposes not to let the ultra-Orthodox and religious nationalist minority that totals less than one-fifth of the Israeli-Jewish population, to dominate the society. The secularists should push harder than ever to strengthen their values and morality as a way of providing all citizens with a life of dignity, security and common identity.

When emphasis is placed on common values like respect for another's beliefs and values and the principle that no person has the right to impose his or her values and way of life on another, as long as the other is not advocating incitement or disobeying the law, we will have gone far on the road towards a pluralistic society which allows self-realisation and freedom of expression for all citizens.

The trend towards rapprochement between nationalists and doves and between secular and religious people, as well as between any combination of the four, has deepened since the assassination. It is based on the strong desire of moderates on all sides to bridge the deep chasm that became glaringly apparent after Yigal Amir fired his shots. But there is still a high wall between the camps because of the ultra-Orthodox and religious nationalist belief that their view of Halakha does not allow for renewal – despite the myriad reinterpretations of Halakha in previous generations. This wall has to be taken down, if we are to achieve a society free of internecine hatred and polarisation.

One encouraging phenomenon in this direction is the increasingly loud call on the part of many religious and spiritual leaders for Halakha to again be open to renewal. In contrast to a rigid attitude that leads to fanaticism and extremism, creative religion provides the opportunity to establish dialogue within oneself and with others, as well as with the historical tradition of God and His Law. In this approach, it is the present that counts, a present with its face towards the future, but based on contact with the past.

Over and above the trends that have arisen or been deepened since Rabin's assassination, there is a growing acceptance for many Israelis that solutions aimed at depolarisation cannot be forced – that we must face the difficulties involved in creating communication and understanding among our various subcultures. We must accept our differences, these people say, for they are not in themselves discouraging; these differences (for example pluralism) give Israeli society its dynamism and vibrancy. The real test of what we have learned, then, is not whether we achieve unity of thought, but whether we can learn to accept legitimate differences of opinion in a civilised manner.

The psychoanalyst Leo Rangell (1992) observes that beneficial adaptive change can and does occur in both the individual and society, despite the relentless onslaught of events in our own lives and that of our society. Rangell stresses that there are not always active ways to attempt change, and he underscores the importance of unconscious decisions that may take place in our actions. Rangell writes about the unconscious 'ego will', the force of ego which actively chooses and then executes behaviour selected so that new solutions to intrapsychic tensions can be considered, defences modified or discarded and kinder and more adaptive outcomes tried (Rangell 1992).

I agree with his thesis and would add that such change can take place not only as a result of psychoanalytic treatments. When individuals and groups can keep in their awareness opposing ideas and paradoxes, to forestall premature closure; when they can change terror and violence into cultural discourse and tolerance, and free themselves from the unconscious defence mechanisms and deployment that fan fanaticism and work against development, there is hope that change will occur in the direction of reconciliation and peace. Thus the traumatic murder that affected the whole nation's life brought Israel to an era in which our deepest aspects of identity – conflicts, values, attitudes and psychological deployments – have been and continue to be re-examined.

Towards Reconciliation and Peace with Palestinians and the Arab World

I would like to conclude this work with a description of Israel's withdrawal from most of Hebron in January 1997 under the government of Binyamin Netanyahu. It was a historical event for most Israelis and a defeat for a minority of Israelis. One of the major difficulties in accomplishing this 'redeployment', as promised by Yitzhak Rabin's government, was that the Jews who lived in Hebron view themselves as the last spearheads of 'real' Zionism and view that city as second in sanctity only to Jerusalem. Since they had waged a battle to retain 'the city of Abraham' and to restore it as a place of Jewish religious pilgrimage, it was a great relief for the majority of Israelis when Prime Minister Netanyahu finally realised that 'the ideological concepts he grew up to believe in, are not within reach anymore, and that as a result of the Oslo Accords, there is now a different reality' (Makovsky, 17 January 1997).

In a conciliatory speech to the Arabs of Hebron on 19 January 1997, Palestinian Authority chairman, Yassir Arafat, told a crowd of some 50,000 Arabs and Jews that 'all the Israeli people have made peace with the Palestinians, and the Palestinians seek no confrontation with the town's remaining Jews' (Immanuel, 20 January 1997). While commending Binyamin Netanyahu for signing the redeployment agreement, Yitzhak Rabin's widow, Leah, added that the Prime Minister should now express his remorse and ask her husband's forgiveness for his contribution to the atmosphere that led to Yitzhak Rabin's murder – this in recognition of the fact that Rabin was murdered for taking the same road towards peace that almost everybody now realises is the only way.

For seventy years and more, Arabs and Jews have struggled over possession of this corner of the world. 'Each side has sought to dominate and possess land totally: land as a source of nourishment, land as a memory, both personal and historical; and land in prayer, in poetry, in dreams; land in which our forefathers are buried' (Hareven, 1983:159).

The Jews of the Yishuv accepted the 1936, 1938 and 1947 partition plans, though reluctantly so, while the Palestinians completely rejected all of them, having felt that Jewish immigration was a threat to their existence and having felt insulted by the Jews' tendency to ignore their rights and to feel superior. The Palestinian Covenant called for Israel's destruction, and in spite of changes brought about in it after the Oslo Accords, it is not clear what exactly has been changed. Thus, the Israeli need to be on constant guard against Arab designs is based in part on the perception that the Arabs were always opposed to the establishment of an independent Jewish state in this land.

During the generations of conflict that followed Israel's establishment in 1948, the attitudes and perceptions on both sides became linked in a closed, seemingly unbreachable circle, both sides collaborating in confirming each other's worst convictions about their adversary.

Since that time, and until Yitzhak Rabin signed the Oslo Accords, there seemed to be no secure way to stop the occupation that brought great suffering to the Palestinians as well as to Israelis: many Israelis felt caught up in a 'moral suicide' of ruling over another people. It is unfair and demoralising and involves compelling our children to carry out tasks that contradict the values on which they have been brought up. The resultant pain, humiliation and suppression for the Palestinians, and the feelings of helplessness, shame and guilt of many Israelis, which were often unconscious and drive them to deployments, seemed to be unresolvable.

Yitzhak Rabin led the way to effecting change in the traumatic relationship between Israelis and Palestinians, as well as with the neighbouring Arab states – after peace between Egypt and Israel had been made by Menachem Begin. In so doing, Rabin freed himself and the Israeli people from the heavy deployments that had been hindering change for many decades. As David Grossman (1996) writes, Rabin's peace initiative created a feeling of freedom in military, cultural and economic relationships that involved a great deal of courage, determination, investment and empathy. He and Shimon Peres succeeded in establishing a tentative partnership between Israel and the Palestinians in which the common desire for peace was coupled with the recognition that there are divergent interests on both sides. 'How difficult it is to create something new, and how easy it is to destroy it,' comments David Grossman (1996).

The year 1996 was a terrible year for Israel: Yitzhak Rabin was assassinated at the end of 1995 by a Jewish terrorist; a Likud government was elected that not only opposed the Oslo Accords, but aggravated the situation between Israeli Jews and Muslims by opening an archaeological tunnel near the Temple Mount in a way that demonstrated a lack of empathy with the Palestinians' feelings, and thus led to clashes with the newly established Palestinian police.

As Larry Derfner wrote (16 January 1997): 'After the May elections we thought that the nationalists and Orthodox hardliners were going to put their stamp on every corner of Israeli life. But it has taken the advent of a reactionary government, of a Prime Minister whose strongest backers were radical settlers and Haredim (and who had no opposition party which would kill the peace process) to reveal the real nature of Israeli society which is much more liberal... than we knew, and much more resilient.' But, although Israel lost a Prime Minister to religious nationalist fanaticism, the peace process that this Prime Minister initiated continues to live.

The fact that Israel's Knesset voted eighty-seven to seventeen in favour of withdrawing our forces from Hebron indicates that Yitzhak Rabin's message did reflect the will of a large majority of Israelis to explore the road towards peace, even if achieving that peace means giving up land that is sacred to many Jews.

But for the 400 Jewish settlers who insist on remaining among more than 10,000 Arabs, the agreement that finally led to the withdrawal of almost all Israeli troops out of Hebron, the last occupied city on the West Bank, represents a defeat for the movement of the Greater Land of Israel. Nonetheless, although this minority mourned Israel's withdrawal from Hebron, and Netanyahu's agreement to further withdrawals from Judea and Samaria by August 1998, this time it was mourning through grieving and not through violent terroristic acts.

Everyone is aware that there are many difficulties to be overcome before we can achieve a lasting peace. But what can we learn from the important stage that we have reached? Have we learned how to avoid the 'psychological deployment' that obstructs the rest of the road to dialogue and reconciliation? The first thing that comes to mind in this connection is that much depends on the capacity to mourn our individual and national losses and tragedies in a constructive and creative way instead of 'deploying' ourselves into the grievances and violence that provide the basis for mistrust, fanaticism and rigidity.

This brings me back to Louis Mallé's film *Au Revoir Les Enfants*, the production of which Mallé said had helped him somehow to mourn his shattering experience in the Holocaust when he saw his Jewish school friend treacherously delivered to the Gestapo.

Tommy Lapid, a well-known right-wing journalist and public

figure in Israel, now leader of a small secular party, was twelve years old when his father was taken by the Gestapo.

As Lapid was sleeping near his father, a German in Gestapo uniform entered their house and ordered his father to get dressed and go with them. His father kissed Lapid and told him: 'Either I shall see you again or I shall not.' They never saw each other again.

That moment, Lapid says, is at the root of his nationalist relationship to the state of Israel whose continued existence is his answer to that traumatic moment. It seems that through his participation in radio and television programmes for social and political problems as well as through his writings, he is working through his mourning of his own and our losses in a creative and productive way.

Amira Hass, a reporter for *Ha'aretz*, the most respected daily Hebrew newspaper, lived in, and reported from, Gaza for several years. In her book, *To Drink from the Sea of Gaza* (1996), Hass describes her personal contact with Gazan political leaders, their role in the Intifada and the peace negotiations, and their struggles for human rights when under our rule. In writing her book, Hass says she was primarily concerned with describing the human reality that would portray Gaza as a place populated by human beings with whom readers would be able to empathise.

Hass's motivation for this approach was based on subjective as well as objective elements. She explains that part of the reason she was driven to put herself in the position of the oppressed by living in Gaza and to tell the story of those under Israeli occupation to the world, relates to the experience of her mother who was transported from Belgrade in Yugoslavia to Bergen Belsen, as a young woman in a packed railroad car. As Hass puts it, she assimilated her mother's story in early childhood, after which it festered and stewed until it became part of her own personal memory. This memory included her mother's recollection of how, when she and the rest of the human cargo were unloaded from the railroad car, she noticed a group of German women nearby. Some of them were walking and a few rode bicycles. These women slowed down and stared at the convoy with indifferent curiosity. It was this image, in particular, that became an odious symbol for Hass of being an onlooker. She decided early in her life that she would never be one of those indifferent bystanders.

By going to live among the people of Gaza, Hass hoped to enter their lives and their world, to live their reality herself as far as possible. Not only might it help her to empathise more completely with her mother, perhaps it would also relieve her feelings of standing on the sidelines when her people were in the midst of oppressing another people.

To be in Gaza, which encompasses and symbolises the tragic history of the Israeli–Palestinian conflict, and which Hass feels personalises her own open sadness – like an open wound; to see it through their eyes, and to communicate that experience, became her mission. For many of those in Gaza had escaped or were banished from their villages in 1948 as her parents had been from Yugoslavia. She remembered how her parents had turned to take one last look at the house they had had to leave. She could empathise with the feelings of sadness when being forced to leave the house in which the family had lived for many years, the house they loved. She could, therefore, well understand why, when her parents arrived in Israel in 1949, they refused to accept housing in a building that had once been the home of dispossessed Arabs.

Until she wrote her book, Amira Hass had only told her closest friends that it was the legacy of her parents, a special autobiographical conglomerate, that had led her to the Gaza Strip. Through the people of Gaza, she has not only learned the taste of occupation but has been able to identify with them, become a witness to their lives and share their suffering with the Israeli people.

As for myself, I feel that writing this book was a way for me to mourn Yitzhak Rabin's murder and everything that it involved for me. By mourning, each in his or her own way, deployments can be softened or removed. The possibility of actualising the realistic dream of peace that is now in the process of being born will improve to the extent that both sides relinquish and mourn their own unrealistic dreams. Only then can the destructive deployments that have been obstructing the road to dialogue and reconciliation be identified.

Israel's Likud Minister of Foreign Affairs, David Levy, wrote on 12 February 1997:

> It is important for us all, both Israelis and Palestinians, to know that neither of us has a better alternative than the way upon which we have embarked, the way that obliges us to commit ourselves to a real partnership, to agreed-upon patterns of work, to mutual trust and the willingness to go forward. We must strive for a peace that is not only the result of a political diplomatic agreement, but a reality in the lives of both of our peoples. I am aware of the task before us, but I am also certain that we both have the capacity to succeed in carrying it out. We must, therefore, create channels of communication to reach agreements and understandings with our neighbours, while guarding the security and national aims of an independent and free people which acts to reach a safe place.

From these words of our Likud Minister (now Foreign Minister in the Barak government!) we can feel the spirit of Yitzhak Rabin. The process of peace that he started to implement continues in spite of all the disagreements and difficulties; and Binyamin Netanyahu – though surrounded by much opposition within his own government – continued, for an important period of his government, to fulfil the legacy of Yitzhak Rabin.

More Grief and National Mourning

Although I planned to conclude this book on grief and grievance with the withdrawal of Israeli troops from Hebron, which represented another step towards Yitzhak Rabin's and our dream of peace, events have moved me to conclude with a new wave of national grief brought about by the tragic deaths on 4 February 1997 of seventy-three, mostly young soldiers killed when two helicopters transporting them to Lebanon at night collided in mid-air. This new disaster, one of the all too common features of life in Israel, where we have been living from calamity to calamity for so long, again plunged the people into national mourning.

This pattern of hurtling from the great joy of most Israelis at the hope of peace represented by the redeployment in Hebron to the agony of a new national catastrophe related to our unresolved conflict with Lebanon, plays a crucial role in our group, self and national psyches. It creates the unbearable tensions that may well be behind many of our less desirable traits, including wild driving on our roads and the high rate of accidents – and death. Since death is so close anyway, too many Israelis seem unconsciously to think 'why be careful or restrained?' Or, this seeming rush towards death on the roads may also, perhaps be a way of relieving unconscious shame, guilt or fears at for example not having died in terror attacks, in war or in the Holocaust.

In this small country, every military casualty is a cause for national as well as private mourning. Although we have lost so many soldiers in the prime of their lives over the years that we have deployed ourselves into being hardened to survive and continue to defend our country, the death of every young man is a deep wound that we all carry within ourselves. At times, this has been compared to Abraham's readiness to sacrifice Yitzhak, as Israelis are ready to sacrifice their – our – children and grandchildren for the vision of our forefathers.

Prime Minister Netanyahu responded to the shock of this sudden mass death by declaring a day of national mourning. Shopping malls, theatres and restaurants were closed. Every school was instructed to hold a memorial service.

They did not fall in the war. It was an accident. But the accident was connected to our state of war with Lebanon: these seventy-three soldiers had been on their way to guard the security zone against the Hamas terrorists who are constantly trying to enter northern Israel. And since there was nobody to blame, to be angry at so that we might discharge our grief through what I would call a 'consoling punishment', it has been more difficult to bear the grief. So once more, we remain helpless with our feelings of loss, the loss of seventy-three unique lives not yet lived.

Throughout the country, families, friends and comrades carried coffin after flag-draped coffin to its grave. With flags at half mast and tears in the eyes of tens of thousands, a stunned nation tried to digest and mourn the helicopter disaster. Seventy-three open graves. Seventy-three funerals. Seventy-three bereaved families beside themselves with pain.

The soldiers who died reflected the mosaic of Israeli society. They came from development towns in the north, to Eilat in the south; from Tel Aviv, Haifa, Jerusalem and Beersheba, from small kibbutzim, settlements and *hesder yeshivot*. They included Jews, Druse and Beduin. The seemingly endless list of those who died in the crash, which grew longer with every newscast as forensic experts identified the remains and families were notified in person before the news was made public, was followed by a popular song 'Let Us Live'. Some people asked where God had been when the disaster had occurred. The media participated fully in the mourning, broadcasting interviews with the families and friends of the dead, as well as with spiritual and political leaders who offered their reactions to the tragedy and their solace to the bereaved.

When Yehuda Amichai, one of our great national poets, was interviewed on television, sorrow suffused his face; he suggested that people could gain solace through poetry, in which emotional truth is given a voice.

Ashkenazi Chief Rabbi Yisrael Lau and Sephardic Chief Rabbi Eliahu Bakshi Doron both pointed out that 6 February, the day on which many funerals were held, is a fast day known as *Yom Kippur Katan* (Small Day of Atonement). The chief rabbis called upon the public to undertake spiritual reckoning and repentance in light of the new tragedy. By so doing, the rabbis were showing the way towards mourning in the spirit of Halakha, and trying to head off the mourning customs that consist in blaming sinners for a disaster.

President Weizman and senior army personnel visited every family that lost a son, a brother, or a father, to offer their condolence in person. 'The soldiers shared something beyond a spiritual kinship, a sense of common purpose. We share the families' grief to the point of tears. In their death, they had shown us, as a nation, who we are or at least who we can be,' wrote journalist Abraham Rabinovich (7 February 1997), in the wake of the latest army disaster.

Thus, although it had been reported that the motivation to enlist in special units of the army was decreasing in Israel as a result of disappointment in government policy – or perhaps the wish to live rather than die, to be a normal people rather than have to sacrifice oneself for the greater Israel – a majority of our youth is prepared to continue fighting for their country. Indeed, many young soldiers stationed in safer locations volunteered to replace their lost comrades in Lebanon.

Every new disaster reminds us of previous disasters, of our private and public losses, just as every new loss reminds the individual of previous losses: the War of Independence in 1948, the Six Day War of 1967, the War of Attrition in the early 1970s, the Yom Kippur War of 1973, the Lebanon War of 1982, and the assassination of Yitzhak Rabin in 1995. The public mourning of these tragedies brings about catharsis for both the individual and society. It is still a question whether intense public ceremonies are a way to mourn together, or whether there is a manic or hysterical element thrown in that prevents us from mourning fully and building internal meanings once the particular form of group mourning dies down.

As with past calamities, all of Israel was united in this tragedy. Indeed, it unfortunately takes a national disaster to bring out the best parts of our national character – solidarity – a solidarity that is otherwise missing or masked by religious and political differences. Since almost everyone knows someone who is touched by a tragedy, when it occurs, there is a strong sense of everyone belonging, of sharing the grief of the bereaved. This represents a healthy departure from past tendencies of survivors to shy away from victims of tragedies or their relatives, out of guilt or shame or embarrassment. Now everyone cares when one of ours is struck down, and fewer persons or families feel abandoned to their solitary grief. 'Why do we learn our lessons only after such horrible disasters?,' asked Uzi Benziman (16 February 1997) reflecting the mood of many Israelis. 'Something in the Israeli education is wrong: From kindergarten on, children should learn how to respect the law and other basic values.'

I will deal with this topic in the last part of this postscript and this book.

Changing Attitudes: Education towards Openness, Flexibility and Pluralism, and Opposing the Dangers of Deployment

The assassination of Yitzhak Rabin has sharpened the need to try to better understand the failure of education both on the individual and the social levels; and the possibilities found to be successful in lessening ethnic and religious strife, violence, racism and terrorism.

One of the conclusions of the committee that investigated the support given to Yigal Amir was that more hours should be given to foster issues of values, to mobilise critical and moral judgement, and discuss, and attempt to resolve, social problems. It was also concluded that teachers be provided with more information and tools to advance the teaching of democratic values (Kashti, 4 December 1996).

In the light of the violence, the incitement to extremism and delegitimisation, the feeling of many is that unless we are able to remove the blind spot that stops us from seeing the whole picture in a more complex and understandable light, it may turn into a black hole that will swallow us all; whereas if we expend more energy, time, resources and creative thinking on exploring the aims of education and ways to implement them, changes in society's cultural pattern as a whole may occur.

In trying to establish what psychoanalysts can offer towards the development of the human factor in education, and therefore in society, I am suggesting several lines of thinking of how to use our professional knowledge and sensitivities to try to find better ways of handling conflicts, tensions, frustrations and the unbearable pressures of everyday life that are the seedbed of grievances, violence and terror.

One direction lies in encouraging attitudinal changes in those who serve any kind of pedagogical, social or psychological function in our society. When the phenomenon of pupils who do not live up to their potential, or who regard their years of study as a series of injuries and failures, boredom and suffering, is widespread, it is an indication that this is not the problem of a few emotionally disturbed children, but that there is something in the educational framework that needs attention and change.

Although I will centre on the need for change in the Israeli educational system, I do think that many of these thoughts can also be applied elsewhere, both in Israel and abroad.

Educational Aims Required to Change Teachers' Roles, Attitudes and Training Needs

Leadership is a transactional process in which both the leader and the led react to each other. I shall focus in this part on transactional processes in the field of education.

Autonomy, self-realisation, openness to basic rights, flexibility, tolerance and pluralism are generally accepted basic values in a liberal, modern society. The feelings of our pupils, their independence and interdependence, their self-image as individuals and their roles in the larger social system are to be regarded, according to my view, as no less important than their mastering knowledge, culture and spiritual education.

Those who grew up on such basic values, which I shall call *democratic*, often find it difficult to behave in accordance with them, to maintain them consistently and to enable our children to realise them. There is a difference between knowing these values, even if they were experienced by the persons themselves, and applying them in practice. It is even more difficult to inculcate such values to those raised with different values, who perceive them as abstract principles. A separate study is needed to reach groups whose scales of values differ from those of the liberal ones, to find the common denominators between different groups and to overcome the reclusive trends of some groups in society.

However deeply divided the Jewish people are, in spite of their shared historical fate and emotional attachment to the myth that 'all Israel are a fraternity' (*kol Yisrael Haverim*), most agree that fanaticism is the real threat to Jewish continuity (Hartman 2 November 1996). Much experimenting and theorising is still needed to enable the different groups to work together, to know each other better, to reduce prejudices, to be more empathic towards each other. Unconscious fear, anger and shame vis-à-vis the cultural threat from different and strange values need to come to awareness, to be felt and understood in order to try and overcome the mistrust and power struggles within and among the groups.

What is presented below is based on many years of teaching and training teachers in the setting of the School of Education, Division of Counselling in the Hebrew University, Jerusalem, as well as from my experience as a school psychologist, my job before becoming a clinical psychologist and a psychoanalyst.

We realised that the change in educational aims involves a greater alertness to the impact of the teacher's attitudes on the reactions of pupils and the educational climate. I think, for instance, that it is the experience of many that an appreciative, trusting attitude on the part of the teacher tends to create an atmosphere of affirmation that encourages a zeal to learn, work and reason for oneself; whereas an attitude of suspiciousness that stresses the deficiencies and mistakes of pupils produces vulnerabilities and resentments that tend to lower the pupils' readiness to participate emotionally and fully in the educational process. The more the teachers – as all leaders – are ready to listen fully, to whatever the pupils feel, think and say, the more the pupils will be open to growth and change; consequently, there will be less need for them to become deployed into grievance, imperviousness to the feelings of others and hatred.

In a letter to his father, Franz Kafka (1919, 1966) masterfully describes the inner damage he felt in response to certain of his father's attitudes, attitudes that are also typical of many teachers.

> You are at bottom a kind and soft-hearted person… As a father you have been too strong for me. You are a true Kafka in strength… in loudness of voice and eloquence. I was quite obedient; but it did me inner harm. This sense of nothingness that often dominates me comes largely from your influence. If I were asked what was your influence on me – it would be difficult to answer. This is so because of a fear of you which I still feel – a feeling of being nothing, a zero which often takes hold of me. Even now, writing, I feel inhibited.
>
> If I could get you to acknowledge this, what would be

possible is not a new life – but still a kind of peace; not a cessation but still a diminution of your unceasing reproaches.

We were so different – in our differences so dangerous to each other. What I would have needed was a little encouragement, a little friendliness, a little keeping open of my road. Instead of which you blocked it for me. Though of course with the good intention of making me go along another road. I was weighed down by your physical presence.

Much has been written about narcissistic factors in the individual and the group (Kohut 1971, 1977; Kernberg 1992), but relatively little of this has been applied to the field of education.

Some pupils tend to react to the hurt or humiliation that they feel their teachers inflict on them with a quick narcissistic rage that helps them discharge their tensions and appear strong; yet it leaves them unaware of their hurt and further emotionally disconnected and deployed.

Many of the narcissistic wounds and shaming that cause the individual to shrink, block or become deployed in aggressive counter-shame strategies could be avoided if educators (and, of course, also parents and other cultural and political leaders) were more aware of the effects of their attitudes on pupils and others. For that reason, I think it is crucial that teachers receive training more focused on the interactive relations between the cognitive and emotional realms, and the interaction between teacher and pupil and teacher and class; and that a better understanding of the circumstances that create dangerous deployments can help them to know and feel the potential damage that the ongoing threat of feeling ashamed and humiliated can bring about.

The well-known psychologist and pedagogue Fritz Redl (1957) – who wrote about the disorganisation and breakdown of behaviour controls and controls from within – was said to start each staff meeting by relating some of his own mistakes. This was one of the attitudes that created an open atmosphere which freed staff members to invest their energy in talking about meaningful events rather than try to conceal their weaknesses or failures, as often happens. This is an example of an attitude (not a technique!) that facilities a freer flow of communication and internal work useful also in other settings. For more about this issue, see my book, *Deployment* (1994 and my paper on 'Remaining in the Bunker Long After the War is Over: Deployment in the Individual, the Group and the Nation' (1996)).

The shift of emphasis towards the combined task of developing the whole personality of the pupils and providing an atmosphere which facilitates learning together with transmitting knowledge and skills involves a change in the way the teachers and the society see the role of the teacher. When the automatic prestige and protection accorded teachers by the existing social order disappear – as they increasingly do in secular school systems the world over – a transition occurs from functioning as an 'irrational authority' (Fromm 1941), to becoming a rational authority, namely being a leader on the basis of merit. We can see how difficult this is, since many teachers who cognitively wished to stop being authoritarian and who were willing to give up their power position in favour of establishing an egalitarian relationship with their pupils in spite of their different roles, felt that they lost their authority altogether and as a result became helpless in many situations.

This is so especially because the teachers did not have enough opportunities to explore their new identities, nor did they have the chance to practise the new tools of building a strong sense of their own self. Thus, they could not use their relationships and attitudes in a way that would restore their self-confidence in their new role of a 'rational authority'. We – the staff of the counselling division in the School of Education – felt that the above implied the need for drastic changes in the selection, training and internal training of those who are to teach our youth and no less for a change of attitudes on the part of those responsible for the entire educational system.

As in Israeli society at large, we can still find a negative attitude towards the expression of feelings (Moses and Kligler 1966) and towards dealing with them appropriately in certain groups of teachers, because to them feelings seem primitive, childish, hysterical or feminine. This is so in spite of the considerable social and cultural changes in Israel and in the Western world. It was our opinion that much change is required in the emotional attitudes of teachers to enable them to feel the importance of a need for change and to be ready and willing to invest in this direction both practically and theoretically (Moses-Hrushovski and Moses 1984). This would then make them more alert to their own attitudes, as well as to the reactions of their pupils and to the educational climate created.

I shall describe several goals that we, the staff of psychoanalysts, clinical psychologists and social workers who participated in the training programme for teachers and teacher-counsellors had in our minds, or in our subliminal minds, and deal with some issues around their implementation. Like Sandler (1996), I shall follow the distinction between process goals which relate to changes that the staff aimed to bring about during the process, and outcome goals which refer to a change of attitudes. One outcome goal is formulated by Nevitt Sanford (Axelrod *et al* 1969): 'In social responsibility, as in every other aspect of personality development, our goal is to expand both the intellectual and the realm of motive and feeling and then to integrate the two in ego-controlled action. To this end, we try to mobilise the student's deeper motives and emotions in the interest of intellectual striving, and at the same time we try to bring the intellect to bear upon the issues he cares more about.'

We felt that being aware of our goals and values helped us to respect the separateness of our students and their differences from us. Thus we presented our conceptions more as questions and suggestions and not as rules and impositions.

As we became gradually more crystallised in our working conceptions, we could also regress more easily in the service of the ego (Kris 1964), be less controlling and more directly goal-oriented and creative. Each meeting was a potentially new learning experience both for our students, the teachers, and for ourselves.

Studying the diverse emotional elements employed in cognitive functioning was one of our process goals. 'Emotion without cognition is blind and cognition without emotion is vacuous,' says Israel Scheffler as he outlines basic aspects of emotion in the cognitive process. He does so with the purpose of overcoming the breach between unfeeling knowledge and mindless arousal (1991).

Many studies show that there are gender differences that arise from constitution, yet primarily from socialisation. Through differentiating masculine and feminine, as well as other opposites within themselves, teachers might be able to become more cognisant of the differential mental sets also in their pupils. We felt that this would enable teachers to accommodate better to different ways of perceiving and learning, as well as creating a more peaceful atmosphere in the classroom. To concretise the differences among various types of mentality, I prepared in one of the courses for teachers a schema that deals with the interrelation between feelings and thinking.

Feeling and Thinking: their Interrelation; or, Feeling our Thinking, and Thinking about our Feelings

There are people that naturally charge their thinking with feeling. It is a kind of feeling from the guts, something kinaesthetic, not only from the head, the brain. It is as if empathy is their natural language: receptivity and openness dwell in them, as it were, from birth.

Before they hurry to organise their thinking, they tend to lose themselves in the process. Their mode of perception is usually inductive. When they light up, their thinking is at times jumpy. At times, it is confused. Often it tends to be creative.

It is sometimes hard for them to plan. How can they know what they will be feeling tomorrow? Affect accompanies their words when they talk with considerable modulation.

A tremor in their voice, when it arises, does not only divulge their anxiety, lest they are not properly understood, but also the fear lest they will not be able to collect their thoughts and feelings in time; this is even more so when they find themselves in an atmosphere in which they tend to freeze or be overwhelmed from inside.

In an atmosphere free from arbitrary interdictions, on the other hand, everything flows from within freely and fluently. A richness then denotes the members of this group. They are sensitive to what they experience as false. What matters to them most is emotional truth, authenticity and sincerity.

Abstract material not based on empirical or experiential data often evokes in them a kind of distrust and emotional distance.

When one listens to a talk they give, as meaningful and interesting as it may sound, it is often hard to reconstruct exactly what they have said. This relates to the nature of feelings.

When they are emotionally charged, they are dramatic and most convincing. When the charge is turned off, it is as if they fade or do not exist.

I have briefly mentioned in what I have described above about twenty characteristics directly or immediately, without expanding on them. Such directness is a further characteristic of the feeling world.

On the other hand, there are people who, as it were, naturally leave their feelings outside themselves when they think. Their thinking is pure and clean. When they speak there is much clarity which may arouse admiration in many. The ideas are well-developed and organised, and can be easily understood and recapitulated. Their way of perceiving is essentially deductive (and not inductive). The speech is fluent. There are no endless qualifications of a different emphasis, of a variation in weight, depending on the context; or a variety of distinctions and subtleties which might make the speech more accurate, but usually disturb the listener and confuse him.

Some sort of distrust is felt in such people when feelings become mixed up with thinking. This is reminiscent of what Rollo May (1953) says about the classicists: 'They expected from the intellect that it would find a solution for every problem and the will-power to actualise it. And what concerns the feelings, well, this is a disturbing factor which has to be controlled or suppressed.'

This schema which portrays two opposing kinds of mentality evoked a lively discussion in the teachers about differences of mentality related to gender differences and ethnic background as they detected them both in themselves and in their pupils, and how they might seek ways to adapt to them. The more attention we gave to affect expression, affect verbalisation, affect tolerance and the interrelationships between the multiple ways of thinking in the training group, the more sensitive they became to the distinct styles of mentality in their classroom.

Fostering one's faculty for empathy was considered by all of us as a major goal both in order to be able to establish meaningful relationships with pupils and to adjust the curriculum to their needs and ways of perceiving, and also for being able to build a climate for productive learning and well-being. I found that what frequently obstructed the teacher's capacity to empathise was related to their being unconsciously threatened by their child parts: 'Childish' impulses, 'childish' longings, or 'childish' ways of perceiving and fantasies.

Some of the teachers tended to be very controlled and controlling. I could feel how defensive and therefore closed they were vis-à-vis regressive ways of behaving, as if the shame to be caught in what they regarded as primitive was still active, and as if they still had to be on guard not to be driven by inappropriate or dangerous impulses (Olden 1953).

At the other pole were teachers who solved this kind of conflict by over-identifying with their child parts. They behaved as if they still are in a battle with their previous authority figures, as if they still had to rebel against values such as obeying or making order, values like efficiency which were so often overstressed in their homes at the expense of attending to their feelings. These teachers tended unconsciously to collude with the rebellious child part in their pupils. They often succeeded in establishing close relationships with their pupils, but found themselves helpless in situations in which frustrated pupils behaved destructively or rebelled against requirements and actually needed a firm attitude rather than their teacher's tendency to forgive.

One of the essential objectives in this workshop was to enable spontaneous emotional expression of their mixed and confused feelings, allowing them to express their inner chaos which inevitably increased in times of having to leave their old ways of thinking and behaving and entering unknown situations. Expressing their inner chaos also helped them to deal with it more effectively.

Along with what Jona Rosenfeld (1995) found, I think that the most salient feature shared by all project directors – their work with families he had described – was an uncompromising commitment to the teachers we worked with and the search for new ways that called upon their strengths rather than their pathology.

What we found during the course of training was that within the two years of studies to become a teacher-counsellor, most teachers succeeded in being more in touch with diverse feelings than they had been before; they became more capable and willing to listen to previously unheard voices in themselves and from others; they were less threatened by 'unwanted' parts in themselves, more ready to take responsibility for them rather than be excessively driven to use projective processes, i.e. ascribe them to others.

When freedom of expression was encouraged in the supportive atmosphere of the training group, when acknowledgement of the difficulties involved in this kind of learning process was given; and when more insight into their conflicts had been gained and a regression in the service of the ego became a valuable goal rather than something to feel ashamed of, a more accepting attitude was established towards the previously suppressed child parts or the rejected adult parts in themselves. Thus, an ongoing dialogue was created between the child and adult part.

Being freer to lower their psychic barriers also permitted a more flexible shift from over-identification to empathy, which is based on a continuous oscillation between total identification with the other and disengagement, as Katz describes in his book about *Empathy – Its Nature and Uses* (1963).

While these intensive workshops became for many a source of growth, creativity and increased empathy towards both themselves and others, there were others who found the work on emotional attitudes to be frightening, confusing and at times even humiliating. For some of them, participating in a team in which teachers, psychologists and interested people from other disciplines and backgrounds met on a regular basis to think about developmental issues, was a more suitable way of increasing their sensitivity and openness to pluralism and to gaining more empathy with people who had previously been considered strangers or opponents.

But while at first glance the nature of change needed for instilling democratic values in their pupils appeared to be feasible and almost self-evident, the more we became invested and the more varied the groups of teachers who came to study were, the more we realised what an arduous and complicated task it was to try and change adults' attitudes. To students who suffered from emotional difficulties and excessive rigidity and anxiety, we tended to suggest undergoing an individual process of psychotherapy or psychoanalysis. In times of disappointment and doubt, we asked ourselves whether changing adults' attitudes towards openness, flexibility and pluralism was at all possible without working through unconscious conflicts and defences.

At times, we felt as if we were, fanatically, fighting for openness and against fanaticism. But when we learned to live with our inner fluctuations between regressions and progressions – without losing hope – there was again an opening of new initiatives and energy. We could then accept the opinion of Nevitt Sanford – one of the authors of the famous book *The Authoritarian Personality* (Adorno *et al* 1950) – who writes that 'modification of unconscious structures and attitudes as well as the changing relations to the conscious ego is not necessarily achieved only through therapeutic activities – unconscious processes may become conscious in the normal course of events and it is possible to speed up this developmental change' (Sanford 1967).

Dvorah Koubovi (1992), one of our senior staff members, has developed a creative programme for teachers and teacher-counsellors to increase psychological-mindedness and sensitivity to psychodynamic aspects of the inner world. She has found during her many years of work along these lines that mental processes of teachers as well as of their pupils can be changed by the use of her instrument.

The project consists of works of literature and Bible that evoke emotional involvement and identification in the children. The teacher-counsellors or teachers who were guided on a regular basis by Koubovi enabled their pupils to learn about the emotional world by discussing the feelings and psychological mechanisms as they were perceived in the characters of the literary pieces and from what reverberated in them.

One of the goals was to deal with basic attitudes. As an example, I will mention attitudes towards mourning. In a country cursed by recurrent terror attacks, wars and accidents – talking about the feelings of shock, anger, grief, helplessness and often guilt that is irrationally involved – it is important to provide settings for 'debriefing'. To talk about the feelings is one way to avoid post-traumatic stress disorders from becoming part of the personality.

Psychiatrists Yitzhak Ben-Zion and Asher Shiber, and the social worker, Mali Herzno, from the Psychiatric Department of Soroka Hospital, claim that the murder of Yitzhak Rabin worsened the emotional state of post-traumatic stress disorder patients. They found that these patients, whose illness was caused by traumatic experiences, such as road accidents, rape or terror acts, reacted acutely to national mourning and connected it with their mental state. (Merav Nesher, *Ha'aretz*, 20 March 1997).

The stories Koubovi selected helped the pupils to mourn. Listening one to the other's horrifying experiences, thinking and reflecting together, transforming feelings, memories and thoughts into words and fostering the integration of dissociated experiences via group processes, is one of the ways of mourning that took place in the classroom.

If mourning means being with the variety and complexity of feelings resulting from loss, neglect or abuse, to express them in affective and verbal ways and let the grief be linked with other emotional experiences until one is ready to separate and reconnect with present life towards the future (Herman 1992), deployment is the antithesis of mourning. To restate briefly some of the features of deployment (see Chapters 3 and 4), let me mention the following: deployment means enlisting much effort in the direction of self-hardening, in a strong refusal to accept the loss and mourn it. It means using violence and counter-shame strategies to control others and sever emotional connections between the person and the unbearable injuring self-experiences; but also from others when they are conceived as threatening to their sense of dignity and wholeness.

To end this chapter, I chose to expand on the problem of violence and education, which is one of the most destructive forms of deployment which is dangerous for the individual, for groups and, as we saw, for the entire nation. In fact, it may imperil democratic policy if we do not check our power motives, our sadism and omnipotence.

People who despair of violence and corruption in political life, turn with hope towards education. Here, they believe, the cycles of violence, vengeance and revenge can be broken – or at least reduced. Perhaps a new chain of events can be started from early childhood on. 'Why should children beyond nursery age settle their differences through jungle tactics?' asks Selma Fraiberg, the author of *The Magic Years* (1959). She claims that often educators do not step in to prevent children from destroying each other through words or subtler forms of sadism. The principle needs to be that whatever the reasons for the feelings may be, one has to find civilised solutions. Violence, Fraiberg adds, must be dealt with on many levels. The right way to solve problems with aggression is through conversation and compromise, not submission, suggests Fraiberg. Children have to be guided to find ways other than force to defuse their anger and frustration.

We all know that there are ample opportunities in the classroom to look into behavioural patterns and motives that contribute to violence. One instance is the phenomenon of power conflicts, be it between pupils and their teacher or among pupils. The attitudes of the teachers are again of great importance. If power conflicts are primarily regarded as a disciplinary problem, when the teacher is mainly interested in finding out who is to be punished and stops the 'wrong' behaviour by shaming, or blaming, while ignoring his own part of responsibility, then defensiveness, aggressive attacks or pathological deployments are often encouraged!

But when the power struggles are used as an opportunity to learn about struggles in families and in wider society, to learn about the hidden grievances that may lead to violence, especially if there is nobody to listen to what hurts and is unfair; if one is capable of using the opportunity to see the complexities involved in democratic as opposed to other policies and ways of life, then it can turn into a meaningful learning experience for both pupils and teacher.

Teachers who have had the opportunity to study group dynamics experientially, and not only intellectually, usually have more skills to use in classroom situations for learning about life. When the training programme and supervision has provided teachers with tools that increase their sensitivity and self-confidence, there are better chances that they will be able to contain their pupils' aggression. At the same time, they can encourage pupils to talk about what they feel and be firm enough to not let incitement and the temptation to be violent be acted on.

If there is a good enough relationship with the teachers, attitudes tend to be internalised and transferred to other situations as well. When power conflicts arise on the basis of ethnic prejudices, pupils who have experienced exploring the nature of conflicts tend to search for pertinent information and to correct their misperceptions.

I shall conclude with an example of trying to overcome prejudices in a successful and original way by a programme of 'Playing for Peace'.

Children, six to ten year olds from the Israeli Agron School in Kiryat Yovel and a Palestinian Lutheran and Catholic school in Beit Sahur, a West Bank village next to Har Homa, have been brought together by 'Play for Peace', a ten-month-old organisation based in Denver, Colorado. Their purpose, according to co-founder Craig Dobkin, is to promote positive relationships among children from conflicting cultures by encouraging them to have fun together. Craig Dobkin quotes a University of Minnesota study that states that 'when I hear something, at the end of two weeks I retain ten per cent of it. What I see and hear, I retain twenty per cent. Of what I see, hear and do, I retain eighty per cent. And what I see, hear, do and teach, I retain ninety-seven per cent.' This is the rationale behind getting teenagers from both cultures to learn and then to teach the games they have learned to younger children.

They form affectionate bonds during their two and a half days of training. It is the common purpose of teaching younger children that creates the bonds, Dobkin says.

Rihab Jaber, sixteen, from Beit Sahur, said she had never talked to an Israeli before her 'Play for Peace' training week. 'I thought it would be impossible for me to talk with them,' she said. 'I was small when the Intifada (uprising against Israeli occupation in 1992) began, and the only image I had of Israelis was of soldiers trying to kill me. But I wanted the challenge. I managed to make friends. I know now that people are not the problem. The people want peace. It is a problem of governments.'

Another participant from Beit Sahur commented that he had thought that 'Israelis and Jews are bad people who come here to steal our land,' but now he sees 'they are people one can play with and make peace with.'

I have described possibilities of bringing about social change through education and the difficulties that are involved in changing attitudes and opposing deployments. What Kernberg writes about the individual may also have relevance for groups and nations: 'A stable ego identity becomes a crucial determinant for the stability, integration and flexibility of the ego, and also influences the full development of higher level superego function' (Kernberg 1994:12). Fostering the capacities of the teacher's ego for dealing with conflict, increasing her or his ability to tolerate frustration, to adapt and find solutions that reconcile inner and outer reality, might have an impact on our children and youth, and thus on the nation. Hoping to learn from the lessons of the tragic assassination of Yitzhak Rabin rather than turning it into a 'Chosen Trauma' (to use Vamik Volkan's term) or to be deployed into apocalyptic thinking, and acting upon it (Ostow 1986) is one of the messages of this book.

I want to conclude this part with Gardner's words which strike an echo within me (1994):

> Human development, whether 'personal', 'academic', psychological, physical, political or other, occurs characteristically in progressive bursts separated by relatively longer stretches of relatively slower change. On the verge of such bursts, individuals or groups become a trifle unhinged and return to earlier challenges, dilemmas and solutions until, in transcendental leaps, they can bring old solutions to new and better conclusions. In these moments of wobbling before leaping, the liveliest hidden questions,

sparked by the resurgence of old tensions and shaped by the current play of inner and outer worlds, press even more importunately than usual for expression. And it is these moments of inquisitive hesitation that mark the largest opportunities for learning and teaching.

The Applicability of the Content of this Book

I strongly believe that many of the descriptions, the details, the studies and the beliefs which I have detailed as I have reported on Israeli society and its particular reaction to the first assassination of a Prime Minister, have a wider applicability. I have tried to make use of my knowledge about the intricacies of Israeli society to understand and assess its social and psychological state, its ways of dealing with trauma, its particular forms of splitting and polarising; and finally the form that violence and its usage takes as a result of all these (and probably more) causes. I believe that this approach and this knowledge can be applied – in appropriate, adapted form – to other societies and to the problems they have with trauma, with violence and with fundamentalistic styles of thinking and behaviour. I think that the concept of deployment and its intricacies can be useful for the understanding of these complexities in any society. This is particularly so when a society 'gets stuck', and processes of facilitation of change and reconciliation – inner and outer – are imperative.

BIBLIOGRAPHY

Abir, Mordechai, 'Islamic Fundamentalism, the Permanent Threat', in *Israel's New Future: Interviews*, ed. Manfred Gerstenfeld, Jerusalem, Rubin Maas, 1994, pp.71–82

Ablon, S L, 1993, 'The Therapeutic Action of Play and Affect in Child Analysis', in *Human Feelings*, Analytic Press, Hillside, New York, pp.127–144

Abramov, S Z, *Perpetual Dilemma: Jewish Religion in the Jewish State*, London, Associated University Press, 1976

Adorno, T W, Frenkel-Brunswik, E, Levinson, D J and Sanford, R N, *The Authoritarian Personality*, New York, Harper and Row, 1950

Akhtar, S, *Immigration and Identity: Turmoil, Treatment and Transformation*, Northvale, NJ, Jason Aronson, 1999

——, 'A Third Individuation: Immigration Identity and the Psychoanalytic Process', *Journal of the American Psychoanalytic Association*, vol. 43, pp.1051–1084, 1995

Alon, G, 'Ben Yair: A View has been Developed in our Society that it is Permitted to Achieve an Ideological Aim in a Violent Manner', *Ha'aretz*, 3 January 1997

Aloni, S, 'The Tragedy of Automatisation', *Ha'aretz*, 9 April 1996

Arens, Moshe, 'The Test of Democracy', *Ha'aretz*, 2 February 1996

Assia, J, 'The Ideology behind the Gun', *Ha'aretz*, 8 November 1996

Aviram, R, 'The Education System in the Post-modern Society: An Anomalic Organisation in a Chaotic World', in *Education in the Era of Postmodern Discourse*, ed. F. Gur-Zeev, The Hebrew University of Jerusalem, The Magnes Press, 1996, pp.103–120

Axelrod, J, Freedman M B, Hatch W R, Katz J & Sanford N, *Search for Relevance*, San Francisco, 1969

Bakshi-Doron, E, 'Education for Openness and Democracy', *Ha'aretz*, 21 November 1996

Baram, Chaim, 'About Tears', *Kol-Hair*, 27 October 1995
Bar-Gal, D, 'The Freedom of the Individual and Cultural Pluralism', *Ha'aretz*, 7 March 1997
Barsilay, A, 'The Democratic Rabbi Cannot Force', *Ha'aretz*, 20 November, 1995
Bartholet, Jeffrey, 'A New Kind of Blood Libel', *Newsweek*, 19 February 1996, p.33
Beilin, Y, 'Fanaticism and Folly', *Jerusalem Post*, 2 October 1996
Ben-Ezer, G, 'Yegan Mevpaht', in *Migration and Absorption of Ethiopian Jews in Israel*, Jerusalem, Reuven Maas, 1992
Ben-Meir, Dov. B. (ed.), *Yitzhak Rabin 1922–1995*, Syndicated International Trade, New York 1996
Benziman, U, 'What Shall We Tell the Kindergarten Children?' *Ha'aretz*, 16 February 1997
——, 'The Call of the Ravens,' *Ha'aretz*, 29 December 1996
Benvenisti, M, 'Across the Melting Pot', *Ha'aretz*, 14 June 1996
Biran, Hanna, 'Fear of the Other', *Palestine–Israel Journal*, vol. 4, pp.44–53, 1994
Bott-Spillius, E, 'On Formulating Clinical Fact to a Patient', *Inernational Journal of. Psychoanalysis*, 75:1121–1132, 1993
——, 'Varieties of Envious Experience', *International Journal of Psychoanalysis*, 74:1199–1212, 1993
Brandes, O, 'Demonization of the Other', *Ha'aretz*, 21 October 1996
Brinker, M, *Shalom Friend: The Life and Legacy of Yitzhak Rabin, Ha'aretz Book Supplement*, 25 May 1996
Brody, L R, 'On Understanding Gender Differences in the Expression of Emotion', in *Explorations in Affect Development and Meaning*, eds. Ablon, S L, Brown, D, Khantzian, E J Mack, E J, Hillsdale, NJ, The Altantic Press, 1993, pp.87–121
Bronner, E, 'After Rabin, Rifts Not Healed', *The Boston Globe*, 24 October 1996
Broshi, Etan, 'Kibbutz Gevat', *Ha'aretz*, 20 November 1995
Brown, D, 1990, 'Affective Development, Psychopathology and Adaptation', in *Human Feelings*, op. cit.
Carter, Jimmy, *Keeping Faith: Memoirs of a President*, New York, Bantam Books, 1982
Cashman, Greer Fay, 'Katamonim: Fear Surfaces Amid Macabre

Humor', *Jerusalem Post*, 4 March 1996, p.4

Cohen, E, 'The Removal of the Israeli Settlements in Sinai: An Ambiguous Resolution of an Existential Conflict', *The Journal of Applied Behavioural Science*, vol. 23, 1 November 1987

Cooper, A M, 'The Unusually Painful Analysis: A Group of Narcissistic-masochistic Characters', in *Psychoanalysis: The Vital Issues*, vol. 2, eds. E K John, Gedo and George Pollak, New York; International University Press, 1984

Dankner, A, 'It's Time to Review Halakha', *Ha'aretz*, 9 February 1997

——, 'Haredim in Our Lives', *Ha'aretz*, 16 September 1996

Derfner, L, 'Happy Days', *Jerusalem Post*, 16 January 1997

Dershowitz, A, 'Extremists Endanger Life of a Great Jurist', *Jordan Post*, 9 September 1996

Diamond, B L, 'Failures of Identification and Sociopathic Behaviour', in *Sanctions for Evil*, N Sanford, ed., Boston, Beacon Press, 1971, pp.125–135

Dror, Yehezkel, 'True-believer' Terrorism', *Jerusalem Post*, 4 July 1996

——, 'Israel's Long-range Prospects: a State at its Best Ever', in *Israel's New Future: Interviews*, ed. Manfred Gerstenfeld, Jerusalem Centre for Public Affairs, Rubin Maas, 1994, pp.35–47

Elon, A, 'Israel and the End of Zionism', *The New York Review*, 19 December 1994, pp. 22–30

Erikson, E, *Insight and Responsibility*, New York: Norton, 1964

Erlich, S, 'Use, Abuse and the Boundaries of Intergenerational Responsibility – A View from Psychoanalysis', Contribution to the Panel of 'Shifting Grounds in the Psychoanalytic Perspectives of the Child and the Parent', presented at the Sigmund Freud Centre International Conference: In the Best Interest of the Child: Contemporary Perspectives, Jerusalem, 6 November 1996

Etinger, Y, 'Mourning', *Kol Ha'ir*, 16 August 1996

Feldman, M, 'Grievance', paper presented at Herzliya at Annual Conference of Israel Psychotherapy Assn: Psychotherapy and Aggression on 23 April 1993

Firestone, R W, 'The Origins of Ethnic Strife', *Mind and Human*

Interaction, vol. 7, 4 December 1996

Fishkoff, 'Their Patience is Running Thin', *Jordan Post Supplement Reports*, 6 August 1996

Fraiberg, S H, *The Magic Years*, London, Methuen, 1959

Friedgut, T H, 'Israel's Turn Towards Peace' in *Israel Under Rabin*, ed. Robert O Freedman, Westview Press, Boulder, Colorado 1995, pp.71–91

Friedman, Menachem, 'Impending Changes for Ultra-Orthodox Society', in *Israel's New Future: Interviews*, ed. Manfred Gerstenfeld, Jerusalem Centre for Public Affairs, Rubin Maas, 1994, pp.199–211

Friedman, T L, 'The Unsilent Majority', *Jerusalem Post*, 20 January 1997

Freud, S, *Group Psychology and the Analysis of the Ego*, S E, 18, 1921, pp.65–143

——, *On Narcissism: An Introduction*, S E, 14, 1914, pp.73–102

——, *Mourning and Melancholia*, S E 14, 1917 [1915], pp.237–258

Fromm, E, *Escape from Freedom*, New York, Rinehart, 1941

Gabai, D, 'The Smile of Yigal Amir Relates to the Contempt He has Toward the Crowd', *Maariv*, 13 March 1996

Galili, O, 'Labour will not Win Unless it Changes', *Ha'aretz*, 8 November 1996

Gal-Or, N, *The Jewish Underground: Our Terrorism*, HaKibbutz Hameuhad, 1990

Gardner, H, *Art, Mind and Brain*, New York, Basic Books, 1982

Gardner, M R, *On Trying to Teach the Mind in Correspondence*, Hillsdale, NJ, The Analytic Press, 1994

Gerstenfeld, M, *Israel's New Future: Interviews*, Jerusalem Centre for Public Affairs, Rubin Maas, 1994

——, 'Introduction', *Israel's New Future: Interviews*, Jerusalem Centre for Public Affairs, Rubin Maas 1994, pp.1–19

Gevirtz, Yael, 'The Servant of the Ebb', *Musaf*, 29 March 1996

Gilligan, C, *In a Different Voice*, Tel-Aviv, Sifriat Poalim, 1995

Goel, Y, 'Don't Silence the Haredim', *Jerusalem Post*, 6 September 1996

Golan, A, 'Arrogance and Its Punishment', *Ha'aretz*, 4 June 1996

Golan, Galia, 'Women in Israeli Society: An Overview', *Palestine–Israel Journal*, vol. 2, no.3, 1995, pp.13–18

Goodman, H, 'Explosive Silence', *The Jerusalem Report*, 14 November 1996

Gordon, E, 'Zo Artzenu as Bad as Terrorists', *Jerusalem Post*, 22 January 1997

——, 'Attorney-General Won't Probe Haredi Attacks on Barak', *Jordan Post*, 15 October 1996

——, 'Petition', *Ha'aretz*, 9 September 1996

——, 'The Haredi Attack on Barak', *Jordan Post*, 27 August 1996

Green, J, 'Reading from Right to Left', *Jerusalem Post Literary Supplement*, 23 January 1997

Grinberg, L, and R, *Psychoanalytic Perspectives on Migration and Exile*, New Haven and London, Yale University Press, 1984

Grinwald, J, 'The Culture of Polarisation: Between Two Cities, Jerusalem and Tel-Aviv', *Ha'aretz*, 22 November 1996

Gross, N C, 'Orthodox Women Rally for Life over Land', *The Jerusalem Report*, 6 February 1997

——, 'Justice on the Firing Line', *The Jerusalem Report*, 10 March 1996

Grossman, D, 'The Peace is in Flames', *Die Zeit*, 4 May 1996

——, 'The Humiliation of Auschwitz', *The Observer*, 21 January 1995

——, *The Yellow Wind*, London, Jonathan Cape, 1988

Grunberger, B, *Narcissism*, New York, International Universities Press, 1971

Hagman, G, 'Mourning 1995: A Review and Reconsideration', *International Journal of Psychoanalysis*, vol. 76, pp.909–925, 1995

Hanley, C, 'On Facts and Ideas in Psychoanalysis', *International Journal of Psychoanalysis*, vol. 76, pp.901–908, 1995

Harel, Z, 'The Psychologist said that Amir does not Suffer from a Personality Disorder', *Ha'aretz*, 13 March 1996

Hareven, A, 'The Price of Humiliation', *Ha'aretz*, 19 July 1996

——, *Can the Palestinian Problem be Solved? Israeli Positions*, Jerusalem, The Van Leer Jerusalem Foundation, 1983

Hartman, D, 'Hearts with Many', *Jerusalem Post*, 2 November 1996

Hass, A, *Drinking the Sea at Gaza*, Kibbutz Meuhad, 1996

Haynal, André, Molner M & Puymege G, *Fanaticism: A Historical and Psychoanalytic Study*, New York, Schocken Books, 1983

Hecht, E, 'Dybbuks Stay Away from Exorcism Ceremony', *Jordan Post*, 13 August 1996

Heilman, S, *Defenders of the Faith: Inside Ultra-Orthodox Jews*, New York, Schocken Books, 1992

Herman J L, *Trauma and Recovery*, New York, Basic Books, 1992

Honig, Sarah, 'Peres Calls for Early Elections', *Jerusalem Post*, 12 February 1996

Hori, R G, 'The Language of a Cold Peace', *Jerusalem Post*, 28 October 1996

Hornik, D, 'Oh, Wouldn't It Be Lovely...', *Jerusalem Post*, 3 February 1997

Horovitz, N, 'People Search a Shelter and Find God', *Ha'aretz*, 23 June 1996

——, 'And the Poet Said You Cannot Force Love on Anybody', *Ha'aretz*, 14 December 1993

Hutman, B, 'Haredim Attack Car Near Rehov Bar Ilan', *Jerusalem Post*, 10 November 1993

Ibrahim, Youssef M, 'In Calamity, Common Ground', *New York Times*, 3 December 1995

——, 'In Calamity, Common Ground', *Jerusalem Post*, Weekly Review, 4 December 1995

Ilan, S, 'Hundreds of Threats Against Reformist from Telephone Booths in big Yeshivot in Jerusalem', *Ha'aretz*, 9 November 1996

——, 'Worries of the Haredi Rabbis', *Ha'aretz*, 3 November 1996

Immanuel, J, 'Arafat: Our Peace is with all Israelis', *Jerusalem Post*, 20 January 1997

——, 'Sons of Abraham', *Jerusalem Post*, 17 January 1997

Kafka, F, *Letters to his Father* (1919) New York, Schocken Books,, 1966

Kapeliouk, A, 'Rabin – un Assassinat Politique', *Le Monde Editions*, 1996

Kaplan-Sommer A, 'Rabin Square Deco: Eyesore or Loving Tribute?', *Jerusalem Post*, 19 January 1996

——, 'Songs of Comfort' *Jordan Post Magazine*, 1 December 1995

——, and Netty C, Gross, 'Unity's Brief Recovery: We All Knew It Could Happen', *Jerusalem Post Magazine*, 10 November 1995

Karavan, Dani, 'A Creative Piece without the Drive of the

Creator', *Ha'aretz*, 29 November 1995

Kashti, O, 'The Commission that Investigated the Students' Support of Rabin's Assassin', *Ha'aretz*, 4 December 1996a

——, 'The Committee that investigated the support of the pupils to the assassin of Yitzhak Rabin', *Jerusalem Post*, 4 December 1996b

——, 'Rabbi Bakshi-Doron: Education for Openness and Democracy Destroyed the Value of Respecting Parents', *Ha'aretz*, 21 November 1996

Kaspi, A, 'Peace Through the Viewfinder', *Ha'aretz Supplement*, 1 November 1996

Katz, L, R, *Empathy – It's Nature and Uses*, London, The Free Press of Glencoe, 1963Kaunber, E, 'Memorising Rabin', *Jerusalem Post Magazine*, 1 December 1995

Keinon, Herb, 'Tears for Seventy-three Families', *Jerusalem Post*, 6 February 1997

——, 'Hebron Jews Unimpressed with PA Peace Rhetoric', *Jerusalem Post*, 20 January 1997

——, 'With Rabin's Death Israel Becomes a Full Member of the Family of Nations', *Jordan Post Magazine*, 10 November 1995, p.4

——, 'Rabin Laid to Rest on Mount Herzl', *Jerusalem Post*, 7 November 1995

——, and Immanuel, Jon, 'Council of Settlements Blasts Secret Settler Dialogue with PA', *Jordan Post*, 4 August 1996

Kernberg, O F, *Internal World and External Reality – Object Relation Theory Applied*, Northvale, NJ, Jason Aronson, 1994

——, 'The Psychopathology of Hatred', in *Rage, Power and Aggression*, eds. R A Glick and S P Roose, New Haven: Yale University Press, 1993, pp.61–80

——, *Aggression in Personality Disorders and Perversions*, New Haven, Yale University Press, 1992

Kishon, E, 'The Trade Union Building has been Destroyed', in Fifty-eight Satires, Israel, Maariv Library, 1995

Klein, Halevi Y, 'Keep the Continuity yet Change', *The Jerusalem Report*, 26 December 1996

Klein, M, 'Notes on some Schizoid Mechanisms', *International Journal of Psychoanalysis*, vol. 27, pp.99–110, 1946

Kleinberg, A, 'The Grief of the Israelis – Doron Rosenblum', *Ha'aretz Book Supplement*, 27 November 1996

Kleist, H von, *Michael Kohlhaas* (1808), Oxford University Press, 1967

Kohnt, H, *The Analysis of the Self*, International Universities Press, 1971

——, *The Restoration of the Self*, International Universities Press, 1977

Koubovi, D, *Bibliotherapy, Literature, Education, Mental Health*, Hebrew University, Jerusalem, Magness Press, 1992

Kravitz, H, 'The Need to Mourn', *Transcultural Psychiatric Research Review*, vol. 32, pp.411–414, 1995

Kris, E, *Psychoanalytic Explorations in Art*, New York, Schocken Books, 1964

Krystal, H, *Integration of Self-healing Affect, Trauma, Alexithymia*, Hillsdale, NJ, The Analytic Press, 1988

Kuttab, D, 'Equal Rights for All', *Jerusalem Press*, 12 November 1996

Langer, S, 'Philosophy in a New Key, Cambridge, Mass, Harvard University Press, 1942

Lasch, C, *The Minimal Self-psychic Survival in Troubled Times*, New York, Norton, 1984

Lazarus-Yaffeh, H, 'Contemporary Fundamentalism in Judaism, Christianity, Islam', *Jerusalem Quarterly*, vol. 47, pp.27–36, 1988

Leon, Dan, 'In Memory', *Jordan Post*, 25 January 1996

Lev-Arie, R, and Dalia Yair, *Don't Just Raise Your Hands*, Keshet, Tel Aviv, 1996

Levi, G, 'A Lesson which was not Learned', *Ha'aretz*, 14 January 1995 & 31 December 1995

——, 'The Twilight Zone', *Ha'aretz Supplement*, 31 December 1993

Levin, S, 'The Psychoanalysis of Shame', *Intenational. Journal of. Psychoanalyis*, vol. 52, pp.355–362, 1971

Levy, A, *The Ultra-Orthodox*, Jerusalem, Keter Publishing House, 1981

Lewis, A, 'Israel's Lethal Mix of Religion and Nationalism', *The New York Times*, 5 January 1997

Lewis, H B, *The Role of Shame in Symptom Formation*, Hillsdale, NJ,

Lawrence Erlbaum, 1987

Littlewood, Jane, *Aspects of Grief Bereavement in Adult Life*, London, Routledge, 1992

Loewald, H W, 'Some Considerations on Repetition Compulsion', in *Papers on Psychoanalysis*, New Haven, Yale University Press, 1973, pp.87–101

Makovsky, D, Immanuel, J and Collins, L, 'Prime Minister: Not All our Ideals are Within Reach Anymore', *Jordan Post*, 17 January 1997

—— and Immanuel, J, 'Hussein Compromise May Clinch Hebron', *Jerusalem Post*, 13 January 1997

Marcus, Raine, 'Friedman, Fellow Soldier Remanded', *Jordan Post*, 3 January 1997

Marks, I M, *Fears, Phobias and Rituals: Panic Anxiety and Their Disorders*, New York, Oxford University Press, 1987

Mason, Ruth, 'Meeting the Other: Israelis are Trying to Bridge the Gaps Uncovered by the Rabin Assassination by Talking to Each Other', *Jerusalem Post*, 19 January 1996

May R, *The Courage to Create*, London, Collins, 1975

——, *Man's Search for Himself*, New York, Norton, 1953

McDougall, J, *Theatres of the Mind*, New York, Brunner/Mazel, 1985

Melamed, A, 'William Styron', *Kol Hair*, 19 January 1996

Melman, Y, 'The Testimony of Yigal Amir in the Shamgar Commission', *Ha'aretz*, 17 January 1996

——, 'What Turns a Regular Person into a War Criminal?', *Ha'aretz*, 28 December 1995

Miller, J, 'Israel Fundamentalist Thing', *Jerusalem Post*, 10 June 1996

Modell, A H, *Other times, other realities: toward a theory of psychoanalytic treatment,* Harvard University Press, Cambridge, Mass., 1990

Morrison, N K, 'The Role of Shame in Schizophrenia', in *Essential Papers on Narcissism*, ed. A R Morrison, New York, New York University Press, 1986, pp.51–87

Moses-Hrushovski R, 'Discussion of Grievance', 1993, paper presented at Conference of the Israel Psychotherapy Association, Tel Aviv, 19 April 1993

——, *Deployment – Hiding Behind Power Struggles as a Character Defence*, Northvale, NJ, Jason Aronson, 1994

——, 'Transference and Countertransference from Deployment against Feelings of Loss – through Psychotic Regressions – to a Better Capacity to Feel and to Mourn, *International Journal of Psychoanalysis*, vol. 73, pp.561–576, 1992

——, 'The Teachers' Attitudes in Creating a Climate of Growth in Counseling in Education', pp.9–16, Hebrew University: School of Education

——, 'The Teacher's Attitudes in Establishing a Climate of Growth in the Classroom', in *Counselling in Education*, ed. R Moses-Hrushovski, Jerusalem, Hebrew University, 1970

——, 'Remaining in the Bunker Long After the War is Over: Deployment in the Individual, the Group and the Nation, in: *Psychoanalysis at the Political Border, Essays in Honor of Rafael Moses*, eds. L Rangell and R Moses-Hrushovski, Madison, CT, International Universities Press, 1996

——, 'Trauma, Mental Deployment and some Therapeutic Aspects of Recovery', paper presented at First Izmir Psychoanalysis and Psychotherapy Conference, Izmir, Turkey, 1999

——, The Inner Story of a Workaholic: as Revealed in the Course of his Psychoanalysis, in press 2000, in *Psychoanalytische Blätter*, Germany

Moses-Hrushovski, R and Moses R, 'The Human Factor in Education', *Readings in Education*, vols. 37/38, pp.32–40, 1984

Moses, R and Moses-Hrushovski, R, 'Reflections on the Sense of Entitlement', in *The Psychoanalytic Study of the Child*, vol. 5, pp.61–78, New Haven, CT, Yale University Press, 1990

Moses, R, 'On Dehumanising the Enemy', in *The Psychodynamics of International Relationships*, eds. V D Volkan, D A Juliks and J V Montville, Lexington, MA, Lexington Books, 1990, pp.111–118

——, 'Unconscious Guilt Feelings on the Israeli Side of the Arab–Israel Conflict', *Segmund Freud House Bulletin*, vol. 7, no.1, pp.2–14, 1983

——, 'The Group Self and the Arab–Israeli Conflict', *Internalional Review of, Psychoanalyis*, pp.55–65, 1982

——, *Persistent Shadows of the Holocaust: its Meaning to those not Directly Affected*, Madison, CT, International Universities Press, 1993

Moses R and Kligler D, 'The Institutionalisation of Mental Health Values', *Israel Annuals of Psychiatry*, vol. 4, pp.148–161, 1966

Munson, H, *Islam and Revolution in the Middle East*, New Haven, CT, Yale University Press, 1988

Nardi, Rivka and Chen Nardi, *Men in Change*, Moden, Tel Aviv 1993

Neminoff, A, Sugarman A & Robbins A eds, *On loving, hating and living well*, 1968

Nesher, Merav, 'The Assassination of Yitzhak Rabin Worsened Their Mental State', *Ha'aretz*, 20 March 1997

Neuman, J, 'The Moonstruck Minority', *Ha'aretz*, 25 November 1996

Newman, J, 'Call for Reconciliation', *Jerusalem Post*, 19 November 1996

Novick, J and Novick, K K, Some Comments on Masochism and the Delusion of Omnipotence from a Developmental Perspective, *Journal of the American Psychoanal Association*, vol. 39, pp.307–332, 1991

Ofir, A, 'Postmodernism: A Philosophical Attitude', in *Education in the Era of Postmodern Discourse*, ed. F. Gur-Zeev, The Hebrew University of Jerusalem, The Magnes Press, 1997, pp.136–163

Olden, C, 'On Adult Empathy with Children', *Psychoanaitic. Study of the Child*, vol. 7, 1953, pp.111–125

Or, K, 'The Committee that Investigated the Support of the Pupils to the Assassination of Yitzhak Rabin', *Jerusalem Post*, 4 December 1996

Ostow, M, 'The Fundamentalist Phenomenon: A Psychological Perspective', unpublished, 1988

——, 'Psychodynamics of Apocalyptics: Discussion of Identification and the Nazi Phenomenon', *International Journal of Psychoanaysisl*, vol. 67, pp.277–287, 1986

——, 'Apocalyptic Thinking in Mental Illness and Social Disorder', *Psychoanalysis and Contemporary Thought*, vol. 4, 285–295, 1997

O'Sullivan, A, 'Inquiry Panel Begins Its Task', *Jerusalem Post*, 6

February 1997
——, Rudge, D, Collins, L and Shapiro, H, 'Nation Mourns Biggest Loss since 1973', *Jerusalem Post*, 6 February 1997
Palgi, A, 'Internalisation of Meaning of Yitzhak Rabin's Assassination in Israel', *Ha'aretz*, 2 July 1996
Peleg, M, 'The Militant Settlers have no Ownership on the Forefathers', *Ha'aretz*, 5 November 1996
Person, Ethel S, *Dreams of Love and Fateful Encounters: The Power of Romantic Passion*, Hammondsworth, Penguin Books, 1988
Pollock, G H, *The Mourning-Liberation Process*, Madison, Conn, International University Press, 1989
Post, J M, 'Terrorist Psycho-logic: Terrorist Behaviour as a Product of Psychological Forces in Origins of Terrorism, in *Psychologies, Theologies, States of Mind*', ed. Walter Reich, Cambridge University Press, Cambridge, 1990
Rabin, Y, 'Article Adapted from Prime Minister Rabin's Address in Paris on Receiving the UNESCO Peace Prize', 1994
Rabinovich, Abraham, 'Our Sons, Our Brothers', *Jerusalem Post*, 7 February 1997
——, 'Power of Disdain to Destroy', *Jerusalem Post*, 3 October 1996
Ragen, N, 'Too Late', *Jerusalem Post*, 24 October 1996
Raine, M, 'Psychologist Testifies Amir was Sane When He Shot Rabin', *Jerusalem Post*, 13 March 1996
Rangell, L, 'Moral Conflicts, Public Opinion and the Political Process', in *Psychoanalysis at the Political Border*, ed. L Rangell and R Moses-Hrushovski, International Universities Press, Madison, CT, 1980
——, 'The Psychoanalytic Theory of Change', *International Journal of. Psychoanalysis*, 1992, vol. 73, pp.415–428, 1992
——, 'Action Theory within the Structure View', *International J. Psychoanalysis*, vol. 70, pp.189–203, 1989
——, 'A Core Process', *Psychoanalytic Quarterly*, vol. 56, pp.240–249, 1987
——, 'The Object in Psychoanalytic Theory', *American Journal of Psychoanalysis*, vol. 33, pp.301–335, 1985a
——, 'On the Theory in Psychoanalysis and the Relation of theory to Psychoanalytic Therapy', *American Journal of*

Psychoanalysis, vol. 33, pp.59–93, 1985b

Redl, Fritz, *The Aggressive Child*, Glencoe, Ill, The Free Press, 1957

Rodan, Steve, 'Inside the Mind of Saddam Hussein', *Jerusalem Post*, 6 September 1996

——, 'King Hussein has Started Putting his Vision of a Real Peace with Israel into Practice', *Jerusalem Post*, 9 February 1996

Rogan, N, 'Too Late', *Jerusalem Post*, 24 October 1996

Rolef, S H, 'When He Wants and She Wants, He Wins', *Jerusalem Post*, 25 November 1996

——, 'People Who Live in Glass Houses', *Jerusalem Post*, 11 November 1996

——, 'People May Live as They Like', *Jerusalem Post*, 2 October 1996

Rorty-Oksenberg, A, *Explaining Emotions*, Berkeley, CA, University of California Press, 1980

Rosen, R, 'The History of Denial', *Ha'aretz Book Supplement*, 15 November 1996

Rosenblum, D, *Israeli Blues*, Tel Aviv, Am Oved Publishers, 1996

Rosenfeld, J M, Sihon, D A and Sykes, S J, *Out from Under: Lessons from Projects for Ineptly Served Children and Families*, Jerusalem, Brookdale Institute of Gerontology and Human Development, 1995

Rosenfeld, S S, 'The Peace that Netanyahu Talks About Isn't Peace', *Herald International Tribune*, 9 October 1996

Roth, S, 'The Shadow of the Holocaust', in *Persistent Shadows of the Holocaust*, ed. Moses R, Madison, CT, International Universities Press, 1993, pp.37–64

Rubenstein, A, 'Also If We Give, They Will Take', *Ha'aretz*, 27 October 1996

Saar, Rali, 'Fundamentalism and Violence', *Ha'aretz*, 22 November 1995

Samet, Gideon, 'The Penetration of the Culture of Restraint', *Ha'aretz*, 23 October 1995

Sandler, J, and Dreher, A V, *What do Psychoanalysts Want?*, London, Routledge, 1996

Sandler S, 'Rabin and the Religious Parties: The Limits of Power Sharing', in *Israel Under Rabin*, ed. Robert O Freedman, Boulder, CO, Westview Press, 1995, pp.169–188

Sanford, S, Nevitt, 'Going Beyond Prevention', in *Sanctions for Evil*, ed. Nevitt Sanford and Craig & Associates, Boston, Beacon Press, 1971
——, *Self and Society*, New York, Atherton, 1967
Sassar, M, 'Chaimke Drukman', *Ha'aretz*, 20 November 1995
Schacht, L, 'Winnicott's Position in Regard to the Self, with Special Reference to Childhood', *International Review of Psychoanalysis*, vol. 15, pp.515–529, 1988
Segal, Z, 'Democracy has to Attack', *Ha'aretz*, 28 October 1996
Segev, A, 'Elections Determined by the Unreal', *Ha'aretz*, 21 June 1996
Segev, T, 'Towards the Future', *Ha'aretz*, 10 January 1996
——, 'After a Year', *Ha'aretz*, 17 October 1996
Shaffer, G, 'Destruction or Normalisation', *Ha'aretz*, 30 December 1996
——, Strange Mistrust of Arabs, *Jordan Post*, 24 January 1996
Shapiro, H, 'Admiring Amir is Antithesis of Judaism', *Jerusalem Post*, 2 September 1996
——, 'Haredi Family Fears for Future after Father is Excommunicated', *Jerusalem Post*, 7 July 1996
Sheleg, Y, 'A New Generation Requires Change', *Ha'aretz*, 6 January 1997
——, 'Terror is Like Terror', *Ha'aretz*, 6 September 1996
Schiff, Z, 'Two To Extradite Noam Friedman', *Ha'aretz*, 17 January 1997
——, 'The Price of Incitation', *Ha'aretz*, 3 January 1997
Shimburska, R, ", *Ha'aretz*, 24 January 1997
Shohat, Z, 'It's Not Spoken about Shabbat-candles', *Ha'aretz*, 29 August 1996
——, 'Fascist Ecology', *Ha'aretz*, 25 October 1996
Shohet, O, 'To Disconnect Now', *Ha'aretz*, 3 January 1997
——, 'The Moment that Determined His Life', *Ha'aretz*, 16 March 1995
Shragai, N, 'Since the Assassination of Rabin the Right Wing Suffers from an Illegitimate Image by Its Traditional Supporters', *Ha'aretz*, 14 February 1996
Simon, B, *New and Renewed Thoughts on Inter-generational Relations and Psychoanalysis, October 1996*, paper presented at the

Sigmund Freud Center International Conference: In the Best Interest of the Child: Contemporary Perspectives, Jerusalem, 6–7 November 1996

Slater, Robert, *Rabin of Israel: Warrior for Peace*, London, Robson Books, 1996

Solan, R, 'Normal and Pathological Narcissism – Flexible or Petrified Envelope for Self-preservation', *Zeitschrift Fur Psychoanalytische Theorie and Praxis*, vol. 12, 1997

——, 'The Narcissistic Vulnerability to Change in Object Relations', in *Psychoanalytische Blätter*, ed. R Moses, 1998, 36–55

Sommer, A K, 'The Case of the Orthodox versus the High Court', *Jordan Post*, 30 August 1996

Staub, E, 'An Ideology of Antagonism', lecture presented at Givat Haviva Teacher's Seminary, 1995

Stavi, Z, 'Yitzhak Whom You Love', *Yediot Ahronot*, 1995

Steinberg, J, 'I Love Yigal Amir: What it Says about Our Schools', *Jordan Post*, 16 August 1996

Steiner, J, 'Revenge and Resentment in the 'Oedipus Situation'', *International Journal Psychoanalysis*, vol. 77, pp.433–443, 1996

——, *Psychic Retreats: Pathological Organisations in Psychotic, Neurotic and Borderline Patients*, London and New York, The New Library of Psychoanalysis, 1993

Stern, D N, *The Interpersonal World of the Infant*, New York, Basic Books, 1985

Stone, A M, 'The Role of Shame in Post-traumatic Stress Disorders, *American Journal of Orthopsychiatry*, vol. 62, pp.131–137, 1992

Tähkä, V, 'Dealing with Object Loss', *Scandinavian Psychoanalytic Review*, vol. 7, pp.13–33, 1984

Tzalal, M, 'The Human Factor in Traffic Accidents', *Ha'aretz*, 11 April 1996

Tzalal, M, *Ha'aretz*, 11 April 1995, 18 October 1996

Tzur, B, 'Education Ministry Issued Guidelines on Dealing with Stress', *Jordan Post*, 7 March 1996

——, Collins, L and Rudge, D, 'Nation Marks a year Since Rabin's Slaying', *Jerusalem Post*, 24 October 1996

Vardi, D, *Memorial Candle: Children of the Holocaust*, Tavistock, London, 1992

Volkan, V D, 'Intergenerational Transmission and "Chosen Traumas": A Link between the Psychology of the Individual and that of the Ethnic Group', in *Psychoanalysis at the Political Border: Essays in Honour of Rafael Moses*, eds. Leo Rangell and Rena Moses-Hrushovski, International University Press, Madison, Conneticut, 1996

——, 'Immigrants and Refugees: A Psychodynamic Perspective', *Mind and Human Interaction*, 4 April 1993

——, on 'Chosen Trauma', *Mind and Human Interaction3:13*

——, 'Living Statues and Political Decision-making', *Mind and Human Interaction*, vol. 2, pp.46–49, 1990

——, *Attitudes of Entitlement*, Charlottesville, University Press of Virginia, 1988

—— and Ast, G, 'Malignant Narcissism', in *Spectrum des Narzissmus*, Vandenhoeck and Ruprecht, Göttingen, 1994, pp.92–103

—— and Harris, Max, *Shaking the Tent: The Psychodynamics of Ethnic Terrorism*, Centre for the Study of Mind and Human Interaction, Monograph no., 1993

——, *The Need to Have Enemies and Allies: From Clinical Practice to International Relationships*, Northvale, NJ, Jason Aronson, 1988

——, *Liking Objects and Linking Phenomena: A Study of the Forms, Symptoms, Metapsychology, and Therapy of Complicated Mourning*, New York, International Universities Press, 1981

Wachsman, E, 'An Abortive Search for Soulmates', *Jordan Post*, 20 January 1997

Weinberg, Carrol, A, 'Terrorists and Terrorism, Have We Reached a Crossroad?' *Mind and Human Interaction*, vol. 3, pp.77–82, 1992

Wheatcroft, G, 'Netanyahu's Hebron Dilemma', *The New York Times*, 17 December 1996

Wheelis, Allen, *The Quest for Identity*, New York, W W Norton, 1958

Winnicott, D W, 'Delinquency as a Sign of Hope', eds. S Feinstein and P Giovacchini, in *Adolescent Psychiatry*, vol. 2, New York, Basic Books, 1973, pp.364–371

Woolf, V, *A Room of One's Own*, Quentin Bell and Angelica Garnett, 1929

Wurmser, L, *Die innere Grenze, Das Schamgefühl – ein Beitrag zum Uberich – Jahrbuch der Psychoanalyse Band*, vol. 18, pp.16–41, 1986

Wurmser, L, *The Mask of Shame*, Baltimore, The John Hopkins University Press, 1981

Yehoshua, A B 'Without the Persecution Complex', *Ha'aretz*, 2 February 1996

——, 'New Components of Israel's Identity', in *Israel's New Future: Interviews*, ed. Manfred Gerstenfeld, Jerusalem Centre for Public Affairs, Rubin Maas, 1994, pp.187–198

Yudelman, M, 'Leah Rabin: Netanyahu Must Now Ask Yitzhak's Forgiveness', *Jerusalem Post*, 16 January 1997

——, 'The Invasion of the Soul Snatchers', *Jerusalem Post*, 5 December 1996

——, 'Left-wing Fascism, Orwell Style', *Jerusalem Post*, 8 November 1996

——, 'Religious and Haredi Knesset Factions Formed a Chorus Demanding the Elimination of Kopatch's Spot', *Jerusalem Post*, 8 November 1996

——, 'Uproar over Attacks on Justice Barak', *Jerusalem Post*, 27 August 1996

—— and Izenberg, 'Widespread Condemnation Greets Amir Fan Club', *Jerusalem Post*, 12 August 1996

Zayyad, Z and Ciegelman, R, 'Seeking Justice', *Palestine–Israel Journal*, vol. 2, no.4, pp.8–14, 1995

——, 'Mutual Recognition of Suffering', *Palestine–Israel Journal*, vol. 2, no.4, pp.25–28, 1995